om f   flap)

JUSTICE

IN

MOSCOW

George Feifer

SIMON AND SCHUSTER

NEW YORK   1964

First Printing

LIBRARY OF CONGRESS CATALOG CARD NUMBER: 64–11199
MANUFACTURED IN THE UNITED STATES OF AMERICA
BY AMERICAN BOOK–STRATFORD PRESS, INC.

To Professor John N. Hazard

Contents

The law, the working of the law, the daily application of the law to people and situations, is an essential element in a country's life. It runs through everything; it is a part of the pattern like the architecture and the art and the look of the cultivated countryside. It shapes, and expresses, a country's mode of thought, its political concepts and realities, its conduct . . . —SYBILLE BEDFORD, *The Faces of Justice*

The law is a mirror of life, a reflection of social relationships. —ANDREI VYSHINSKY, *Concerning the Situation on the Front of Legal Theory*

The emergence of a complex judicial system applying formal rules worried many Soviet jurists, so they sought to differentiate the system they had created from that of other lands, to claim that it was unique in all the world. —JOHN HAZARD, *Settling Disputes in Soviet Society*

Introduction

THE FIRST HEAVY SNOW had fallen, the tourists had gone home, and elderly women strangers had started scolding me on the streets—"Young man, you had better put on a scarf and a hat immediately." It was, I understood then, a winter city, warmed in spirit now that the frosts had come. From the window I could see the early morning skaters, flat-faced lusty college youth reveling in a section of sporting grounds which had been flooded a month before. Sweet-sad peasant songs sounded softly over the loudspeakers and diffused quickly in the brittle-cold air. Beyond the hill was the icy river Moskva, and in the distance lay the city, the sun glinting gold on the cupola of the Bell Tower of Ivan III. I was still childishly exhilarated, because I could look upon the Kremlin in the morning while my roommate Valerii made tea and sausages for breakfast.

But that morning was especially exciting. On my desk—our room was on the ninth floor of the giant gingerbread dormitory of Moscow State University on Lenin Hills—lay my reading for a year, about thirty-five books recently published by the State Publishing House of Juridical Literature. They had been assigned by my adviser at the university, the dean of the Juridical Faculty. I was living in Moscow by arrangement of the U.S.A.–U.S.S.R. Cultural Exchange Agreement, gathering material for a doctoral dissertation on Soviet criminal theory. This meant a year at the university as an *aspirant*, roughly the Soviet equivalent of an American graduate student. Research in the libraries, courses and seminars, meeting with professors, reading cases and decrees—that is what I had been doing in the six weeks since I had arrived, much the way I had done it in the six months before I left New York. And to tell the truth, it was not overwhelmingly exciting. But that morning I had decided to quit the books and sample the pudding, instead of reading the recipes—I was going to court.

The address of the nearest courthouse lay in my pocket, and I was going there instead of to the Lenin Library. I was on my way to find out about socialist legality in the flesh, not on paper; to seek the ways of living Russian law and the workings of Soviet justice.

I remember my anticipation as I walked across the crunchy snow to the bus stop against a stream of commuters hurrying to the university. For me it was to be the consummation of a long search and study, a test of personal preconceptions, and a quest. The quest had started six years before, when as an undergraduate at Harvard I first made remote contact with the Soviet legal system. It seemed then in many ways a good system, and I suppose that because I was just becoming aware of the faults of the American system, socialist legality became a passion. I learned Russian and went on to study Soviet law in traditional ways at Columbia University; and what I found out about it fired my interest. My reading led me to expect that I would track down justice, unqualified by "Soviet," in Moscow's courts. Nothing less than justice is what I set out to find that Monday morning.

This sounds high-flown; I shall try to explain. It was not the Rule of Law, the Four Freedoms, Constitutionalism, Liberty or Democracy, not the Great Shining Things, the bold steps forward to new decencies or the courageous defenses of old ones—all of which Western courts produce in their best moments—that I expected to find. Political rights must be defended to their limits, and the central fact about Soviet political life, I knew, is that the limits of everything are set by the Party. When policy and precedent are made, the courts fall into line —and not even near the head of it. They have no independent source of authority; they are not an impartial arbiter between government and citizens; they do not—even in Soviet theory— transcend the interests of the Party. "Today skillful Party direction of the courts takes on more significance than ever before," the Central Committee announced in 1962. To look for the rule of law in a one-party, one-press, one-explanation, one-art-form state where not a single dissenting vote has been cast in the Supreme Soviet in thirty-five years and every deviation from the current reading of Marxism-Leninism is considered heresy would have taken more naïveté than I could muster. In Russia the Party rules; that, the Party tells us, is as it should be.

But the rule of law is not always the same as justice, and it was the latter that I was looking for. I was interested not in cases defining the fringes of political rights, but in all those ordinary cases in the middle: the daily cases that deal with common crimes and disputes; the great mass of cases that have nothing at all to do with state security or ideological purity; the kinds of cases that American courts—there is no denying it if you have served on a jury or have read the law journals or if your uncle is a lawyer—handle so badly when there are no constitutional principles to fight for; the kinds of cases Americans never hear about (Soviet terror and political trials make so much better news copy) but which most directly affect Ivan, that average fellow. I wanted to know what happens to *him* when he falls afoul of the law, his wife, or his boss.

And I wanted to test for myself whether in these cases Ivan gets a fair trial. Soviet times had changed not a little since the Moscow Trials of the 1930s which, classic example of perversion of the law that they are, had become the Western symbol of socialist legality. And although by dwelling on that bygone era (as some American writers did in discussing the trial of Francis Powers) it could be proved that the Soviet people have suffered and that Our Cause is just, not much could be learned about the average day of the average Muscovite in court.

In preparing for the trip to Moscow, I was struck by the thoroughness with which Soviet law had been reviewed since Stalin's death and by the fact that its really objectionable features had been eliminated. Conviction by "analogy" had been repudiated; "social danger" had been narrowed to mean only crimes specifically described in the criminal code; and the class origins of the parties before the court was no longer a matter for consideration by judges. Civilians were no longer tried in military courts, except in cases of espionage. Unpublished criminal statutes had ceased to be the practice. The M.V.D. boards, which formerly convened secretly on the basis of secret procedure and issued secret, nonappealable decisions, had now been abolished; all crimes were now tried in the regular court system. The procurator's obligations to the accused had been clarified and increased throughout the criminal process. In court, the burden of proof was more clearly on the prosecution, and the standards of proof had been raised; confession alone could no longer convict the accused.

From the decrees and the literature, the post-1953 reforms seemed impressive indeed. No one could be sure, of course, that the changes were complete, but the improvement was unquestionably great. Two principal tendencies underlay the changes: elimination of extralegal terror which complemented the regular court system, and liberalization, rationalization and humanization of both procedural and substantive laws within the legal system. (In my first week at the Juridical Faculty I had some talks with a youngish professor who worked in the procuracy during the 1940s. "Even then we had good laws and fair judges," he would say. "What went wrong had nothing to do with the codes or the courts; it was Stalin's personal affair. But I'd say that even in those days ninety-nine per cent of the cases were decided legally and correctly.") In a word, every aspect of the criminal trial had been reviewed and improved. Campaigns in the legal press and instructions by the Supreme Court emphasized that the rights and interests of defendants must be protected—*in practice*. High Party officials spoke about the great importance of justice and promised that "the criminal violations of legality which existed in the past will never again be repeated. . . . The shortcomings of our courts linked to the cult of personality of Stalin can never again be part of Soviet life."

This is what led me to expect that the Soviet court had become an understandable, accessible, workable institution which settled disputes through standard procedures; that the Soviet citizen was likely to get as fair a trial as Western citizens; that in the ordinary cases, socialist legality served him well.

Some features of Soviet law, even after the reforms, remained objectionable to American lawyers; however, these are not a function of totalitarianism, or even of socialism, but of the tradition, common on the Continent, of Roman, or Civil, law. Many European countries combine judge and jury. Since Civil law procedure is not adversarial and the trial is less a contest of the strength and skill of the parties than a search for truth by all, many countries limit the role of defense lawyers. Many require a thorough pretrial investigation.

When I first began reading Soviet law it seemed, on the basis of what I had learned of American criminal procedure, that Soviet courts sometimes convicted defendants on the basis of extralegal considerations. But later I read cases in which these same considerations—the personality of the defendant, his previous record and experiences, his reputation in the community, the emotional circumstances surrounding the cases—

served to help some defendants, even some accused of counter-revolutionary crimes. This was because Soviet courts tend to judge the "whole man," not just carefully selected evidence pertaining to an isolated episode in his life.

I assumed that the Soviet people would see nothing sinister in this; judging the "whole man" appeared fundamental to their concept of fairness. The Swiss people too regard it as proper; Swiss courts, for example, are likely to ask a defendant whether he was beaten as a child by his father—a totally irrelevant question in a common-law court. This is standard practice on the Continent: "Judge the criminal, not the crime." The courts of many Western nations go far beyond what British and American jurists, bred on the common law, consider relevant and material.

Similarly, the difference between Soviet and American practice, as regards the role of the judge, is the difference between France and England more than that between dictatorship and democracy. The Soviet judge, like his French counterpart, does not remain behind the plate while prosecution and defense have their innings. He is an active player—the *most* active, questioning and examining, carrying out the Civil law tradition that the court itself must direct the search for truth rather than limit itself principally to the evidence offered by the "sides."

Of course, this approach to the trial places great reliance on the judge. And I knew there would be abuses. But isn't the abuse as great in America, where reliance rests on ambitious prosecutors, greedy lawyers and bigoted or intimidatable juries? And on judges placed by political favor? Habeas corpus, warrants, and strict rules of evidence fail to protect too many Americans who do not understand these principles or are too poor to engage an able attorney or to purchase their way out. Both systems, of course, can work poorly or well in practice, but it seemed to me that in the petty cases

advantage lay with the Soviet. I had watched American courts
at work. I had seen the influence of the dollar, overheard the
deals, sensed the dishonesty, and I was disappointed by the
callousness and crudeness of the lower courts. Perhaps there
was a chance of finding something better in Moscow.

I had often heard commentators say that dictatorship is incompatible with fair trial, that fair trial is a danger to political
control. On the contrary, it seemed to me, fair trial has great
value to dictators. Even if "the interests of the state take un-
questioned precedence over those of individuals" and Soviet
law "has no other function than to carry out the policy of
the state" (as Western commentators have written) doesn't
this mean precisely that the ordinary cases must be handled
equitably? The present Soviet leadership seemed to have
learned that legality is far more effective than arbitrariness in
cultivating a loyal citizenry and in running an efficient society,
and that a stable legal order is a *sine qua non* in a complex industrial society. Every Party pronouncement I have read indicated that its leadership was very eager to have the common
crimes and disputes settled fairly and humanely. No other
policy would make sense. Whom would it serve to convict an
innocent factory worker for stealing? Or punish a guilty one
cruelly? Soviet texts constantly emphasized the harm of such
wrongs, and this seemed only the logic of things. Of course,
the same could be said of American society, but too much in
America is left to chance and to free enterprise. I assumed
that if the Party wanted fair trials, the Party, with its effective
controls, had the means of providing them.

There remains the matter of Marxism. Years ago I felt that it
was somehow incompatible with the law. I wish the relationship seemed so simple now. In graduate studies I had to spend
months with the black-bound tomes of socialist philosophy,
and more than anything else, I learned from them that the re-

lationship between Marxism and the law is a bewildering one. But let me say "two words," as the Russians say, about that.

"Marxism scientifically illuminated the whole of human history, all areas of the life of human society, discovered and explained the laws and the genuine meaning and genuine essence of all social phenomena . . ." et cetera, et cetera. So wrote Vyshinsky* and every other Bolshevik jurist who followed him. In the Marxist *Weltanschauung*, law, like everything else, from the movement of planets to marital infidelity, has an appointed place and an exact explanation. Law is a reflection of the material world, for material (matter) is the ultimate reality, the source of everything. Men's thoughts, ideologies, spiritual values, constitutions, religions, ethics—and their laws—emanate from matter.

I understood the scheme to be roughly this. Material is primordial, and the basis of society, the "foundation," is determined by the relationships into which men enter in dealing with it: in earning a living, in producing goods. The relationships, therefore (to go one step further), are determined by the forces of production, and the forces of production— pastoral, manorial, industrial, and so on—group men into classes. Classes are the crucial division of society.

It is the class division, therefore, that determines the "superstructure"—attitudes toward life, society, religion, philosophy, morals and laws. For law, like the state, is a product of the class struggle, a weapon of the class which dominates the means of production. "Put as simply as possible, state and law always contain fully expressed class character, arising out of economic relationships—out of the war of the classes."

Therefore, there is feudal law, bourgeois law and socialist law, but never universal law or natural law founded on

* Andrei Vyshinsky (1883–1954), before being appointed Stalin's Foreign Minister and head of the Soviet delegation to the United Nations, was an important early Marxist legal theoretician.

"higher" moral, religious or human values, since justice cannot rise above the interests of the class it serves. A Soviet jurist explains that "law is always the will, written into laws, of those classes in whose hands, in accordance with the economic relationships prevailing in a given society, state power resides. The history of law testifies that there never was and never can be law with some kind of 'eternal' or 'universal' content. Every law has always been and is the law of a definite class and historical type. It is always a part of the superstructure over the productive relationships of class society."

Marxist jurists have always argued that "bourgeois" law, far from providing equal protection for all, protects only the diabolical exploitation of the many by the few, and that all the fine words about universal principles and common standards are only a façade veiling its class essence. Marx and Engels announced this discovery in the famous passage in the *Communist Manifesto:* "Please do not argue with us by using your bourgeois notions of liberty, culture, right, et cetera, as the standards for judging the abolition of bourgeois property. Your ideas themselves are the outcome of bourgeois methods of production and of bourgeois property relations, just as your 'right' is only the will of your class writ large as law. . . ."

Steeped in this cosmology, worshiping it as a faith, the early Bolsheviks made strong statements and took strong action with respect to the law when they seized power. The law was politics; it was power; it was a weapon "we" must use against "them"; it was the mailed fist of the proletariat. "The highest law is the good of the revolution." Tsarist codes were scrapped, the old courts were abolished and illiterate judges were directed to exercise their "revolutionary consciousness" to suppress the enemies of the proletariat—that is, of the Party. The laws were flexible and were flexibly applied, and it all smacked of terror. "The court is an organ of power," lectured Lenin. "This is sometimes forgotten by liberals. But a Marxist commits a sin if he forgets it. . . . Our court is an organ of the rule of the proletariat and the poorest peasantry. . . ."

Not equal justice for all (which Vyshinsky called "that children's comedy"), but the repression of class enemies and recalcitrants was the function of the new courts. For Soviet rule was no bourgeois-liberal democracy of phony equality, but the dictatorship of the proletariat, described by Lenin as "unrestricted power, beyond the law, resting on force in the strictest sense of the word." The state was "a machine in the hands of the dominant class for crushing its class enemies"; the Soviet state was "the legally unlimited dominance of the proletariat over the bourgeoisie, resting on violence."

In 1938, an official definition of law was adopted, preserving the class flavor. "Law is a combination of the rules of behavior (norms) established or sanctioned by state authority, reflecting the will of the ruling class—rules of behavior whose application is assured by the coercive power of the state for the purpose of protecting, strengthening, and developing relationships and procedures suitable and beneficial to the ruling class."

Why look for justice—I was often asked before my trip—in a society where legal thinkers glory in terrorism, militarism, naked force, class justice and dictatorship?

Because, for one reason, the days of naked force were over. They had been largely a product of the revolution—every revolution must turn to force over the law—and of Stalin's "dialectic" theory (now loudly denounced) that as the country advanced toward socialism, class war and repression must intensify. Besides, the discourses on legal theory did not explain how class justice was *applied*, and I was not convinced that the concept was inherently pernicious. Injustice can be administered in the name of any theory of law; it has been, and is, by governments and men who talk of the universality, immutability and sanctity of law under God. "Absolute justice" can be a dangerous ideology too, nicely suited to justifying wrongs in the name of higher goods.

What is more, class justice had been abandoned! This was a recent development: the dictatorship of the proletariat was declared superseded by an "All-People's State" and an "All-People's Law" in 1961. "With the final victory of socialism, the conditions requiring the Dictatorship of the Proletariat disappeared entirely. There are no antagonistic classes, or even elements, in Soviet society, no segment of society which must be restrained, and therefore no reasons whatsoever for a dictatorship of one part of the harmonious Soviet population over any other. The proletariat is now juridically equal to all other strata of the population. The Soviet state represents and defends the interests of all Soviet citizens identically and equally; Soviet law provides for no preferences whatsoever. All are equal before the law. This is the highest development of democracy ever attained by man."

It was a recent development, but inevitable; Soviet law has gradually, if unevenly under Stalin, been moving toward "classlessness" since 1917. For class justice has no place in a classless society; the very success of the revolution and of building socialism doomed the dictatorship of the proletariat. The half-life of "revolutionary" and "class" law is inversely proportional to the progress of the regime toward its goals, and when the antagonistic classes have disappeared and no one is left to suppress, the *raison d'être* of class justice disappears. It made no sense to talk about the suppression of the bourgeoisie after the bourgeoisie had long since been eliminated from the social scene—and less sense still (Soviet courts had stopped this decades ago) for a judge to favor a worker over, say, the director of his factory, a *Soviet* engineer, the product of Soviet education and incentives. Otherwise, who would become the directors?

The crucial difference between socialist law and bourgeois law, Soviet theory now explains, is that the former is *classless*, while the latter continues to serve a single, owning class. The canon has come full circle.

I could say much more about the Soviet theory of law but I am not sure that it would help anyone picture a Soviet court. One fact helped me cut through the ideological haze: that the single central movement in legal practice since 1917 had been a steady development toward West European traditions. Soviet writers had always proclaimed their law to be something entirely new, better than, "higher" than, in every way diametrically opposed to, bourgeois law; but the laws themselves—the codes, the crimes, the articles—were mostly repetitions of bourgeois laws, of the tsarist norms in fact, which borrowed from the German and French codes. In the end, the Party wound up with a system which operated much like Western ones. Almost all of the legal paraphernalia were patterned after European models; more important, the very concept of legality based on statutory norms, prescribed procedure and nonarbitrary, impartial decisions was common to East and West. Statutes, evidence, codes, terminology, procedures, norms, institutions, principles—all these, in the everyday cases, were used in a familiar way. Soviet lawyers had become lawyers as I understood them; judges, judges; and courts, courts.

How Soviet jurists replaced talk of the "withering-away" of the law under socialism with arguments that its "greatest flowering" takes place only under socialism makes a fascinating story. It has, too, a labyrinthian plot, but the principal point is that they had come full circle again. From contempt of law —law in general, as well as bourgeois law specifically—Soviet writers had swung around to admiration. "Socialism alone develops the law fully and permits a genuine respect for legality."

Introduction

It came, then, to this: similar procedures and similar laws, and Marxism reduced largely to *saying* that socialist legality differs entirely from bourgeois because under socialism the factories are owned in common.

That, anyway, is what I knew and assumed as that cold, crowded bus rattled into town, and that is why I felt one ought to take a look at socialist legality and judge it by his own standards. These remarks are an introduction less to Soviet law than to my preconceptions about it; at least I was not looking for the worst. Now, at last, I had the chance to explore, to look over the top of the iceberg, if only to help speculate about what lay underneath; to hear the judge's voice and watch the defendant's face; to see the dossiers and talk with the lawyers; to try to find out by looking and listening— not reading—what is meant by "justice" in Moscow.

The courthouse that I was visiting was a sagging two-story wooden structure, once—well before the Revolution—the showy home of a merchant. Somehow it had survived from the days of wooden Moscow. A weatherworn plaque at the entrance read "Ministry of Justice, Russian Soviet Federated Socialist Republic, People's Court, Kropotkinskii District." Everything was startlingly homespun.

I went inside to find an ordinary case.

Part One

THE
PEOPLE'S
COURTS

I

The Average

THE ROOM IS Number 7 in the rear, small and square and shabby; layers of paint have petrified the look of fatigue. Perhaps the merchant's daughters slept in this part of the house, but it is hard now to picture it gay. The walls are faded, the wood is worn, and three bare bulbs harden the stale gloom. Only the portrait masters the drabness—above the dais a smiling-frowning likeness of Lenin, challenging the living. It is the young Lenin, eager and confident, in a stylish suit; probably he had not long before won his law degree from a reluctant tsarist examiner. Grayed chips of plaster reach out from where the nail has been banged into the wall. From the office next door—someone has forgotten to close the door—a telephone jangles unanswered.

"Defendant, we are waiting. The court is waiting to hear how you explain your unsatisfactory performance as a worker."

He is standing in the dock, heavy, rough hands behind his back, shaking his head slowly, looking up plaintively at the disapproving judge, and again at his feet. He does not answer.

"I repeat, how do you explain your record? You misbehaved, you systematically violated work discipline. Why? You were a burden to the administration and your fellow workers. What prompted you to act that way?"

No answer. He looks away; he does not want to begin.

The judge clears her throat, flips the pages of the record and finds her place with a stout finger. She is prim and plump, a schoolteacherish woman over forty, a matron in shapeless dress, with rimless glasses and hair combed back into a tight bun.

"Have you been reprimanded for truancy at the factory?"

"Yes."

"Absent from work with no good reason—that is your attitude toward your work, toward your responsibilities. And rebukes for appearing drunk in the factory—did you get any of these?"

He does not answer.

"*Did* you?"

"I think . . . well, yes."

"How many?"

"I don't know. I don't remember."

"Four?"

"Maybe. I didn't count. Sometimes it was on a holiday, when everybody was drunk."

"Four reprimands! That's an unheard-of attitude toward work and life in our socialist society. Disgraceful! It started with disinterest in work; then drinking and hooliganism—and led from that to stealing; of course it led to stealing, naturally to stealing—do you understand that? Why were you repeatedly late? Why did you continue to violate work discipline in spite of your warnings? You ignored them. You drank on the job. You were truant. And then you stole. Logical."

"I . . . never drank on the job."

"You came to work drunk; it's the same thing. You knew that you may not appear on the job in a drunken condition. Your attitude is quite clear."

He shakes his head again and looks away, sunk in resignation. But then he glances at a woman in the rear of the room who is nervously clasping a swaddled infant in her arms, and a smile makes quick, deep wrinkles in his cheeks. The woman, apparently his wife, tries to smile back.

"I don't consider myself a bad worker. Not worse than average; I've a decent record. You're just collecting all my sins."

"You have a record of consistent violation of discipline and have had plenty of opportunity to pull yourself together. Evidently you are not interested in leading an honest life as a Soviet worker."

"I admit I was wrong. I'm sorry. But all I did before was to drink sometimes. I admit that; I'm not perfect."

"But don't you see where that drinking led you? And the ignoring of the warnings—your attitude? Do you understand that now? That's what this court wants to know."

In the early stages of the trial the court seeks what it wants to know in this dialogue. Judge and defendant have a talk. The judge works almost singlehandedly; other voices rarely intrude. The other members of the court, known as lay assessors —in this case they are an abstracted, mousy young woman and a tieless, frayed man of middle age—shift uncomfortably in their unaccustomed high-backed chairs. The relatives and spectators, bundled up in overcoats and babushkas in spite of the suffocating heat of the room, look on with noises of protest, resignation or despair. The pretty young secretary looks at nothing and does not cover her yawns. No prosecutor or defense counsel has appeared; the case is too unimportant and too simple. Eleven persons in all are present, plus two ham-faced policemen in huge blue greatcoats alongside the dock.

As the judge and the defendant have their talk, the story— the plea, the protest, the excuse, the explanation, the denial, the confirmation, the confession, the appeal—spills out in words as simple as the setting.

"You did not intend to take the galoshes? Strange. What *did* you intend? How did they get under your coat?"

"I don't remember, I was drunk. I just know I didn't mean to steal."

"We are not here to listen to what you intended. Are you going to deny now that the galoshes were found concealed under your coat?"

"No. I must have done it. I just don't know why. I never stole anything before in my life."

"Never stole anything, or never was caught? Well, let's start from the beginning again. Exactly what time did you get to work?"

"At about eleven-thirty P.M.; I was on the night shift."

"You arrived drunk?"

"I must have been fairly high."

"So you knowingly, willfully broke the rules, in spite of all previous warnings . . ."

This was the average of averages. The charge was violation of Article 96: Petty Theft of State Property. A pair of woman's rubber boots; they sold for four rubles and sixty kopeks* in the stores.

I saw about fifty such cases in all, and this one was closest to the common denominator among them. The excuses of the defendant, the didacticism of the judge, the slow movement toward an inevitable end, made those two hours typical of those that occupy the People's Courts, Monday through Saturday in Moscow. I would like to describe it, therefore, in some detail and as carefully as possible. For this is what I was

* Sums in rubles will appear often in this account; I have not rendered the dollar equivalents because there is no sure way of doing it. The official exchange—the Soviet government's exchange—is: one ruble = $1.11. International and domestic black markets value the ruble at from one third to one fifth of that. What a ruble is *worth* in Moscow is a tricky business too, because a respectable pair of leather shoes costs 50, and a respectable apartment 8 per month. A skilled worker earns about 100 per month; a fine restaurant meal costs 3 or 4. All in all, I used to think of a ruble as *about* a dollar, remembering that they were much less easy to come by. There are 100 kopeks to the ruble.

looking for on the hard wooden benches in those dusty rooms.

An air of informality prevails from the start. The little blue card at the door indicates the trial will start at 1 P.M.; at 1:25 three of the witnesses have not arrived. Those who have come chat distractedly and wait, as Russians are used to waiting. A secretary, lips reddened and young voice already thickened with *burokratism,* bellows the roll; the others pay her no mind. Without the high-backed chairs embellished by crumbling Soviet emblems, they might be waiting for the milk train in a provincial station.

At last, a man in worker's garb—rumpled jacket far too short in the sleeves, faded flannel shirt—is marched down the corridor and into the dock by two booted policemen to the directions of a third. A tall, gaunt, wordless man, probably blond; his features look too large against a shaved head. He sits behind the railing against the wall and looks out the double window.

Some time later the court appears unannounced: three ordinary citizens in ordinary office-drab dress, and before everyone understands that he is to get to his feet they are in their places on the dais and the case has started, without a hint of flourish. No costuming or ceremony, no magic words or mystery; the judge slips on her glasses and opens the dossier. "The People's Court of Kropotkinskii District is in session. The case of Kondakov will be heard."

The first few items of routine are quickly completed. The participants are identified, the witnesses are sent to wait their turns in the corridor, and the judge is at her accustomed work.

"Defendant, stand. Your name?"

"Kondakov."

"Christian name and patronymic?"

"Vyacheslav Sergeyevich."

"Date of birth?"

"August 14, 1933."

"Nationality?"

"Russian."

"Education?"

"Eight classes [of primary school]."

"*Partiinost* [Party affiliation]?"

"*Bezpartiinii* [Not a member of the Communist Party]."

"Married?"

"Yes."

"Children?"

"A daughter, five months."

"Occupation and place of work?"

"I'm a stitcher in a factory, the Red Hero."

"You earn?"

"Eighty rubles [per month]."

"Ever convicted before?"

"No."

"No criminal convictions whatsoever?"

"None."

"But you were sentenced for petty hooliganism."

"Yes."

"How many times?"

"Once."

"And that was when?"

"About a year and a half ago."

"May 25, 1961? Drunk and disorderly in the metro?"

"I think so."

"When were you arrested on the present charge?"

"October 12."

"And received a copy of the indictment?"

"I don't remember. A few days ago."

"December 16?"

"Yes."

Soviet trials begin with a short biography of the accused—

his "introduction" to the court. A Russian judge would think it silly to deal with Ivan Ivanov, a stranger off the street. Who is this fellow? What is his record at work? In the courts? What about his personal and family background? And so, information about the character and history of the defendant—information which is usually kept secret in English and American courts until guilt or innocence has been decided—is sought and aired at the outset.

"Kondakov, you are the accused in this case. As the accused, you have the right to make explanations concerning the accusation against you, to present evidence, submit petitions, participate in the hearing, challenge the composition of the court, and appeal its actions and decisions. You have, also, the right to the last word. Are these rights clear to you?"

"Clear."

"You entrust the present members of the court to hear your case?"

"Of course."

"Have you any requests at this time?"

"What kind of requests?"

"Anything to ask of the court?"

"I do. I ask the court to call Shisko and Vorabiova. They know me from the factory, they can tell how I worked on the shift. The investigator questioned them, but they're not on the list of witnesses. . . ."

"You saw the list. Why didn't you request this earlier?"

"I didn't think it was important."

"Well, you *ought* to have thought." The judge pauses. "The court will postpone decision until after the other witnesses are heard. If necessary, we will call them later."

". . . under his coat and excused himself, saying that he was going to the bathroom. The galoshes made an unusual

35

bulge, attracting the attention of the guard. Kondakov was stopped and . . ."

"He was very drunk, to the extent that his speech was impaired. He has a record of such intoxication at the factory; he has been reprimanded repeatedly for . . ."

"According to the witness Markova, Kondakov left the shop at about three A.M. Several minutes later she saw him in the stitching room; a pair of black, woman's galoshes had just been removed from . . ." This was confirmed by witnesses Stonkov, Delyenko and Kaminskaya, who also testified that . . ."

"Kondakov himself at first denied that he had hidden anything under his coat, and later denied an intention to steal, but the accusation is proved beyond doubt by . . ."

". . . that is, actions proscribed by Article Ninety-six, Paragraph One of the criminal code of the Russian Soviet Federated . . ."

The judge has proceeded to a reading of the indictment, and although she reads rapidly, it takes her a full five minutes. For the indictment in Soviet procedure is so detailed and so seemingly accurate and complete—so *long*—that there seems little left to be heard afterward. It is not merely an accusation, but a detailed, repetitious account of the crime as reconstructed by the investigation, a summary of the testimony of each witness called, a résumé of the defendant's "explanation," a description of his personality and the relationship of the crime to his past behavior, and a juridical qualification of the acts charged under the code. The indictment tells the story and sets the tone—and leaves little to the imagination or to suspense.

Stripped to the plot—which it repeats seven times—it is a simple charge. On the night of October 11–12, Kondakov reported for work drunk, behaved suspiciously, excused himself to go to the toilet and was stopped by the guard at the gate with a pair of finished boots stuffed awkwardly under his jacket. The guard called the foreman; the foreman, the police. Kondakov had no excuse.

"Defendant, stand. Do you understand the charges against you?"

"I understand."

"Do you admit your guilt?"

"I . . . suppose so. Yes, I admit my guilt."

"Tell the court exactly what happened that night—everything you know."

"Comrade Judges, what can I say? I don't remember much about it. I guess I took the galoshes, I don't know why. I had too much to drink, I suppose; it was my wife's birthday, we've been married three years. We observed the occasion; had some friends over, you know—a little celebration. I guess we celebrated too much."

"What were you drinking?"

"Vodka. Wine."

"How much?"

"Not very much. I don't remember. A few glasses of vodka, a few of wine."

"I can imagine. Go on, what happened then? Were you very drunk?"

"I didn't think so; a little bit high. But maybe I was. Well, I was at my place, stitching; we were working hard on the winter stuff. Then I had to relieve myself and—well, you know the rest. I don't remember anything about it, I have no idea what the galoshes were doing there. I was on my way to the toilet and the guard took my arm and they found this pair of woman's galoshes I was carrying. I honestly don't know to where. 'What have you got under your coat?' he said; I thought he was joking. Honestly, Comrade Judges. This is very shameful to me; I've never stolen a thing in my life. I ask the court to forgive me, I had no intention at all to steal. It's not true that I resisted efforts to stop me."

"So you admit that you were taking the galoshes out under your coat?"

"Yes, I must have done it."

"Then why did you deny it when you were stopped?"

"I don't know . . . I don't remember. Perhaps I really didn't know they were there."

"Then why did you try to run away?"

"I . . . don't know."

"You don't know? Do you know that it is wrong to take for yourself the fruits of your collective's labor? Do you know that that is stealing?"

"Of course I do."

"And what do you think about it, about the way you behaved?"

"It was very wrong."

"Yes, we agree. Very wrong. With whom were you operating—to steal footwear?"

"Not with anyone. You don't understand, this was a mistake, an accident."

"Are you sure? We have had a lot of trouble lately at the Red Hero; a lot of shoes have been missing." The judge's voice is professionally dry.

"It was absolutely unplanned."

"What did you intend doing with the galoshes afterward?"

"I didn't intend anything. Honest, I'm telling you."

"Then why did you take them? The court wants to hear your explanation."

Kondakov hangs his head; he does not answer. The judge, squinting, peers steadily at him through her glasses. The assessors look faintly ashamed.

"*Why did you steal?*"

"I was drunk, that's all; I didn't know what I was doing."

"Were things difficult for you? Did you live badly?"

"I lived O.K.—like everyone else."

"You earned eighty rubles; not bad. And your wife? Where

does she work? What does she earn?"

"About the same—ninety rubles. She's a bookkeeper."

"So you were not suffering. Life was not bad for you. Was it necessary for you to steal? *What did you lack?* Did you lack something? What was your *reason?*"

In this vein, inquisition continues. Not about the galoshes; that is known from the first. About other things—the drinking (one of the neighbors had revealed during the investigation that Kondakov was sometimes tipsy in the apartment); about the affair in the metro eighteen months before; about language (several witnesses had said that he was free with strong words) —about the "whole man."

But one part of the whole is given special attention.

"How long have you worked at the Red Hero?"

"Just over a year."

"And before that?"

"I had a number of jobs."

"A number of jobs? You had four in three years, is that correct?"

"Yes."

"Why such an unsatisfactory record?"

"No reason. I didn't plan it. I just couldn't find a job to suit me."

"That's not right. What about the job at Mosstroi? You were fired from that job, is that correct?"

"Well, technically I was fired. It wasn't my fault."

"What was the reason?"

"My foreman didn't like me. We didn't get along. It was personal."

"Not according to the record. You were fired for drunkenness and absences, isn't that the case? You were warned several times, then fired when you didn't show up for three days."

No answer.

"That was in May 1961. And your next job was at the Red Hero, which you took in September. Is that correct?"

"I think so."

"For four months you were without a job? You did nothing?"

"Well no, not nothing. I had odd jobs. And we had a place in the country—I worked on the vegetable garden."

"Four months without a job. Doing nothing, living off others. A parasite. And that's the way you treat your obligations as a Soviet citizen; no interest at all in your work. A man without a job is a man without a soul. No wonder you stole, it was just another step, with that attitude. Don't you understand that a man needs a steady job—for his own sake, not only for others? Or are you interested only in vodka? Where did you get the money for all that drinking when you had no job?"

"I didn't drink that much, you are exaggerating. You are blowing everything up. I drink average. Not so much at all. Average."

After Kondakov, the witnesses are called. "You must tell the court only the truth. If you give untruthful testimony, you will be criminally responsible; the punishment may be deprivation of freedom. Sign this paper indicating that you have been warned . . ."

In Anglo-Saxon law, the case would have ended with Kondakov's admission of guilt; in fact, the great majority of such cases end this way. But the great majority of Soviet trials *begin* with "I admit my guilt"; for here it is not a plea, but merely an answer, and it does not relieve the prosecution of the obligation to present further proof. It is a humane rule, for it protects against false confession. And it is an essential one for a court concerned as much with repentance and reform as with retribution.

The witnesses testify from the rickety, three-sided, almost-black wooden box near the center of the room. Their testimony seems superfluous; everyone knows what they will say. The judge knows; the record of the preliminary investigation is in her hands. Kondakov knows; he has read the record. Even the spectators know; they have heard the substance of the testimony in the indictment. Excitement at a Moscow trial is like excitement on a roller coaster: the real suspense is repetition. The witnesses confirm, they do not report. Sometimes a witness forgets, sometimes he adds new details. But rarely—very rarely—does he produce evidence not expected of him.

The defendant was caught in the act. When the old guard spied and stopped him, Kondakov was finished. Everyone saw the galoshes and heard the stammering excuses. Three fellow workers are called, in addition to the watchman and the foreman, to confirm the story.

"Tell us all you know about this case. . . ."

One by one they describe the incident: Kondakov drunk, acting strangely, leaving for the toilet, with the bulge in his coat, denying, admitting, protesting . . . The evidence is overwhelming; the repetition wearying.

The fourth witness is Polyanskaya, Vera Petrovna, a slight girl in her early twenties who stands easily in the box, with her hands in the pockets of her overcoat.

"What do you remember about this case? Tell the court everything you know."

"What do I remember? Not very much. I remember it happened on the night shift, sometime in early October—"

"The night of October 11–12?"

"That's right. Kondakov"—she glances in his direction and smiles at him—"arrived about twenty minutes late for work. It was quite clear that he had been drinking. He was pretty drunk. He kept on getting up from his table—I worked next to him—and singing the first stanzas of folk songs. And getting up to congratulate us, I don't know for what. Ordinarily he is a quiet sort.

"Well, at about three-thirty he announced loudly that he was going to the bathroom. Of course, I paid no attention. But a few minutes later there was a commotion in the next shop. Everyone ran out—I did too. There he was with the galoshes. He had stuffed them under his coat and the guard noticed it. Well, that's all I know. The police came and took him away. He seemed confused. Embarrassed. He kept saying, 'I never stole a thing in my life.' "

"Did he swear?"

"Not while I was there. He just muttered to himself, sort of."

"Was he stealing shoes before this incident?"

"I don't know, I have no idea. I don't think so."

"Why do you think he committed this act?"

"I haven't the faintest idea. He was quite drunk."

"But not so drunk that he didn't know he was stealing?"

"I can't say. I don't think so."

"Was he often drunk at work?"

"Not often."

"But he *has* been drunk; did you know he was warned about that?"

"Yes, I knew."

"What can you tell us about his character?"

"He was all right. Decent. I never had any unpleasantness with him."

"But you know that he had 'unpleasantness' with the administration."

"Yes."

"Did you know that he was fired from other jobs and arrested for petty hooliganism?"

"No."

"You didn't know that. Perhaps you ought to have interested yourself in your neighbor. Well, what kind of man was he at work? Did you expect that he might steal? What can you say about his working habits?"

"He wasn't a bad worker. Or unusually good, either. He did his share. I'd call him normal."

"You mean that a normal worker is late and absent and drunk on the job?"

"Uh, he worked well—"

"Worked well! He *stole* well. What about the reprimands he kept getting?"

"During the last couple of months, he worked very hard. I don't think he had any reprimands."

"If you don't count thieving."

"I think he was trying to—"

"Such people have got to be taken under control, they have got to be shown. He drinks, he fails to appear at work, he creates scandals—and now look where he ended. The logical end; he didn't want to heed the warnings. Well, we have a job to do: the people of Moscow need shoes and the Red Hero is trying to supply them. We don't have to put up with people who deliberately stand in the way."

The judge puts back her glasses.

"Now is there anything else you would like to add? Can you tell us anything more about his intentions?"

"I don't know anything more. It was a surprise to me."

The judge turns to the assessors. "Have you any questions?"

They shake their heads, No.

"Does the defendant want to question the witness?"

Kondakov has no questions.

There is no defense in the special sense of the word. No one to pick at the flaws in the indictment, to discover the escapes, to suggest that Kondakov had intended to return the galoshes, to ridicule the idea that a man would intentionally take an almost worthless pair of boots, to break down the guard's story, to argue that the procurator had classified the crime under too drastic an article of the code. Even had a lawyer been present, these tactics probably would not have been used, for when facts seem obvious in a Moscow court, they are usually taken as such. In a way, the judge herself represents the defense, for even though most of her questions point in the other direction, she does make clear that Kondakov served honorably for three years in the Soviet Army and that he did social work in his apartment house.

The accused too has a turn at questioning each witness (he may do it even when a lawyer defends him) and Kondakov makes greater use of his right than most defendants.

"Do *you* think I intended to steal? . . . Would *you* call me a bad worker? . . . It isn't true that I deliberately ignored warnings, why do you say that to the court?"

And when the last witness is testifying, there is help from another, unexpected source. A voice in tears breaks into the questioning. "You are twisting everything to the worst. He is a good man, not a thief."

It is Kondakov's wife, round and red-faced, looking ten years older than he, rocking her infant while she sobs. The judge demands silence—"This is a court!"—but when she does not get it, she listens without interrupting. The trial stops for the stricken woman's plea.

"It's not fair. I tell you it's not fair. It is my fault. It was my birthday, I arranged the evening, I poured him his vodka. He didn't mean to get drunk, he didn't mean anything wrong. He is an honest man. He gives me all his wages. And the child —what are we to do now? He is a good man, and you are making of him a thief, an ordinary criminal. Why are you doing that to him?"

The judge waits until the woman, sobbing, ends her plea.

"Defendant, you have heard the testimony. Have you anything to add to it before your last word?" The judge's voice softens again, but remains detached. No play of emotions between confessant and confessor; this is her job, she has handled hundreds of cases like this before, and there is another one scheduled for late afternoon.

"I would like to say that I did not intend to steal, I don't understand myself why I did it. I've tried, at least, to be an honest man."

"An honest man does not put galoshes under his coat. Well, enough. What will you say as your last word?"

There is a short pause which seems long. Kondakov looks up at the judge, but she keeps her gaze now to the record book.

"Comrade Judges, what can I say? I committed a serious crime, of course, I fully understand that now. But I ask the court to remember my family—my daughter. Let me redeem myself! Let me show that I can work honestly and be a useful member of society. This will never happen again. I ask the court not to deprive me of my freedom."

The judge has closed the record book and is on the edge of her chair. "Is that all?"

"Yes."

And the court steps out quickly to deliberate, as unceremoniously as it entered.

The hearing lasted not quite an hour. Then there is half an hour of waiting, of strong cigarettes puffed in resignation rather than anxiety, before the defendant is marched back to his place and the court takes theirs.

"The sentence is announced. In the name of the Russian Soviet Federated Socialist Republic, on December 20, 1962, People's Court, Kropotkinskii District, People's Judge Volochova presiding in association with People's Assessors Kuptsov and Sidorenko, heard the case of Kondakov, Vyacheslav Sergeyevich, twenty-nine, Russian, *Bezpartiinii*, married, with eight years of education, living at . . ."

The details of identification once more, exaggeratedly precise.

And the story again, too, a final time, hardly changed from the wording of the indictment. Again intoxication, strange behavior, the toilet, the coat, the bulge and discovery, the galoshes, the record of tardiness, absences and drunkenness, the ignoring of warnings . . . "Kondakov denied an intention to steal, but according to witness Markova, who said . . . and Polyanskaya, who testified . . . and T. and Zh., who confirmed . . . The court considers the accusation fully proved, considers that Kondakov concealed the galoshes intending to steal them, considers the qualification correct under Article Ninety-six, Paragraph One, considers . . ."

Kondakov, at last, is guilty.

"In determining measures of punishment, the court took into consideration a history of unsatisfactory attitudes toward work and responsibilities as a citizen, and also the absence of previous criminal convictions . . ."

The sentence is one year in a labor colony.

At the worst moment, Kondakov, still calm and awkward, still somehow impervious to his misfortune, looks at the windows. The judge finishes quickly and does not look at him again, but the assessors cannot refrain from staring.

"Kondakov, is the sentence clear to you?"

"It is clear."

"You have seven days in which to appeal . . ."

And it is over. The court is through with him; as if in a hurry now, it leaves the dais hastily. Kondakov is again the ward of the police. A year for a pair of galoshes. His wife rushes to him and he kisses her before he is led away; and as he is marched down the corridor from where he came, he orders her not to worry about him.

II

Ten Days' Normal Fare

In capitalist society the court was primarily an apparatus of oppression, an apparatus of bourgeois exploitation. Therefore, it was beyond any question an obligation of the proletarian revolution not to reform court institutions . . . but to destroy them completely, to sweep away the old court and its apparatus to the foundations. The October Revolution fulfilled this task, and fulfilled it successfully. In place of the old court, it began to create the new people's courts . . ."   —VLADIMIR I. LENIN

Truth is straight, but judges are crooked.
Fear not the law but the judge.

              —OLD RUSSIAN PROVERBS

I BEGAN an unhurried, unguided tour of the People's Courts, bottom rung in the Soviet judicial hierarchy. To the great mass of Russian people, the Law means the People's Courts, for almost all civil and criminal cases are heard here first. Here, where the printed words on the page—the articles of the code, the rules of socialist behavior—are translated into terms of human conduct, where the living law is germinated.

There are seventeen People's Courts in Moscow, one to

each city district: Kalininskii, Leninskii, Oktyabrskii, Kirov-skii, Dzerzhinskii, Moskvoretskii, Krasnopresnenskii, Pervo-maiskii. . . . The courthouses are scattered about town in buildings of every sort. Most of them, however, are worn and dry, mournful and bare. They reminded me of the ancient, soulless city hall in the town where I grew up: no comfort anywhere to mitigate the civic gloom.

Each court has eight to twelve judges—"People's Judges" —and a "chairman" in charge. The judges have a courtroom more or less permanently assigned to them and, adjacent, a tiny, sparsely furnished office which serves as chambers, lunchroom, deliberating room and, for some intimate personal cases, courtroom. Somewhere in the building is a larger office for the court as a whole, dealing in the inevitable exaspera-tions of petty bureaucracy. Somewhere sits a duty lawyer on watch, offering on-the-spot consultations for a trifling fee.

Here, in these plainest of settings, the coating of mystery, enigma and mumbo jumbo surrounding the law dissolves, leav-ing the commonplace.

The corridors of all the People's Courts offer similar joyless scenes. A crowd, made up of quiet couples waiting their turns, bunches outside the room in which suits for divorce are being heard. Police lead defendants, heads bowed and hands clasped always behind their backs, to and from their trials. Inquisitive time-wasters open doors, peek in, search for a good case. Wit-nesses pass around cigarettes and the morning's *Pravda*. Rela-tives—mostly older, black-clothed, wrinkled relatives—wait out the writing of verdicts. Lawyers between cases prepare their next speech, or answer queries of prospective clients. A queue forms haphazardly to see the judge, who is giving con-sultations about alimony, the necessary papers, the procedure for appeal, the insults of a neighbor or a foreman.

Opening a door along one hallway, I would come upon a

typical scene. The first impression of a court in session was of drabness and routine; had I been seeking sensation, I would have left soon. I stayed a long time, however, even after my understanding of trial procedure was clear, for here was exposure to Soviet working-class life that a foreigner can get nowhere else. Here was detailed scrutiny of life in a country where such material is not much publicized.

Behind a door picked at random, the case on trial was likely to be minor, one I had seen many times before. For there is no summary procedure in Soviet criminal law, and the simplest cases are tried under the same general rules of procedure as the most serious and complex. The People's Judge—who is more often than not a woman—would be questioning the defendant or a witness in tones that reached the back of the room as a drone. The lay assessors would simply be in attendance, like bodyguards for the judge. The court secretary, often a fresh young girl just out of school, would be jotting down essential facts at a desk alongside the judge's bench. A small, dark group of spectators smelling of pomade, strong tobacco and uncleaned wool—mostly the family and friends of the parties involved—would be listening glumly, whispering their comments and sometimes shouting them to the bench. The door would creak as stray spectators or extra policemen would wander in or out.

Probably there would be no procurator, for he, the Moscow equivalent of an American district attorney, is overworked and cannot afford to assign his men and women to minor trials. (Or, as a procurator explained to me, he does not want to—for the law requires that when a procurator prosecutes, the accused *must* be represented by counsel, and "dragging a lawyer in makes unnecessary difficulty for everyone; it is better to keep him out, to keep a simple case simple.") More often there would be a defense counsel, for defendants *may* be represented whether or not the procurator attends, and Muscovites seem to value representation, even when the facts are obvious.

Sometimes the accused would be in the dock, watched by a surprising number of policemen. His head is shaved (in accordance with Russian prison rules), and in all respects he is a marked man, silly- or sad-looking. Among certain middle-aged Russian men a shaved head is still a mark of fashion, but for prisoners it is humiliating, a badge of guilt which keeps the head hung low. Sometimes, if he has not been taken into custody but has appeared at the trial still a free man, the defendant may sit in the first row of public benches and testify from his place.

In the first weeks, I was surprised by the informality, the lack of legal phraseology, of practiced, self-conscious precision, of esoteric procedural niceties and devotion to form. Much has changed since the early years of Soviet rule, when judges drew upon their "revolutionary consciousness" as the new law. But something of that amateur spirit has remained. A Soviet trial is informal by any standards; there is nothing a layman cannot understand. The rules of the game (or compulsions of the ritual) are not treasured like intricate, ancient plumage. What the people in court have to say is more important than how they must say it. In the trials that I observed, when an interested observer had some relevant information to give, he gave it, even if it would have been inadmissible as evidence in a foreign court and even if he was not, at the moment, in the witness stand.

As time went on, I sensed a lack of excitement and suspense—though not a lack of drama and emotion. There was a matter-of-factness, an everydayness, a quiet sadness, a weariness. All issues seemed to move, very slowly, to their fated ends, and the sameness of the cases and the repetitiousness of the "story" compounded the feeling of *déjà vu*. Heard once, the events sounded like a crime, but like fiction; heard ten times at each trial, through a hundred trials, they became heavy with some sort of personal meaning—inevitable, inexorable, confessional.

I was reminded in these courts of what I had read and seen of peasant Russia—of strength, simplicity and endurance; of human tragedy, official severity and personal compassion. For the People's Courts are enclaves of old Moscow, tucked away among the modern, optimistic façade of the new capital.

People's Court, Dzerzhinskii District. The courthouse is the second and third floors of a narrow old office building on Srentenka, a busy central shopping street. Its façade is nineteenth-century Russian classical, the pasty-yellow plaster surface of most of downtown Moscow. The interior is dark and in need of paint. Just inside the entrance is a red banner with an inscription lettered in white: "THE TINIEST ILLEGALITY, THE TINIEST VIOLATION OF THE SOVIET LEGAL ORDER IS A CHINK WHICH IS IMMEDIATELY USED BY THE ENEMIES OF THE TOILERS. —V. I. LENIN." A tinted portrait of Lenin hangs in every room.

Open a door along one of the corridors . . . I am selecting from ten days' normal fare.

*Article 144: Theft.** The accused is a muscular young man,

---

* The articles are those of the Criminal Code of the Russian Soviet Federated Socialist Republic—Russia. Soviet criminal and civil law falls under the jurisdiction of the constituent Republics, and each of the fifteen—Russia, Ukraine, Georgia, Estonia, Moldavia, Armenia, Kazakhstan, Uzbekistan, et cetera—legislate their own codes.

These fifteen codes vary only slightly, however, because they all conform to general principles established by the central, All-Union government. The federal principles, called "Fundamentals," settle all major problems of criminal theory and outline the law in considerable detail; the Republics are left to fill in the gaps and adjust for local peculiarities. This is the way balance between local and national interests is sought.

The current Fundamentals were enacted by the Supreme Soviet of the Union in 1958; the Russian code by the Supreme Soviet of the Russian Republic in 1960.

As it affects the courts, Soviet federalism is far less confusing than born in Moscow but, like so many, reeking of peasant ancestry. He has admitted stealing a *papakha* (a tall fur hat popular in winter), which had been lying on the seat next to his, late one evening in the metro. Next to it, dozing, had been a hatless man, obviously the owner. This man, the complainant, works for the K.G.B. [secret police].

"What do you do there, if it is not a secret?" the judge asks. "Do not tell us anything you shouldn't."

"I am a driver. I don't know *anything* secret."

The accused has been convicted of crimes twice before, for hooliganism and for theft of a watch.

"Now this is the third time, Solovyev. What's it all about? What are you doing with your life? Do you want to be a common criminal? That's where you're headed, you know."

No answer.

"What is your explanation, if you please?"

No answer.

"I don't understand. You know there is nothing romantic about this—you know jail. Do you like it there?"

An answer is formed but not spoken.

"Now look, you are a trained worker, you were taught a trade valuable to Soviet society, you have a decent income; your mother and father are both on pension. *How do you explain this thing?* Were things difficult for you? I would like to understand what made you steal again. I cannot. *Why?*"

"I did it, I told you that, I admit I took it. I already told you everything." The youth half whines, half defies.

"I'm trying to find out *why*."

"I . . . didn't know it was his hat."

"Why didn't you ask? Why just take it?"

American. The court structure resembles a simple pyramid, local arrangements moving up to national. There cannot be any conflict between national and state law in a given territory, nor any conflict of jurisdiction. Organizationally, it is a simple, logical system.

"I don't know. I didn't know who to ask. I thought . . ."

"In February, a man walking around with a bare head, and on the seat next to him an unattached hat. Nonsense! Do you think anyone is going to believe that?"

"It's not so strange. There are lots of people without hats. *I* don't always wear one."

"Maybe you'll think this over a minute and tell the court what really happened. Don't think I'm talking you into anything. But if you have made mistakes in life you yourself must be the first to recognize them; then things will go better for you."

Solovyev winces. "I didn't intend to steal it."

"But it's still theft. When you take someone else's things without asking, that is theft. Do you understand that?"

"I understand . . . but I wasn't trying to steal."

"What *were* you trying to do? For heaven's sake, isn't it the normal thing to ask before you walk off with a hat that belongs to someone else? What did you have in mind?"

"I don't know. I really don't know what I had in mind. I just did it."

"Come on, tell us now. What were your motives? We want to hear what you were thinking in that metro."

"I wasn't thinking anything. I just picked up the *papakha* when I came to my station and . . ."

"You *stole* the *papakha*. Look, Solovyev, I want to hear one thing from you. When you take a hat from a seat without asking, do you understand that that is a *crime*, that you are stealing?"

"Yes, I do understand."

A second lesson remains to be taught. It turns out that the young man, a lathe operator, had not been working for some ten weeks before the incident. He had quit his job, drifted around, gone to movies, met his buddies in the park, done odd jobs, drunk in the afternoons and evenings, and lived principally on doles from his parents. Hearing this confirmed by the offender, the judge berates him.

"How could you permit yourself to go for weeks without work? Why did you quit? Why didn't you get a new job? Where is your honor as a Soviet citizen? How could you, a healthy young man with strong hands and an honest profession, refuse to work, disregard your civic duty for the sake of loafing? Aren't you ashamed of yourself? Do you understand how wastefully and decadently you spent your time? Do you understand that there is a direct correlation between not working—the idle hours, the drinking, the loss of self-respect—and the crime? What right have you to expect the support of society without your support of it?"

Solovyev seems indifferent. He replies in words of one syllable.

"And how do you regard your actions now? What can you say about the way you behaved?"

"Not very good."

"That's all? 'Not very good'?"

"Terrible."

In appointing punishment, the court takes into consideration the defendant's disrespect for his obligations as a citizen as evidenced by his unwillingness to work. The sentence is one year in a labor colony, normal regime.

Article 211: Reckless Driving by a Professional Driver. The defendant, thirty-two, clean-cut, Driver Third Class, bounced the factory's *pik-ap* ("pickup truck") over a curb one icy February evening, slightly injuring two schoolgirls who had been playing in the snow. He had been rushing home from work "terribly upset" by a telephone call informing him that his brother, a tuberculosis victim, had been taken to the hospital after a relapse. He had dashed to the store for some things for his brother, forgetting his license in another jacket, had gulped a few swallows of vodka for his nerves, and then had skidded on the ice in the truck.

His own lawyer, counsel for the defense, grills him determinedly. Had he behaved well? No, very badly. Not *badly*, the lawyer says, but *criminally;* does he understand that he committed a serious crime, not only in hitting the girls, but in sitting behind the wheel with vodka in him? Does he know that every Soviet life is sacred? Will he do it again, will he drink and drive? Will he promise he will never, never do it again? Does he understand that that kind of irresponsibility cannot be tolerated in Soviet society?

The driver, voice unsteady and hands stiff at his sides, is too upset to play a part; he manages only a look of sincere shame and a simple apology. "I behaved very badly." While the court is out, his relatives pounce on him for his weak performance and for not emphasizing that he helps support his mother and invalid brother. "I couldn't say more; I am guilty, I hurt those poor girls. The court must decide what to do with me."

It decides mercifully: corrective labor* and loss of driving rights for a year, but no imprisonment.

Article 154, Paragraph III: Petty Speculation. At the famous outdoor market-fair in Luzhniki, alongside Lenin Stadium, a young man, the picture of innocence, had sold his place near the head of a queue for Polish raincoats to a Georgian—the latter had been 465th in line—for three rubles. When he had successfully made his sale, the accused realized another ruble profit by selling to his victim two pairs of men's socks for six rubles instead of the five he had just paid. He had a history of such speculation: a camera bought and sold, jazz records, a rug; and once he peddled a trip to Leningrad that his brigade

---

* Corrective labor is performed by the penalized person in his regular place of employment, at his regular job. A part of his salary—from 5 to 20 per cent—is deducted. Otherwise he is a free man, living a normal life. *See* Appendix I.

had been awarded for outstanding production.

The Georgian glowers menacingly, seemingly galled for having been taken in. His excuse is that he had wasted the entire previous afternoon standing vainly in line for a sweater; the supply had given out before his turn came up. The judge gives him a lecture, and to the speculator a look of disgust and a year's corrective labor.

Article 96: Petty Theft of State Property. Dozens of packs of Dukat cigarettes, totaling twenty rubles in value, had been filched from a tobacco factory in several installments. The accused is twenty-eight; like many Russian workers, he looks ten years older. He had been caught stealing before, had been warned, and had been reprimanded by the factory's Comradely Court. Now he can offer the judge no excuse other than vodka. He agrees that his wages had been sufficient for a comfortable life and that nothing had forced him to steal.

When the court retires, the man's wife turns on him. "Oh God, Andrei, why did you pretend we are not lacking for anything? You *know* that we hardly manage each month, with the children and everything. You were never able to speak up for yourself, you! Why didn't you say that your father and brother are sick and that you have helped them all these years? Oh, God. Or that our girl is weak and constantly needs milk? Besides, you earn sixty rubles, not seventy. The children ask already, 'What are we going to do without papa?' We will go hungry, that's what we'll do. Oh God, Andrei."

The children are with them in the courtroom, two well-formed blond cherubs, too young to understand. They have a grand time, playing peek-a-boo behind their parents' motionless forms, giggling quietly, forming their newly learned words, and crawling up on the bench from time to time to embrace *mamachka* and *papachka*.

Then mother and father embrace, before he is led away to begin a two-year term in a labor colony.

Article 145, Paragraph II: Robbery. "I was on my way home at midnight," recounts the victim, a plump woman in her thirties, "when he grabbed me, took my watch, and searched my bag. I told him I had nothing besides the watch. When he unbuttoned my coat, I screamed—hard. Lord knows what he had in mind. I'm a married woman."

The attacker, an unskilled laborer, does not know himself what he had in mind. He was drunk. Now he admits his guilt "fully and completely," is eager to explain how it happened, and keeps repeating, "That's correct, that's correct," to all the charges. "Yes, it was a stupid, criminal action."

He looks up plaintively. "Comrade Judges, what can I say?"

"That is your affair."

"I have nothing to say."

This was his third robbery in three years. The court, "considering that the earlier sentences had no educative effect," orders deprivation of freedom for four years.

Article 211: Reckless Driving by a Professional Driver. A woman was slightly injured by a truck and spent three days in a hospital. The driver had been drinking.

The judge informs her that she is entitled to make a claim against the driver.

"Do you mean money? Oh no, I don't want any money."

"Are you sure?" the Judge asks. "Nothing?"

"Well, perhaps enough to replace my stockings and skirt which were ruined. But money has nothing to do with it; my claim is only that such an untrustworthy man should not be allowed to drive in our socialist society."

Article 206: Hooliganism. The code defines hooliganism as "intentional actions grossly violating social order and express-

57

ing obvious disrespect to society." Rowdyism, in other words; being drunk and disorderly and disturbing the peace.

Predictably, it is the most frequent single charge; twenty-eight cases fall under this article during the ten-day period —more than one third of the total calendar. The defendants are mostly men, mostly seedy, mostly repeaters—and mostly drunk. After drinking followed scenes, slaps, street fighting, or swearing—foul language in public is also hooliganism.

"Hooliganism" is an indispensable word in Moscow. A mother tells her young son to stop "hooliganizing"; a procurator says it can be grounds for capital punishment.

The criminal code provides a wide range of punishments: social censure, fine up to fifty rubles, corrective labor up to a year, detention up to five years (when the defendant has been convicted before of hooliganism or has resisted the police or has behaved really outrageously). The twenty-eight cases here fell in between: from six months' corrective labor to two years' detention in a labor colony.

Articles 91, 144, 145 and 146: Armed Robbery with Intent to Seize State Property; Theft; Robbery; and Armed Robbery. Ten thin seventeen-year-old boys, their faces already hardened by vodka and factory work, sit on two benches in the dock, watched by nine policemen in boots, belts and pistols, five facing the boys, a foot away.

The youths formed a neighborhood gang, which grew spontaneously, and spontaneously went wild, beating up and robbing people (with a 1903 German pistol that did not work), to keep themselves in vodka, or just for the fun of it. There were nine incidents in a three-week period. The victims were boys they disliked, random boys, a taxi driver, a policeman, salesgirls, and watchmen.

The judge is old enough to be their mother and acts as if she is.

With tender concern, she asks each boy to have respect for the court, and then: *"Why?* What made you do it? What were your thoughts? Tell the court how you feel about it now. It is your future we are concerned with. Do you realize what you have done with your young life?"

Two boys got ten years; the others, eight, six, and five.

Suddenly, in an ordinary case of hooliganism, a drunken voice and meaningless whistling disrupt the orderly routine of the judge. "Yea Castro, Onward with Castro! Hurrah for Lenin! Give it to him like Lenin." It is a disheveled, red-nosed spectator, sprawled out on the rear bench, announcing his political creed. Some old women near him try to hush him up, but the soused man, who had been dozing, bellows on. "Let him have it like Castro and Lenin." He whistles and smirks.

The judge looks up calmly, stops the trial, and quietly orders a recess while the secretary fetches a policeman from the corridor. The big man is led away by the ear, protesting to Lenin's portrait. No one is surprised or outraged; it has happened here many times before.

Article 147: Swindling. A young Gypsy couple are charged with fortunetelling and shortchanging drunks. Their entire tribe, it seems—about fifty persons, of three generations—have come to the trial to encourage the accused. During the deliberation they wait in the corridor—on one side, men; on the other, women, each with at least one infant, some of them nursing openly while squatting on the floor. There is no mingling of the sexes.

The Gypsies are dark and colorful, wretched and filthy. They are openly resentful, sneering at "this court, this law." When Russians pass by for a look, the women swear foully and make obscene gestures with their hands and bodies. "What are

59

you looking at, you dirty Jew," one screams at an astonished blond onlooker.

"I'm not a Jew," he assures me. "I'm one hundred per cent Russian."

I cannot push my way past the tribe into the courtroom to hear the sentence.

Article 206: Hooliganism. The accused is not present; he is not permitted to leave the mental hospital where he is confined. He is charged with systematically creating disturbances in his apartment house, swearing vilely, distributing foul letters, frightening children, shutting off the electricity, chasing women with knives—for no apparent reason. His neighbors* confirm it, each standing about two minutes in the witness stand. Various remedies have been tried in vain.

The procurator says that psychiatrists have found him mentally unbalanced, and he urges that the accused be absolved from criminal responsibility. The defense counsel agrees, referring to war wounds and a medical history. The court is out eight minutes: it finds the accused guilty, but applies "enforced medical treatment" in the hospital, instead of criminal punishment. For how long? I ask. Until the doctors say he is well.

This is the shortest case, thirty-five minutes in all. Obviously procurator and judge had settled everything beforehand on the strength of the psychiatric report.

Article 196, Paragraphs II and III: Forgery and Counterfeiting of Documents, Stamps, Seals and Forms. A year and a half earlier, a thirty-two-year-old bus driver in Odessa stole two tires from a parked car. He was discovered, and while his

---

* Throughout this account, "neighbor" usually refers to someone sharing the same multifamily apartment with the person involved. He is, literally, a next-door neighbor, since the rooms in most of Moscow's pre-World War II apartments are split up into separate family units and the kitchens and bathrooms are shared.

case was under investigation—he was not taken into custody—
he fled to Moscow, moving in with an old army buddy and
his wife, trusted friends. "I don't know what happened to me.
I never had anything to do with the police before and I was
frightened, frightened to my depths. And ashamed."

He sold his suit and raincoat and—"What does a man do in
such a situation?"—wandered the streets and drank. Soon he
was broke. He could not apply for work because his documents remained in the hands of the Odessa police. He feared
that his friend would become suspicious of his unexplained
idleness and his depression. He prepared to return to Odessa.

One day, at his wit's end, he spilled his sad story to a man
with whom he happened to be sharing a bottle of vodka at a
café. The man told him to relax, that everything could be fixed
—for a fee, of course—and that he would never have to go
to jail.

Two weeks of intense work followed, under the direction of
the mysterious man. Passport, labor book, draft card and registration in a Moscow reserve unit, health card, permission to
reside in Moscow, driver's license (second class), certificates
—all the documents necessary to make a Muscovite—were
forged by the two men. "I can't do it, I just can't," said the
bus driver at first. "*Nichevo,*" said the older man. "You'll
train a bit and you'll learn." He learned so well that it became
his hobby, and on his own he forged twenty-six supplementary
documents, whose quality flabbergasted investigators when he
was finally discovered.

Armed with new papers, he started a new life. Aleksandr
Akimovich Bobrenko became Aleksandr Akimovich Bobren-
kov. "I wanted to work, to begin again, to pay for my crime
and then forget it." His friend found work for him, driving a
truck on a construction project, and a bunk in the dormitory
at the site. Soon he moved again—in with a woman in her
twenties and her seven-year-old son. He worked well, ac-
cumulating letters of recommendation and awards. His circle

of friends grew. He became an outstanding Soviet toiler. He took his new family to visit his old mother in Odessa. He was appointed brigade leader of a section of the new circular superhighway around Moscow. Only good was said of him.

How he was found out is not revealed at the trial. Nor how much he paid the counterfeiter who started him on his way, nor what happened to the counterfeiter, nor where blank documents were obtained . . . "We are not interested in such details," the judge explained afterward in his chambers. "They're not important. Maybe he was lying—lying about the whole story of how he got the documents. Everyone in trouble meets some 'man in a café.' "

Bobrenko-Bobrenkov is deeply penitent, confessing in great streams of self-accusation and apology: "I stole and I lied and I falsified. I don't know whether I shall ever be able to redeem myself." Some of his Moscow friends who have come to the trial weep; and his army buddy and the buddy's common-law wife testify that they did not believe the investigator when the accusation was made, so honorable had his conduct been. "Comrade Judges!"—counsel for the defense begins his plea—"a little over a year ago, there was a fine Soviet worker . . . what made him stray? Fear and shame over a minor crime which, considering his heretofore exemplary life, would have been punished lightly . . . This proves that he is not a hardened criminal; on the contrary . . ."

The sentence, incorporating the year meted out for the two tires in Odessa, is four years in a labor colony, strict regime.

Article 89: Plunder of State Property by Means of Theft. A civil suit for eighty-five rubles—the value of a defective refrigerator which had been trucked out of a local factory by two enterprising workers between shifts and sold to a fence—is attached (as it may be in Soviet law) to this otherwise ordinary criminal prosecution. The lawyer presenting the fac-

tory's claim is a diffident young woman, who stumbles and
falters as if it is her first case. (It is one of the rare times that I
have seen a participant, other than defendants, self-conscious
and inarticulate in court.) Although both men sit as defendants in the dock, the eighty-five-ruble claim is brought against
only one. This puzzles the judge.

"You consider only Yegorov guilty?" he asks the lawyer
gently.

"No . . . I . . . suppose not."

"You consider that *both* defendants are guilty as described
in the indictment?"

"Yes . . . I think so."

"Then the court does not understand your reasoning. Why
is your claim directed only against Yegorov?"

The embarrassed girl tries to think. The second defendant,
having confessed voluntarily soon after the theft to factory
administration and police, was still at his job; most likely she
excluded him because he seemed *less* guilty than criminal-
looking Yegorov, who denied all knowledge of the refrigerator
and was taken into custody awaiting trial.

"I don't understand. If you consider both men guilty, you
should bring your claim against both."

"Oh . . . well . . . all right . . . I'll make it both. In
equal amounts?"

*Articles 112 and 130: Intentional Light Bodily Injury, and
Insult.* These two charges, plus petty slander, are the only
"private" crimes in the code: they must be initiated by the
offended party (rather than the procuracy) and may be
dropped by mutual consent if the parties are reconciled before
the court retires for deliberation. The judge, moreover, is
obliged to seek reconciliation; and this one—in his black shirt
and yellow knit tie looks as if he belonged on the opposite side of the bench in a third-rate gangster film—does his

best. "This is a shameful thing—Soviet adults behaving like children; it ought never have come to court. Now, we can dismiss the charges and forget everything if you will settle amicably and promise to stop this childishness. Otherwise you are going to have criminal records, and that would be sad—especially for the Communists among you."

The defendants are four respectable-looking, suited Ukrainian *gentilhommes*, all well-educated professional men, and all members of the same family. Three of them are co-occupants of one apartment—seven adults and four children in three small rooms and a kitchen—and the fourth is a frequent visitor. For months the apartment has been a circus of snarlings, fracases and sieges, with everyone worn to a fine edge in the close quarters. "Positively childish," says the judge, "a family of your background slapping and swearing at each other like guttersnipes!"

After the sermon, the accuser-defendants agree to reconcile. The judge has them sign a pledge: "In the future we obligate ourselves not to insult and hit each other, and to observe all the rules of socialist communal living. If anyone violates this pledge we ask that he be given maximum punishment. We request that the present case be dismissed."

The judge dismisses it. "But may I come back again if they keep annoying me?" whines the youngest man. "You may come back tomorrow if you must," the judge retorts. The oldest man says soulfully, "This is embarrassing, I am deeply ashamed. You will never see us again. Thank you, Comrade Judge."

But as they reach the door on their way out, the old antagonisms suddenly ignite. Insults, pushing, swearing—". . . purposely making noise when my baby is sleeping . . ."; ". . . if you ever throw a teakettle at me again . . ."; ". . . bully and boor . . ."; ". . . calling my wife a cunt . . ." The judge stuffs the pledge into the record book, hurries from the

64

dais into his chambers, and shuts the door before they can come back.

Articles 92, 170 and 172: Theft of State Property by Misusing an Official Position; Misuse of an Official Position and Criminal Carelessness. The case is in its third week; seven bulging tomes of records lie on the judge's desk; four expert witnesses sit alongside the procurator; mountains of testimony have been taken down (will the court take time to review any of it when making its decision?), and much remains to be given. Two stories of an apartment house under construction in the suburbs collapsed, and during the investigation a plethora of financial, organizational and technical irregularities by the construction firm came to light. The administrators of the firm, a few key foremen, and officials in the trust to which the unit was subordinate had been getting rich in a platitudinous variety of ways—skimping on materials and selling them elsewhere, taking kickbacks from workers, beefing up costs, hiring relatives, neglecting finishing touches . . .

"*Vryad li* [Not a chance that] the case would have come to court had the building not collapsed," the procurator admits downheartedly in the corridor during a recess.

Articles 96 and 206: Petty Larceny of State Property and Hooliganism. The defendant is a frizzy-haired, thin-lipped, hard little woman, an ex-convict, guarded by a policeman and a policewoman. When, as her rights as accused are read to her, she is asked whether she has any petitions, she requests counsel. "Gimme a lawyer."

The judge is annoyed—"Why didn't you ask for one earlier?"

"Because I didn't think it was important."

This is an open-and-shut case, and bringing in a lawyer is going to waste time. Nevertheless, he grants the petition. The appointment of a lawyer will be at the expense of the court in this instance, since she is penniless, and the law requires that every defendant who requests representation must have it.

Article 206: Hooliganism. The judge is disturbed: there is something amiss in the record. The defendant insists that he has been in jail only once before and seems to be telling the truth; the judge seems to believe him. But the dossier lists two previous convictions.

"Look, I've admitted everything here. Why should I lie about this? You can believe your papers if you want, but I know that I was sentenced *once.* I told that to the investigator, but he wrote down the other conviction anyway—said it wouldn't make any difference."

The judge rummages in the record, puzzled and unhappy; this is the kind of uncertainty—a slip-up in the *dokumentatsiya* —that most disconcerts them.

Articles 147 and 198: Swindling and Violation of Passport Regulations. The defendant, a skinny, dark, itinerant Azerbaijanian born in Baku, grins uncontrollably. (Is it the pleasure of confession, or the embarrassment of being caught, that forces that grin on so many defendants' faces? It is the grin of young boys found at mischief and not entirely ashamed. Defendants realize, of course, that they ought to look contrite; but the confessional grin operates on its own.)

He has admitted guilt on both charges. The swindling was attempted in a local *rinok* (an open market where collective farmers are permitted to sell produce from their private plots). With a fellow Azerbaijanian he worked a variation of an old confidence game, known in both the East and West as the "pocketbook drop," on a dashing Uzbek soldier on leave in Moscow. Promising to split the contents of a wallet they supposedly found, the two accomplices enticed the victim to part with his own fortune of sixty-three rubles. (The mustached soldier, a Lermontov character, carried his money in a clip under his tunic, next to his golden skin.) A plain-clothes policeman became suspicious when he saw the transfer of money. The soldier had to be restrained when he realized he had been duped.

The second charge is illegal residence in Moscow: the accused has no *propiska* (a residence permit, issued by the police). This permission, which is stamped in the citizen's (internal) passport, is required in the major Soviet cities—Moscow, Leningrad, Kiev—and in the coastal strip along the Black Sea and in other popular areas. A Soviet citizen cannot simply take up residence in these areas as he could, for instance, in Irkutsk. For a newcomer, permission to stay usually depends upon his having a job which would entitle him to a *propiska;* but for most jobs—to complete the vicious cycle—possession of the *propiska* is a prerequisite. The purpose is to deter migration to already overcrowded cities. Thus, the Azerbaijanian, having no steady job, has no legal right to live in Moscow; he has been warned four times during the past two years about his being there.

The judge is a ponderous man who plays with his words and his fingers. "Young man, you have got to get a job, you have got to find yourself an honest place in our socialist society. And you cannot do it in Moscow. Do you understand that you are living at the expense of society? Young man, you are a piece of fungus. You have done nothing with your life but practice the bourgeois creed of getting something for nothing. Why didn't you go back to your homeland and work, like a Soviet man?"

Grinning, the skinny defendant asks for mercy. He knows that he must be punished, of course; he understands that he did wrong—but could the court please make it as light as possible? You see, he has a sick mother in Baku, he has asthma, and he has a burning desire to reform. . . .

But the sentence is four years in a labor colony, strict regime. The Azerbaijanian is stunned; the grin becomes a mouth agape, then a grimace of hatred.

"Defendant, is the sentence of this court clear to you?"

"Yes, your great humanity is very clear. Thank you"—and under his breath, but loud enough for the fat judge to hear —"you bastard."

Four youths stole three rolls of tar paper from their factory: three years each. A drunk sneaked a mirror from a grammar school on Election Day: two years. A sober man took the windshield wipers and mirror from a parked car: one year. An obviously imbecilic old lush insisted on annoying strangers at a metro station: one year. A waitress had been pouring each glass of wine a few drops short and taking home a bottle a fortnight for herself: two years. A man rolled a drunk for his greasy jacket and scruffy shoes: one year. The punishments are astonishingly severe.

Much is written in Soviet legal literature about the need to re-educate and reform, rather than simply to punish, criminals. Lenin's pronouncement that it is the inevitability of punishment, rather than its severity, that is crucial to the elimination of crime, is everywhere quoted. And the penal policy seems to conform to this enlightened spirit. In labor colonies, at least under normal regime, the lot of prisoners is said to approach the level of ordinary backwoods life. Men live in barracks, work at jobs that are not humiliating, receive wages, and are visited overnight by their wives. It is a far cry from the rot of jail, which in Russia is reserved only for the most dangerous criminals.*

Yet, in the courtroom, the doctrine of rehabilitation seems to evaporate. Judges are simply impatient with the wrongdoer

* See Appendix II.

and quick to hand him a stiff sentence. "We are building Communism," they seem to say (and often they do say it), "and if you are not willing to help after we have given you every opportunity to do so, then you are not worth our effort and we are not willing to help you."

In these ordinary trials the cardinal concern is much broader than the facts and the juridical significance of a single crime, or even a single criminal. A greater task faces the court—no less a task than the remaking of a society. Remaking society means work, toil, labor, in its most direct sense, on farm and in factory. The task of the court is to put every man behind his machine.

But these defendants, like defendants everywhere, are mostly society's outcasts, those who do the least to improve it. Rarely are they the capable, respectable, steady citizens who keep the wheels turning. Usually the wrongdoer has an indifferent history of employment at an unskilled trade. "No established place of work" is mentioned often in indictments and sentences. And much is made of this; for these undesirables, the law is harsh.

Article 211: Reckless Driving. "You know the rules," the judge says with a snort. "What do they read? Why didn't you see him earlier? Why didn't you use your brakes in time? Why weren't you looking ahead? You know your responsibility in this perfectly well."

The accident took place in November, four months ago to the day. That afternoon there was snow mixed with rain; the streets were slick, driving was treacherous. At 4:30 P.M. a Volga taxi hit a seventy-two-year-old pedestrian on the Krimskii Bridge, which spans the Moskva River, near the center of town. The old man was seriously hurt; he could not leave his bed for the trial.

The indictment, laden with figures in meters and kilometers, in rates of speed, braking distances, average times, and references to the Rules for Traffic Safety, the Driver's Manual and the Code for Moscow Chauffeurs, charges that the driver failed to exercise proper care and observe traffic safety rules, and that he was, therefore, guilty of a crime.

The driver's lawyer argues that the elements of a crime are missing in his client's actions, that the old man brought the injury on himself by wandering unexpectedly and inexplicably from the pedestrians' path of the bridge—midway across—in snow and rain. It was an accident, he pleads, not a crime. The driver had practically stopped at the moment of contact; such a blow would hardly have bruised a younger man. Besides, the lawyer continues, even if it *were* a crime, it would warrant only a reprimand, because of the defendant's perfect past, his previously unblemished driving record, and the victim's contributory carelessness. "This one unhappy incident must be contrasted with the defendant's exemplary family and working life."

A single witness testifies that the old man stepped suddenly onto the roadway, into the path of the approaching taxi; that the driver did all he could to stop, blowing his horn and applying his brakes as soon as he saw the pedestrian; and that heavy traffic from the opposite direction made it impossible for the driver to swerve.

The victim himself—his testimony to the investigator is read aloud by the judge—remembers only that he was walking along the bridge and desired to get to the other side . . . and then he awoke in the hospital with a broken hip.

The decisive testimony is delivered by an expert witness, a beefy man with a flushed face, the police specialist in traffic problems. He reads from a technical, highly detailed report, heaped again with references to page and paragraph of various manuals—a man of seventy-two walks at so many meters per second and a Volga automobile proceeding at 35 kilometers per hour requires so many meters to come to a stop. (No mention of bad driving conditions; the driver is expected to allow for these.) Then he submits an elaborately drawn diagram and, finally, delivers his opinion: the crucial question is whether the driver could have stopped in time to avoid hitting the pedestrian; and the figures indicate that that was possible; the driver should have seen the pedestrian at a distance of seventy meters, ample room in which to stop. The conclusion is, therefore, that the defendant is criminally responsible for the accident.

The bulky figure plumps at last into his chair, happy to be finished.

"Comrade Expert, will you tell us, please, what rules the *pedestrian* violated?" It is counsel for the defense, an ample, self-assured woman.

"No, I am afraid I cannot do that."

"You cannot? I think the question is a simple one."

"The movements of the pedestrian were not the subject of my concern."

"But you can tell us now; after all, you do know the case."

"I know the case as I am supposed to. It was not my duty to analyze the pedestrian's actions. I did not investigate that question."

"Well then, on the basis of the facts you know in general, what safety rules did the victim violate? Can you tell us that now, without an investigation?"

"I cannot."

"You do not understand the question?"

"It does not fall within the area of my competence in this case. My job was the driver."

"Surely you are *competent* to answer the question. Did the pedestrian violate rules of safety?"

The expert replies angrily. "I did not investigate the matter from that point of view. What the pedestrian did is not to the point here; the responsibility and opportunity of the driver to

71

stop is clear. That is what I had to determine."

"But you are a traffic expert, are you not? You know the rules that apply to this case as well as any other. Surely you know the regulations for pedestrians."

"I repeat—why can't you understand?—that was not a subject within my competence. I am not required to answer such questions in court—only questions related to the study I carried out."

"I am asking an elementary question, based on your general knowledge . . ."

Unaccountably, the judge does not intervene. A nervous man, he fumbles for a *papirosa* (a Russian-style cigarette) and lights up.

The lawyer, bristling, continues. "This is not a matter that needs investigation, but a simple question pertaining to your general expertise. I want to know whether the pedestrian was right in stepping into the road in the middle of the bridge as he did." It is a classic confrontation with bureaucracy, and the lawyer knows that she has a chance if she does not let up.

Eventually, the expert gives way. "All I can do is to read from the rules for pedestrians."

"Will you do that, please?"

With a grunt, he digs out the appropriate manual from its place next to the lunch in his briefcase and reads: Pedestrians are obliged to cross streets only at properly marked crossings.

"And is there a crossing at that point in the bridge?"

The expert answers with a sullen *"Nyet."*

"Is there a crossing at that end of the bridge that the pedestrian started from?"

"Da."

"Thank you."

But this was all in vain: the verdict is "Guilty. His guilt has been proved in court," declares the nervous judge. The defendant shakes hands quietly with four fellow drivers who have come to the trial to offer comradely support, and he is led away to his year in a labor colony.

Three weeks later I watched the appeal of this case in a higher court. The same lawyer made the same arguments: it was an accident, not a crime, and in any case the punishment was incomprehensibly severe for a man with so sterling a record. The appeal court rejected her arguments and ordered the sentence to stand.

Article 206: Hooliganism. A party of four, drunk in a café in the wee hours (in Moscow cafés this means 11:30 P.M., closing time), started singing bawdy songs. "Aren't you ashamed of yourself?" the judge asks one of the witnesses, who had been sitting at a nearby table. "You, the single Communist present—what did you do to stop the nonsense? Paid no attention, just like all the others. And only a year after the Twenty-Second Party Congress and the new Party Program! What do *they* require of a Communist in keeping our Soviet moral order?"

Article 154: Speculation. "The buying up and reselling of goods or other articles with the intention to make profit." Speculation in sweaters: they bought them from a mysterious woman "wholesaler" for sixteen rubles and fifty kopeks, and sold them for twenty rubles; the normal retail price, as established by the investigation, was thirteen rubles. Usually they peddled them in railway-station waiting rooms. They had been warned and fined several times during the past year for operating there. (One of the fines had been dismissed because the offender was in her last month of pregnancy.)

The defendants are two married women, neighbors, close friends; one of them was once a beauty. They sit together on the first row of benches holding hands. It is after lunch, and one of the assessors gives up her struggle to keep her eyes open.

"The court would like to hear why you persisted in speculating after being repeatedly warned. Has anyone told you that you may be expelled from Moscow as a parasite?"

"No," one of the women answers.

"What would you feel about it now?"

"I have no real excuse; I acted wrongly. I'm sorry."

"Plus the fact that you're not working. What's this record of not working? Why do you avoid work? I suppose you plan to go on living on your profits?"

"No, I've just weaned my son, you see; I'm waiting to find a place for him in a nursery. If he were settled, I would go to work today, that's the truth. Comrade Judges, I hope you believe what I told you. I had this one sweater left, it was the last one. It didn't fit me; I couldn't use it; I wanted to get rid of it. After that I was going to drop this business—forever. I said to myself I was not going to do it again. I knew it would come to no good. It was stupid and wrong and I promise never to do it again. If you forgive me I'll never take part in such things as long as I live."

"Do you recognize this document? It is the pledge you signed for the judge who fined you in December. You promised *then* never to engage in this activity again."

"I know," the woman says with a sigh. "And I really meant it. But there was just this one sweater—"

"Did you honor your pledge?"

"No."

"Why not? What forced you to break it? I suppose you thought such a pledge needn't be taken seriously."

"I feel very badly about breaking my promise."

"You wrote here, 'I shall never engage in such activity in your station again.' *Your* station. Exactly! And you just went to another station to sell your sweaters. Very clever."

74

"They told me to write it that way."

"Who told you?"

"The administration in Leningradskii Station. They asked me why didn't I go to some other station to do my business?"

A pause; the judge is momentarily nonplused.

"Why were you so often caught selling these sweaters?"

"Because I'm a poor speculator—not experienced."

The judge again looks blank, then takes another tack. In good time, the women are sentenced: a fine of fifty rubles for the naïve or artful mother, and corrective labor for six months with a 20 per cent deduction in salary for her companion. The sweater is confiscated.

Article 144: Theft. A man earning handsomely at two jobs is accused of stealing the coat off the back of a drunk in a park. He claims that the drunk pleaded with him to trade his coat for a bottle of vodka. The victim, brought in under guard (he is awaiting his own trial for hooliganism), cannot remember whether he made the agreement, but admits that he sometimes sells belongings when he is on a spree. The principal witness is a woman who says she saw the whole thing; but she has not appeared for the trial. About a quarter of the witnesses called to the People's Courts do not show up, for unexplained reasons, and the trials almost always go on without them. But in this case the judge is vexed; he orders a postponement so that the woman can be found.

Articles 198 and 206: Violation of Passport Regulations and Hooliganism. As I was leaving the courthouse on Saturday, the last of these ten days, a remarkable scene drew me back. People look poor in Moscow, but one rarely sees utter down-and-outs even in the courts—partly because of the intense pressure to get everyone to work, and partly because bums, beggars, alcoholics and prostitutes are weeded out of the city and

75

transplanted in the provinces by a variety of administrative methods. But here, dragging herself up the stairs on a stick (between two policemen), was as bedraggled a creature as I have ever seen—a weird witch, a Hogarth hag. She had an ugly scab on her nose, a filthy scarf on her head, and a putrid bandage, which flapped over the top of her crumbling boots, around her leg. Her dress was a smelly rag. She could hardly walk.

I followed her into a courtroom.

The woman kept up a steady stream of lamentation—cursing, sighing, crying, ranting, screaming to herself and the world, muttering, "Oi, my head, my poor head, my aching body," and "*Uzhas, uzhas* [horrible, horrible], what a stinking life." She kept pulling her matted hair in front of her face and crying into it.

She had been ordered many times to leave Moscow because she had no *propiska*, and no legal right to be there. When she was recently ordered again to leave the city, she swore foully at the police and when taken to the procurator's office—the witnesses testified—she threatened some officials with her stick and promised vengeance for being misused. Now, in the courtroom she screamed and raved as the evidence mounted against her, and defied the judge, who was trying to get on with the trial.

"Don't hurry me! Don't interrupt me! My head hurts, I'm not well. I'm trying to explain what really happened; why won't you listen, why is everybody against me?" And she berated the secretary. "Young lady, stop your laughing, this is not a laughing matter."

It was not a laughing matter, but it was hard not to laugh. When she called the procuracy a *kolkhoz* (literally "collective farm," but figuratively "chaotic incompetence") even the judge laughed outright. "You've got it inside out. The procurators were rude to *me*, *they* were going to beat *me*. I thought the procuracy was supposed to listen to workers'

claims, not laugh at them. I was fired illegally from my job"—
she had been employed in a fish storage plant—"and I have a
right to stay in Moscow until I am reinstated."

Alternately she screamed and whined and spoke intelli-
gently. "I've worked since I was thirteen. Washed dishes. Carried garbage. I'll do it again if I have to. I'm a working woman,
genuine working class. And you treat me like a dog, send me
to jail, where I'll learn to be a criminal. It's very easy to send
someone to jail all right, but you're supposed to be helping
the toilers, not trampling on them. Let me go to the Kremlin.
If Khrushchev is busy, I'll speak to his secretary. *Uzhas!* And
you don't even let me explain what really happened. Oi,
treated like a dog, after an honest life!"

Was she mad or clever? A psychiatric examination had
found her responsible—and suggested she was given to sham-
ming. She herself clutched the latest edition of *Court Psy-
chiatry* in her grimy hands.

The judge somehow managed to finish the trial in spite of
her outbursts. In an hour she was on the stairs again, this time
hobbling down with the aid of her greasy stick. Her bizarre
stream of sounds had not let up.

"Four years?" she suddenly asked her guards between rant-
ings, looking up at them innocently.

"No, two."

*Articles 89, 156, 145, 96, 122: Plunder of State Property by
Means of Theft; Deceit of Customers; Robbery; Petty Theft
of State Property; and Malicious Refusal to Pay Alimony.*
These are cases in Dzerzhinskii District. The indictments, the
stories, the excuses and the sentences this week are much like
what they were the last. In ten days, patterns form, and every
new case is partly repetition. The same faces seem to be in the
dock, the same court on the bench. If there is in Russia such

a thing as a criminal mentality, there is even more noticeably a juridical mentality.

The trials run aground on universal human frailties: a judge misses the crucial point in a defendant's testimony because she is fuming at her secretary for opening the window. A witness remembers, after he sits down, that he has forgotten to mention the most important fact. A court is so annoyed with a lawyer's nasal interruptions that it deafens itself to his client's appeal. And trials run aground, too, on the limitations of the trial form itself; no code, indictment or summation is exact enough to recapture the subtleties of even the simplest case. A trial is an attempt to reproduce episodes and circumstances from life. But where to stop and where to start? How deep to probe? What to simplify and what to leave out? A woman defendant wants to talk about her family troubles, her husband's drinking; a mother thinks she can explain why her son went wrong; a witness struggles to remember who insulted whom first, who bought the vodka, why blows were reached . . . But the court has neither time nor means for exactitude of that kind. It is a cardinal principle of Soviet legal theory that the sentence in every criminal case should reflect *material-naya istina*—"material," or "objective," or "absolute truth." But it is a regular condition of Soviet trial practice that judges are satisfied with much less in dealing with the oral testimony. Even to the untrained ear many facts go undisclosed, and seemingly essential questions go unasked.

These are the People's Courts. After some months in them one feels the absurdity of the notion that "there is no law in Russia"—even though the law is harsh in these ordinary cases and the judges seem to place a subordinate importance on ascertaining the facts. And in time, the drab little chambers seem not inappropriate as courtrooms; whether because of the bareness or in spite of it, they preserve that dignity and solemnity that means a court. People, not furniture or ornaments, dominate those rooms; simple people, unintimidated by pomp and polish, tell their stories and make their excuses in a setting natural for them, and they seem stronger for it.

One feels, too, a sense of social (if not professional) equality in these courts, a real absence of class distinction that is more than a propagandist's invention. Equality between those on the bench and those below it: the judge is not "your honor," and there is no obsequiousness to his person as to someone of higher social stuff. He is, if not always a comrade, then at least a *prostoi Sovietskii chelovyek*—an "ordinary Soviet fellow"— made of the same stuff and stock as his prisoners. No one is embarrassed, awed or frightened by him.

And equality, too, between the defendants. Every statistic confirms that in American courts it's "the rich what gets the mercy and the poor what gets the blame." But it is no longer the same the whole world over. In the People's Courts, money talks softly, when at all. It can buy a better lawyer, and it has been known to bribe a weak investigator; but this is less common than the Soviet tendency to set an example by punishing the more affluent wrongdoers more severely.

In the People's Courts it is poor work in the factory, rather than a poor purse, that puts a defendant at a disadvantage.

III

Preliminary Investigation

*Soviet criminal procedure deals with the "whole man," but
it deals with him in a particular way, as a teacher or parent
deals with a child. The court is interested in all aspects of
his development, and especially in his mental and psychological orientation, because it is its task to try to "remake"
him, or at least to make him behave. . . . The Soviet
criminal trial has the atmosphere not so much of our regular criminal courts as of our juvenile courts.*
—HAROLD J. BERMAN, *Justice in Russia*

THERE ARE some points of Soviet law which cannot be gracefully avoided, even in reportage.

The first concerns the jury. It does not exist in Russia. A
few liberal law professors suggested recently that it be re-
established—fused to the court, like some of the juries of
Western Europe—to decide questions of fact in the most
serious cases. Their recommendations met overwhelming dis-
approval as "bourgeois."

Who, then, makes the decisions in Russia? Trial by whom?
The two men flanking the judge at every trial are "lay assessors," direct representatives of the People, workers. They are
the cream of workers, elected by the trade unions at their factories and offices (less often by general meetings at places of resi-

dence) to sit two weeks a year for two years at the bench. In the words of an official commentary, they represent "one of the forms of drawing the broad toiling masses into the conduct of government in the area of administration of justice . . . an essential guarantee of the completeness, comprehensiveness and objectivity of the trial."

"Lay assessors"—now I am quoting the law itself—"enjoy equal rights with the presiding judge at the trial in deciding all questions which arise during the hearing of the case and the forming of the verdict." Judge and lay assessors decide all questions together by majority vote based on absolute equality, and when the sentence is drawn up the judge must vote last.

Assessors are, of course, of every sort, although almost always a cut above the ordinary factory worker in intelligence and education. Some grin foolishly, look out the window, or doze. A very few are intellectuals, seemingly more capable than the judge. But the vast majority sit quietly and awkwardly in their places as if embarrassed by their superfluity. Overwhelmed by the knowledge, experience and professionalism of the judge, they look on passively, like spectators with good seats. Important guests—but still outsiders. Occasionally they nod their assent in response to a question from the judge, answer "No" when asked whether they have any questions to put to the witnesses, or try to get a glance, over the judge's shoulder, at the dossier in front of him.

Some judges treat them respectfully, taking pains to whisper right and left before announcing any determination during the trial. (This little pretense seems only to intensify the embarrassment of some of the more sensitive assessors.) Other judges all but ignore them and conduct the proceedings as if they were alone on the bench. "Furniture!" said a young lawyer contemptuously, pointing to two fat, bewildered-looking women assessors after a trial during which they uttered not one word and which ended in severe punishment for his client.

How assessors conduct themselves during the deliberations only they themselves and the judge can know, for it is a strict rule that no one else ever is permitted in the little room while the verdict is being reached. One assumes, however, that the ascendancy of the judge prevails, perhaps even more markedly than in the courtroom, where the publicity of their relationship encourages some deference to the form of equality. An elderly lady next to whom I once sat at a concert had served as an assessor the previous year. "What did I know?" she remarked. "I agreed with what the judge suggested. I know nothing about the law and crime, and I did not want to make a fool of myself. Naturally I followed along."

Assessors need not follow along, however. They are, after all, a majority, and when determined they *can* make the important decisions. Here is a story I heard from a trustworthy source.

When the court withdrew, after hearing the testimony in a case of rape, the judge sat down at his desk and began writing rapidly on some sheets of lined blue paper. After a smoke one of the assessors asked, "Say, Pavel Pavlovich, what the devil are you writing so furiously there?" The judge was writing out the sentence. The assessor, an eccentric old individualist, got up stiffly, put on his glasses and read over the judge's shoulder. "Oh no," he said hoarsely, "that won't do—I won't vote for that. Let's talk this over. *I* don't think he is guilty." Annoyed, the judge kept writing. "That won't do," the old man repeated, "you had better rip it up." Rip it up the judge did indeed, after a violent exchange, because the assessor would not be swayed and had won the support of his colleague against the judge. Enraged at the interference, the judge ripped up his second attempt too, which would have softened the punishment but retained a guilty verdict. Then the three sat down together and wrote an acquittal.

Years after the incident, when he was telling my informant about it, the judge admitted that "I still boil over when I think of it." The story was told to me in all seriousness, and from what I saw outside the deliberating room, it has the ring of authenticity. Even when I chatted with the court informally in that room, before and after trials, when it reverted to office-and-chambers, the assessors were largely mute, listening to the judge hold forth as reserve officers might listen to their skipper.

From every outward indication, "the court" means "the judge" in the great majority of Moscow trials.

Who is the judge? He is "elected" in universal, equal, direct, secret balloting. I use "elected" in quotation marks because the electing is done in the Soviet manner, one candidate to an office (even though the Russian verb *vybirat* means "to choose" as well as "to elect"). The idea of appointed judges does not seem sinister to me; I have too often seen the corruption of elected judges in American settings. But it is annoying to read sanctimonious Soviet explanations that this election of judges guarantees their objectivity, independence and quality. What hypocrisy! The judge serves at the pleasure of the Party. This does not mean, on the other hand, that popular pressure never influences the Party's pleasure. In social work, lectures, and meetings of all sorts, as well as in the courthouse, the people of a district come to know their People's Judges, and in this way the judges' superiors learn of instances of exceptional arrogance and incompetence. The chairman of one large People's Court told me that two of his twelve judges were not again "nominated" during the last election, because of grass-roots unpopularity. Such is Soviet democracy.

The judge's term of office is five years. In theory, he may be relieved of office by a vote of his electorate.

Judges too are of many shapes and sizes, but they run generally to one social type: middle-class and middle-minded.

In another setting they would be schoolteachers and insurance salesmen, churchgoers and readers of the *Saturday Evening Post;* working intelligentsia, with frayed, instead of button-down, collars. Most of them wear ties of the clip-on type. Some of the old-timers have had no formal education but got their legal training in night courses and refresher programs, as well as in experience on the bench. All of the younger judges—there are some of these, for like their European counterparts generally, Soviet judges do not need a long apprenticeship at the bar—have had five years of higher education, combining college and law school. In an election year, many newly graduated law students go directly from the university to a judgeship in a provincial town.

As in Soviet life generally, the younger judges seem better trained and better intellectually equipped. And they are more relaxed and sophisticated than their heavy-handed elders.

By my rough count, about two thirds of the judges were members of the Party. But this made no apparent difference in the competence and style with which they handled cases. It did make a difference in the extracurricular social work required of them, and it seemed to make a difference in terms of promotion and career. But it would have taken a sharper ear than mine to detect any difference in "line." They all seemed to ask the same questions.

What stood out most about the judges was the look they had of doing a job like any other job, although harder than many; an everyday, ordinary, unpleasant job like addressing envelopes. As with envelopes, the cardinal criterion of doing this job well was absence of returns—reversals by the higher courts.

I come now to the investigation. It is in the wings of every trial, like the *souffleur* at an amateur play. That is why it is deceptive to talk about courts without explaining how the dossier is compiled.

My great hope was to follow one defendant from the very moment of his arrest to find out what happens before he faces his trial. But such exploration proved to be out of the question. The blue-and-red paddy wagons marked MILITSIYA which were parked outside the courthouses during the working day marked the limit of my line of sight to pretrial procedure. What I learned about it came secondhand.

To start at the beginning, both the police and the investigators are empowered to detain a man if they have reasonable grounds to suspect him of a crime. But the procurator must be informed within twenty-four hours and he, within another forty-eight, must decide whether to sanction the detention or release the suspect. In the former instance, detention becomes arrest. A man may be arrested, too, by order of a court, but this rarely happens. (I saw it happen once. A woman defendant had come to her trial so drunk and was swearing so foully that the judge arrested her on the spot and remanded the case to a new investigation.) Arrest is almost always the procurator's affair—that is to say, the vast majority of arrests are made with his sanction and one of his principal duties is to ensure that "not a single citizen" is arrested without good cause. Soviet jurists refer to this as their habeas corpus.

How well it works as protection against illegal detention, and how carefully the inviolability of the person proclaimed in the Constitution and restated throughout criminal legislation is observed, I cannot say with authority. My supposition is that illegal arrest is not a matter of general practice, but, because of police insensitivity and procurators' laziness, it happens somewhat more often than in northern American cities. Scrupulous observance of form was not characteristic of any of the publicly visible stages of the criminal process, and I guess it was no more characteristic in behind-the-scenes stages.

Investigation follows arrest. It is hard to overemphasize its significance in Soviet procedure. (Perhaps the American jurists who smugly call the Soviet trial "an appeal from the pretrial investigation" have succeeded.) According to law, it is what is established at the trial—in direct, oral testimony—that counts. But what is established at the trial is almost always what has been prepared at the investigation. And if the oral testimony in court diverges from what was written in the dossier—if a witness changes his mind, alters his story, reneges or forgets—the oral testimony is regarded with great suspicion.

At the trial, there are frequent references to the investigation. "At the investigation . . . the investigator said . . . you told the investigator . . . we know from the investigation . . ." Hardly a witness leaves the stand without mention being made of the investigation. To render faithfully the atmosphere of the cases sketched in this account, I should have to interject a caveat into every third paragraph: "Remember the investigation!" To an observer it seems that the trial is a reconstruction not so much of the crime as of an earlier reconstruction of it, that it has all been said before. For it has. Detailed testimony of all the witnesses, explanations by the accused, evaluations by his colleagues and superiors, pertinent documents of every kind, results of expert examinations, conclusions of the investigator—it has all been taken down and lies thick and authoritative between flimsy blue covers in the judge's hands. The *tabula rasa* approach to the trial is entirely alien to the Soviet notion of fairness. On the contrary, the closer the investigation resembles the finished script, the better the chance that the state's interest (not a single criminal must be acquitted) and the people's (not a single innocent man must sit in the dock) will be resolved compatibly. "That court will be ideal from which no one will leave acquitted," said a Soviet jurist in the Party's journal *Kommunist*.

86

What about the investigation? Who conducts it? Under what conditions? What can a suspected man expect?

There are two kinds of investigation: *doznaniye* ("inquiry"), handled mostly by the police; and *predvaritelnoye sledstviye* ("preliminary investigation"), conducted by the investigator, who is subordinate to the procurator. When military or state crimes are involved, the investigation is conducted by military and state security (K.G.B.) investigators, but they too report to the procurator. Inquiry is used only for minor charges, when the circumstances are not complex—for the simple one-act crimes when the suspects are caught in the act. One of the complaints made by proceduralists after Stalin's death was that, although inquiry was supposed to be limited to a fixed category of minor crimes, the police in fact investigated almost everything more or less as they pleased. This seems to have been corrected; the police have been put in their place.

If approved by the procurator, the material of the inquiry becomes, in the words of the procedural code, "the foundation for examination of the case in court."

Investigation is more formal. It may have been preceded by inquiry, for the police are responsible, as they are everywhere, for immediate "operative" measures to uncover crimes and criminals. But when there is reason to believe that the crime under consideration requires *predvaritelnoye sledstviye*, the case must be transferred to the investigator within ten days. (I am still using the rules of the R.S.F.S.R., applicable in Moscow.)

The investigator, of course, investigates. On paper, it is marvelously thorough and fair; the idea, repeated *ad nauseam*, everywhere, is that "every person who commits a crime is punished justly, and not a single innocent person subjected to criminal proceedings is convicted." The investigation is comprehensive—autopsy, search, confrontation, medical and psychiatric examination, subpoena of documents . . . and, of course, examination of witnesses. And the accused—he *must* be questioned. "At the beginning of the questioning, the investigator must ask the accused if he admits his guilt in the accusation made against him, and then ask him to give testimony on the substance of the charge."

Nowhere is it explicitly stated that the accused may refuse to talk, and he is not so informed. However, neither at the investigation nor at the trial is he criminally responsible, as ordinary witnesses are, for refusing to talk, or for giving intentionally wrong testimony. (I feel sure, though, that most defendants know nothing about this protection.) Whatever is said is taken down in rough by the investigator, and when the examination is completed, both he and the accused must read and sign each page.

That the accused is available for extensive questioning by the investigator is the great difference between Soviet and common-law procedure. Under the latter, a man charged cannot be further examined; the prosecution must build its case without him. In Moscow, a man charged faces a long inquisition, and while the prosecution may have a great deal of other evidence to draw upon, it is evident from what goes on in court that that inquisition contributes heavily to the preparation of the state's case.

The time spent under investigation and awaiting trial is not unduly long; two to four months seemed average. Complex cases and those requiring special investigation—such as psychiatric—sometimes take longer.

It should be remembered that not all persons in this suspended state, even those against whom a formal accusation has been made, wait in jail. The investigator is permitted to take a man into custody only when there is danger that he will hide, engage again in criminal activity or obstruct the investigation, and only when the crime of which he is suspected may be punished by deprivation of freedom. These rules are flexible enough in interpretation, however, to allow the investigator wide discretion, and it seemed to me that he decided rather freely who had to wait in a cell and who might wait at home.

The other means of ensuring that the accused will be present at his trial include: his own written promise that he will not leave home; parole in the custody of his collective or of a private person; and bail. But these guarantees seem to be seldom used. More often an accused, if he has not been taken into custody, is merely told to appear at his trial.

The advantages of the Soviet system (the European inquisitorial system in general) are obvious enough. An innocent man, able to present evidence on his own behalf, is almost certain to be released at some point during the investigation and is spared the strains and humiliations of a trial. A guilty one, although his chances of winning an acquittal are narrowed, gets a clear picture of the charge against him and the evidence on which it is based. (An accused can find out much more about this in England than in America.) In any event, he will not be surprised by some last-minute revelation by the state; the prosecution is not permitted to introduce evidence with which the accused is not acquainted. Everything possible within the limits of time and conscientiousness is done so that all of the facts and circumstances and their possible meanings and qualifications are known to all of the participants.

In a word, less is left to chance, or to cleverness, at the trial.* "The organs of investigation," a Soviet jurist has explained, "conduct all their work before the trial and for the trial in order to present the case to the court in a sufficiently

---

* Sybille Bedford has recently put it precisely. "The sporting spirit, the notion of the law as a game of skill with handicaps to give each side a chance, is entirely absent on the Continent." *Tant plus* in Russia.

investigated form so that the court has the opportunity to examine and evaluate the circumstances in their entirety and reach a sentence which is fair in its essence."

It usually takes time for those reared in the Anglo-Saxon legal tradition to overcome the notion that a thorough pre-trial investigation is sinister in itself. Properly executed, it may be humane. It was to avoid the evils of the *old* inquisition, the methods of an unscrupulous Crown, that the English safeguards, so precious to us now, were slowly pieced together. But these strict rules isolating the accused, excluding this and that, making simple stories intricate, may be out of date in an age of civilized civil servants, welfare governments and enlightened citizens. An impartial and efficient investigation may serve everyone's interests—except, to be sure, the criminal's.

"It is forbidden to solicit testimony from the accused by means of force, threats, or other illegal methods. . . . The examination of the accused may not take place at night, except when it cannot reasonably be put off."

But how does it *really* work? How is the accused treated? What are the methods of *dopros* ("questioning")?

I am on shaky ground here, because direct knowledge was denied me. Still, I have a feeling that, harsh as Russian prison life may be (I remember an article in a legal journal urging that it remain harsh to keep the lazy from living at the expense of the state), strong-arm methods, brutality and terror are not used.

I base this on what is said about the *dopros* at the trial. Complaints about investigators' behavior are frequent enough, but the very nature of those complaints suggests that violent mistreatment is not the rule. People protested against rudeness, against being dragged away without a chance to make a telephone call or change a shirt, against jailers' refusal to deliver warm clothing sent to the prisoners by their relatives, against the stupidity, coarseness and stubbornness of investigators. Sometimes there were complaints of beatings, but these seemed to come as excuses, usually from the most disreputable types— the types, however, most likely to be beaten.

But mention of physical violence was rare and incidental. People are not afraid to speak their minds on a certain range of subjects in the Moscow courts. One of these subjects is bureaucracy, especially police bureaucracy. That is why I assume that if outright mistreatment had been practiced I would have become aware of it in court. Or heard about it from the lawyers, who did talk often about the narrowness and one-sidedness of investigators, but not about their brutality. Besides, I met a few graduate students in law who had worked as investigators before entering advanced studies. (In Russia, no one except the brightest scientists goes on directly to graduate work; at least two years of work experience is a prerequisite, just as two years of work separates high school and college, except for physicists.) They too felt that physical pressure was not applied.

Perhaps I can reasonably suggest that although Russian police and investigators are not distinguished by compassion, gentleness, or patience, they are only a grade rougher than police and investigators elsewhere. Then too, Russian life in general is a grade rougher. Whatever the nuance, the blinding lights of *Darkness at Noon* are not turned on in ordinary cases.

The complaints most often made about the investigation concern not physical mistreatment but more subtle pressure, the kind to be expected from a prosecutor—pressure to confess, in order to clean up the case. In a group crime, an investigator promised one of the accused not to jail him if he would confess to just one bribe. In another bribery case, the accused requested a confrontation with his accuser; the investigator refused. A woman with a sick child admitted one incident of theft but repeatedly denied another. Finally her investigator said that she would not go home to her baby unless she confessed in full. She did. A man awaiting psychiatric examination after he created a disturbance on the street, caused another similar scene. The investigator of the second incident was informed about the impending examination, but brought his case to trial anyway and got a conviction. Incidents like these were frequent.

And more frequent were references to dictation. The accused knew he had "done wrong" but did not know exactly what. The investigator explained, then dictated a statement. It turns out at the trial that the defendant confessed to incidents about which he knew nothing. Why? the judge asks suspiciously. "I didn't know the law. The investigator wrote it out and I signed."

What encourages this and keeps the *predvaritelnoye sledstviye* below the standards one would like to see for investigation in an inquisitorial system is not dark doings but more obvious shortcomings.

For one thing, there is the mentality of investigators. I met just two; if they are typical, the system is far from what it could be. They were thick and blunt, uninterested and out of reach. A sharp *nyet* seemed always poised on their lips. Anyone who has dealt with Moscow officials (even those who regularly deal with foreigners and are generally far more civil than the rest) knows what I mean. Soviet bureaucrats are of a certain breed: theirs is a carefully developed resistance to interest in others, to the reasoning of nonofficials, and even to common sense. It can be trying enough to be alone in a room with a bureaucrat when the investigation concerns only travel from Moscow to Leningrad and one already has a half dozen signatures in his hand. Until Soviet officialdom acquires some idea of the meaning of public service, I should hate to entrust my fate to even the most objective Russian investigator. There

seems to be little resemblance between the tactful, understanding Porfiry Petrovich of *Crime and Punishment* and the pres-
ent-day Soviet investigator.

Then there are limitations of procedure itself. In France and
Germany the investigation is conducted by a judge responsible
to the court, and this seems essential in a system where the
investigation counts for what it does. But in Russia, although
the investigator is formally quasi-independent—he was given
greater independence in 1958; he now may refuse to accept
the procurator's interpretation of the investigation, in which
event the record goes to the next higher procurator to decide
in favor of one of them—he is really the procurator's man.
Investigator and procurator usually share the same office, and
promotion for an investigator generally means appointment as
a procurator. Naturally, disagreement is rare; naturally, the
procurator dominates the relationship. "In other words, he is
dependent," said one of my ex-investigator friends. Dependent
upon the procurator. Thus, investigation and prosecution are
joined; and this seems, in Western judgment, unwise. (I shall
try to show later that the Soviet procurator is far more than
prosecutor; he is a figure unknown to Western law, responsible for legality in every sense. Still, he prosecutes.)

A second shortcoming is probably more serious: the accused
(unless he is a juvenile or is mentally or physically sick) may
not be represented by a lawyer at the investigation. There has
been improvement here too since 1958. Counsel for healthy
adults is now admitted after the investigator has completed his
work, but before the case goes to court—that is, in time for the
accused and his lawyer to read the record and request additional evidence and investigation (which the investigator may
refuse). Still, in the ordinary case, the suspect faces the investigator without legal help; and this strikes one as unacceptable
at this stage of legal history. A man alone, whose contact with

93

the world is limited to an investigator who may question him repeatedly, can easily lose his sense of balance and become dependent on his examiner.

Occasionally investigators turn to methods more repugnant than psychological pressure. I was introduced to the kind of foul play that can be practiced when the system works badly, at a meeting of the criminal section of the Moscow Collegium of Lawyers which I managed to attend one evening in November. The gathering was an informal affair held in one of the innumerable banner-strewn "agitation points" of Moscow. It was the counterpart of the "production meetings" scheduled periodically in factories and shops to overfulfill production norms. In the case of the lawyers, the goal was higher standards of defense. As an example of the lawyers' art, a remarkable story was told by four defense lawyers who had participated in an unusual case.

In 1958, a twenty-year-old *studentka* was found dead near a rural railroad platform about twelve miles from Moscow. She had been abused. In two months, the police and investigator were unable to produce a suspect, and the case was closed. After press and public complained about police ineffectiveness, however, a man and a woman appeared unexpectedly at police headquarters, offering information which led to the arrest of one Boris Antonov. The man said he heard a cry, "Don't, Boris, please," at the scene of the crime, and the woman said that she saw Antonov hurry away with scratches on his face. The blood on the girl's dress was of Antonov's type. One expert determined that Antonov had definitely been scratched by the girl; another that the murder weapon was Antonov's heavy key ring. The investigator produced evidence that Antonov's alibi was false.

Based on this, Antonov was sentenced to death by Moscow Oblastnoi (Regional) Court. But the lawyer found so many lapses and contradictions in the principal prosecution witnesses' testimony that the Supreme Court of the Russian republic, on his appeal, reversed the decision and ordered the case reinvestigated and retried. (The procurator protested the reversal to the Praesidium of the Supreme Court, but his protest was rejected.) Again the investigator gathered the same facts—adding this time the testimony of Antonov's neighbor that the latter had begged him to say that they spent the murder evening together—and again Antonov was sentenced to die. But again the Supreme Court was bothered by inconsistencies in the testimony and again it reversed, ordering a third investigation. (Again the procurator protested to the Praesidium of the Supreme Court that the death sentence should stand.) This time a new investigator was appointed, and he revealed what the lawyer had suspected from the first: all of the evidence against Antonov had been fabricated by the police and the original investigator. The principal witnesses were paid police agents with long criminal records and some of the others had been bribed. The script was concocted by the investigator and sloppily rehearsed under his direction. After fifteen months, Antonov, who was entirely innocent, was freed.

(This, incidentally, was not the end of the case; at the time of the meeting in November 1962, it was still in the courts. The second investigator indicted four suspects, all of whom admitted killing both the *studentka* and a passerby who supposedly had witnessed the rape. All four were sentenced to be shot before it was discovered, again in appeal, that the passerby had died accidentally and that the investigator had promised to spare the defendants' lives if they confessed. Wrapped in perjury, worthless expertise, malpractice of every sort and plain mystery, the case went to the Supreme Court of the Union for some semblance of a fair solution.)

The reaction of the audience at the meeting—the lawyers

95

who first worked on the case had been frustrated at every turn by investigator and procurator—was of mild indignation. It was obviously not the first such narrative they had heard.

"The Investigator," the law states, "is obliged to take all measures provided for by law for a comprehensive, full, and objective investigation of the circumstances of the case, bringing to light circumstances both incriminating and vindicating the accused, both aggravating and extenuating his guilt." The Soviet explanation for the absence of the right to counsel at the investigation (counsel *is* permitted in Western Europe) is that the investigator is not an accuser but a researcher. His function is not to "get his man," but to uncover *all* the facts and circumstances, and in this a lawyer would be at best superfluous. Safeguards for the accused are ensured by the investigator himself: he must inform the accused of his rights, help him to defend himself against the accusation, and protect his civil and property rights. He must release him immediately when convinced of his innocence. He seeks the truth, not a conviction. Objectivity is inherent in his job.

That is the theory, but is it any wonder that the practice is sometimes different, that the investigator is sometimes not altogether impartial? It seems utopian to expect an investigator *ever* to shed completely the accusatorial spirit. At least until the standards of investigation are improved, forms of protection more tangible than exhorting investigators to work well must be given the accused. In the first days—these are quite often the most important ones—he is entirely dependent upon his inquisitor. No one is present to give him comfort and a sense of proportion, to say nothing of help with the questioning. Everything that follows these days, therefore, is tinged with suspicion.

In the long run, just administration of the law always depends on the competence and good faith of its administrators, but here too much is asked of them and too little of rules and institutions. True, the legal press constantly encourages investigators to be objective: criticism is aired of the "accusatorial tendency" of "certain" investigators and exhortations are made to do the job as prescribed in the code. The criticism is certainly a good omen. Progress has been made. But the problem is inherent in the office: it is too hard to be both accuser and defender; a man tends naturally to be one *or* the other.

A criminal investigation in any system combines two elements: opportunity for the investigative organ to get the facts and make an accurate indictment, and safeguards for the accused against unethical coercion. To a certain extent, these are like the characteristics of a warship: to strengthen armament or armor, speed must be sacrificed, and vice versa. The presence of a lawyer at the investigation would probably increase the guilty accused's chances of getting away with something—and that is what Soviet legislators fear. But it would also build up the armor against foul play and human error.

But the balance has swung in recent years toward greater protection, and may continue to swing that way. Of all the issues debated by Soviet jurists before adoption of the 1958 reforms, representation at the investigation got the most attention. For a time it seemed that those who urged full representation from the moment of arrest were going to win. Several prominent Soviet jurists told me that before long the debate will be resumed and counsel permitted throughout the entire investigation. "It must be done."

By purest accident, I was able to watch a police detective (not an investigator) at work one Saturday evening in the Sixth Precinct station house near the center of town; but he was questioning a victim, not a suspect, and the matter was very minor. Still, I offer it for what it is worth.

97

It happened unexpectedly, when anything but criminal procedure was on my mind. We—myself, an American friend and two Russian college girls—had been spending the evening in the Prague, a grand downtown restaurant. One of the girls and I returned from the dance floor to find the maitre d'hotel and two coarse men in overcoats waiting at our table. Svetlana froze. Where is your pocketbook? they asked. Her pocketbook was missing from the table, of course. We were told to follow the men.

Svetlana (that, of course, is not her name) was panicky; she feared that it was some kind of trick to find out who she was and punish her for cultivating foreigners. *"Mnye budet plokho*—it will be very bad for me." I knew what she meant: various kinds of unpleasantness are still sometimes contrived for girls who demonstrate "unhealthy" interest in Westerners and bourgeois pleasures.

To put things in perspective I ought to say, however, that by that time I was meeting all sorts of Muscovites freely all around town, having dinner in their homes and making trips with them to the countryside; and although Russians themselves assured me that "they" knew always where I was, I was not once aware of being followed. Earlier that evening at the restaurant—an evening which by that time seemed utterly natural and ordinary—Svetlana happened to muse that had she been dancing with a foreigner under Stalin, the next day she might be packing her things for Siberia.

I didn't know what to do: my presence might harm Svetlana, but it seemed worse to leave her alone. As soon as we reached the cloakroom, however, it became obvious that this was not a trick. In a corner, four policemen and as many *druzhiniki* ("volunteers" with red arm bands who patrol the streets, especially on Saturday night, and help the police keep order; they represent one of the ways in which

*obshchestvennost** participate in the administration of justice)
surrounded three suspicious-looking young men, who hung
their heads in abject surrender. They had been caught by the
cloakroom attendant and the doorman as they were rushing
out of the restaurant, one of them with Svetlana's black bag
poorly concealed under his jacket. As we approached them,
they were begging forgiveness in drunken phrases.

Svetlana was told to make a statement at the station house,
and while she seated herself in the cab of the paddy wagon, I
squeezed into the caged part with the suspects and policemen.
On the way, the driver lashed out at her. "What were you
doing in a restaurant anyway, you dirty little tramp? Where
did you swipe the money to live it up at the Prague, eh?
You're so drunk you can't even hold on to your pocketbook."
(She had had one shot of vodka and a glass of wine.) "Don't
tell me that you didn't expect thievery in a restaurant—don't
you know that people here steal? I suppose you flew in yesterday from America, huh?" (This last had nothing to do with
me. "America" figures in several widely used sarcasms, like
"to discover America." The police, I am sure, took me only for
a laconic Muscovite.)

We were ushered into the main hall of the station house.
There, behind a high counter, sat the duty sergeant, looking
only a shade more formidable than a police sergeant anywhere
else. One of the gloomy young men inched furtively over to
Svetlana. "Please, say you knew us, that we were together, that
you knew about the bag. Please, I beg you; we'll get five
years . . ." Then the three young men were led away.

There was nothing unusual about the questioning of Svetlana, and that is the point I want to make. It was conducted in
a cubbyhole furnished with a giant portrait of Mikoyan, a
decaying desk and two chairs. The detective was brusque but

* The "community," or "ordinary citizens," collectively. See following
chapter.

not unkind; he kept telling Svetlana to relax and have patience. Patience was needed to compose two statements and a receipt for the bag and its contents, all of the papers being slowly written out longhand, slowly read back, and signed in triplicate. The detective, a provincial bureaucratic type, did not seem like a man given to roughing up suspects, and in this seemingly open-and-shut case he observed the procedural regulations scrupulously. For the life of me, I could not find anything to criticize in his manner.

Incidentally, I never saw the trial. Back in the Prague—the police took us back in a motorcycle with a sidecar and escorted us inside so that we would not have to wait in the perpetual queue—Svetlana assured me that there would be none. I was surprised at her sudden self-assurance and the certainty with which she told me this. Then she explained that since her (internal) passport was not in her bag, she had given the detective a false name and address. (This had escaped me because I never knew her last name or address; among the younger generation, last names are rarely given at introductions.) Svetlana wanted no part of police and courts even as a complainant.

I used to wonder how, in a totalitarian society, people could be missing, crimes go undiscovered and things like this —with the police!—go wrong. Quite simply, I found out.

This little affair at the Prague reminds me of another incident which, although it did not involve a criminal investigation as such—perhaps legally it ought to have—offers some suggestion of the tone of the *dopros* in Moscow. This time Natasha was involved, a law student, as it happens, and I have the story directly from her.

Natasha arranged a *svidaniye* (rendezvous) one Saturday in early June with Viktor, an old school friend. They planned to

see a film. She arrived first at the meeting place, the entrance
to one of the lesser-known hotels near her room, and to avoid
an unseasonably strong afternoon sun she retired to the lobby
to wait. After some minutes a burly, stolid man seized her
by the arm.

"Come with me, *dyevochka*."

Natasha is a peppery girl. "What's this? Who are you? Let
go of my arm!" But her heart sank instinctively; he was an
official type. The doorman took her by the other arm and she
was led through a corridor behind the lobby into an empty
room with a desk. The doorman left, snapping the lock.

Showing no identification, the big man began to grill
Natasha. Who was she? How old? Where did she work?
Live? What was she doing in the hotel? How long was she
there? Where did she get her (obviously Western) blouse?
Where was her passport? Natasha was not carrying her passport and at first she declined to answer. "What right have you,
whoever you are, to question me?" But when the man reacted
ominously—"Listen, girl, you'd better answer"—Natasha told
her simple story in detail. Thereupon the man became civil
and advised her not to worry; he would not, however, explain his behavior. Leading her back to the lobby, he gave her
an address at which to report at a certain hour on Monday,
"as a matter of formality."

Natasha was literally sick with fear the remainder of Saturday and Sunday, because the address, known to every Muscovite, is a fearful one: Petrovka 28, the headquarters of state
security. What had she done? Had it something to do with the
hotel? With the French student she had been seeing the year
before? The books she had been reading in French? On Monday she was terrified. Instinctively again, she scrubbed her
face red, put on her oldest school dress, braided her hair, took
off her brassiere, did everything she could to conceal her natural glamour, and appeared, trembling and praying, at Pe-

trovka. Again she was taken to a small room along a long, dark corridor.

Her examiner this time was a slight, bureaucratic type who listened attentively and questioned her courteously. She was still half panicky and half furious when, two months later, she related the episode to me, but she took pains to emphasize that the questioner was decent, even friendly. The interview lasted fifteen minutes. The official took her passport, checked some papers—there was obviously nothing in the files about her—and jotted down her story of that Saturday again calmly and thoroughly. Before dismissing her, he assured her that it was all an unfortunate incident that would come to nothing. After Natasha pleaded to be told what had happened, the investigator explained simply that the man at the hotel had suspected that she was a prostitute, and it was his job to keep prostitutes away from that hotel, which was patronized almost exclusively by visitors from the East European satellites.

"I'm sorry," he said, with apparent sincerity, "that you were taken for a prostitute just because you are so pretty. But go home and get some sleep now—you have absolutely nothing to worry about."

Svetlana and Natasha have diverted me somewhat from the preliminary investigation as such, but their experiences coincided with my general impression of the investigation gleaned from the courts. There *is*, obviously, something to worry about; not the knout or the thumbscrew so much as the enormous power and lethargy of the administrative bureaucracy in a country where the tradition of protection for the individual is still feeble. This is not Stalin's doing so much as Peter the Great's and Nicholas I's, and even the Mongols'. But there are grounds for optimism—Russia is chipping away at the rusty yoke. One is beginning to hear "You've no *right* to do that to me in this country."

IV

Obshchestvennost

In ONE of the first reckless-driving cases in Dzerzhinskii district the accused driver was represented by two defenders, one a Remnant of the Past, the other a Harbinger of the Future, and this double defense, which I later saw often, is one of the idiosyncrasies of contemporary Soviet law that give it a socialist flavor.

The Past, a plump, middle-aged *Frau*, was counsel for the defense. Engaged by the driver's parents in the normal manner through her College of Advocates, she participated in the trial roughly in the way Russian lawyers have participated in trials for about a century.

The Future, a graying Trevor Howard, spoke too in the driver's cause even though he was not a lawyer at all but a senior driver at the defendant's taxi garage. He had the next shift at noon and came to court in his overalls. He is called an *"obshchestvennii* defender" and personifies one of the few Soviet innovations in trial procedure.

"Obshchestvennost" is one of the first Russian words to learn but one of the most difficult to render into English. Variously, "the community," "society," "the public" or "the opinion-makers" suggest its meaning. In Sovietese it has come to mean principally "public but nongovernmental," or "pertaining directly to the people." Thus the *obshchestvennii* de-

fender in that case of reckless driving was neither a private figure nor a governmental one, and he represented not the defendant but a group of people: the defendant's community, the collective of drivers and mechanics at the taxi garage.

When the collective was informed of the accident and charges against one of its drivers, it scheduled a discussion of them for its next general meeting. At the meeting the driver's character and working habits were informally reviewed, those who knew him best speaking up in turn from the floor. Most of his peers agreed that he was a steady, reliable worker who consistently fulfilled his work norms, and a good comrade who volunteered for social work around the garage. A mechanic mentioned that he had a fine record in the Soviet Army. Several drivers said that he had a solid family life. The trade-union secretary reported that his driving had never before led to any incidents.

In the end, they voted to defend him—to ask the court to reinstate him in his job (he had been demoted to nondriving duties after the accident) and free him from punishment. And they elected the senior driver, who knew him well, to make their will known in court. I emphasize that it was *their* will because this was beyond the desires and control of the defendant. In almost all cases, an accused in Soviet law may refuse the services of a lawyer, but not of an *obshchestvennii* defender, because the latter represents the collective, not the defendant.

The *obshchestvennii* defender (he may be just as easily, it is important to remember, an *obshchestvennii* accuser) rarely knows much about the law, and although on paper he has almost the same procedural rights at the trial—to question, to petition, to comment, et cetera—as the professional lawyer, he rarely talks about it. Usually he talks simply about the accused as a man—his character, his rate of production, his attitude toward his work and his fellows, his family life, his crime in the perspective of his everyday life. It is an institutionalization of the "whole man" approach to the trial. For better or for worse the defendant's community accompanies him to his day in court—almost always his working community, for Bolsheviks have always felt that a man's nature reveals itself most clearly at work.

Obshchestvennost has a venerable tradition in Soviet law but it has come to life in the courtroom only in recent years. For—Soviet theorists explain—it is both symbol and agency of a society advancing toward a not-too-distant Communism where government and courts will have withered away, where physical coercion by the state will have become superfluous, where society will discipline itself—simply, without codes, lawyers or appeals, without the cumbersome formal machinery, like courts, required by the state. It will all be done by *obshchestvennost* itself, by society, the community, the public.

Thus, we are told, the introduction of *obshchestvennost* to the courtroom is a movement forward in the direction of the Great Goal, a bridging of the temperamental distance (even in Soviet society, where state and people are one) between the complexity of state bureaucracy and the simple, natural habits of the collective.

About one trial in ten is attended by an *obshchestvennik*—a representative, in working clothes and with working-class speech, of factory, garage, warehouse or department store— who takes his commission from the collective seriously. "Ivan Ivanovich is a fine (poor) worker; he has been praised (warned) many times; he is respected (disliked) by his fellow workers; he works hard (does not do his share) to fulfill the plan; he drinks moderately (intemperately); he lives a respectable (shameful) life; this incident is an accident, an excusable loss of control (a natural outcome of his deviant ways); he represents little social danger (his record shows that he is a constant annoyance and a menace); we ask the court to give him the minimum sentence and if possible hand him over to the collective for re-education (we think he deserves strict punishment)."

Judges are not conspicuously attentive when these standardized opinions are offered.

The participation of lay defenders and accusers in trials, and the street patrols of voluntary *druzhiniki* to supplement the police, are but two phases in a massive campaign to draw *obshchestvennost* into the work of law enforcement. In the official declarations, "It is essential that the functions of maintaining social order and safety be discharged by *obshchestvenniye* organizations parallel with such state institutions as the police and the courts," and, "A constituent element in the building of Communism is the active participation of all *obshchestvennost* in the strengthening of socialist legality, the safeguarding of the Soviet state and social order, the observance of state and labor discipline and also in the elimination of despicable survivals of the past such as hooliganism, drunkenness, bribery, speculation and similar vile actions."

Many are the forms—at least on paper—of participation by *obshchestvenniye* organizations. They aid the procuracy, police and investigative bodies in a variety of ways. They assume the duties of parole over minor offenders. They supply the lay assessors. They may petition for conditional sentences, or apply measures of social censure in lieu of criminal punishment. "The drawing of *obshchestvennost* into battle with crime," a Soviet jurist wrote recently, "is one of the most important and topical questions in the theory and practice of Soviet criminal procedure, because in the conditions of full-scale building of Communism there is taking place a transformation of socialist *étatism* into Communist *obshchestvennoye* self-administration."

One of the central tasks of *obshchestvennost* is, as one would expect, *prevention* of crime and of noncriminal violations of

"Communist norms," work discipline, "rules of socialist communal living," and so on. Preventive work, prophylactic work, protective work—these terms appear again and again in Soviet legal literature. And here the work of *obshchestvennost* coincides with another of the literature's central themes: the educative role of the court. For the Soviet court, say its makers, is primarily educative and only secondarily punitive. It teaches rather than punishes, persuades rather than coerces. Its principal task is to re-educate the errant and instruct the waverers; this is established by law.*

Moscow courts fulfill their educative functions in a variety of ways. They open their doors to the public, lecture defendants and spectators directly and indirectly from the bench, and hold public evening seminars on crime prevention. But their principal teaching method is more straightforward. They simply take about a fifth of the criminal cases from court to the heart of *obshchestvennost*—to the headquarters of the collective whose members are involved in a crime. This institution is called a "traveling session," and I wanted to find out how it works.

One November day I followed three women, the judge and

* "In all of its activity the court educates citizens of the U.S.S.R. in a spirit of dedication to the Fatherland and to Communism, a spirit of strict and steadfast observance of Soviet laws, of concern for socialist property, of observance of labor discipline, of honest acceptance of state and social responsibilities, of respect for the rights, honor and dignity of citizens and for the rules of socialist living and behavior." (Article 3, Federal Fundamentals of Court Structure.)

"The criminal process must further the strengthening of socialist legality, the prevention and eradication of crime, and the education of citizens in a spirit of steadfast observance of Soviet laws." (Article 2, Federal Fundamentals of Criminal Procedure.)

"Punishment is not only a penalty . . . but has the goal of reform and re-education of the convicted person in a spirit of honest attitudes toward work, of precise observance of the laws, of respect for the rules of socialist living and behavior and also the prevention of the commission of new crimes by the convicted as well as by other persons." (Article 20, Federal Fundamentals of Criminal Law.)

two lay assessors, as they traveled—after lunch, on a four-kopek trolley ride—to a red-brick mill ten minutes from the courthouse. It was a printing plant of the Ministry of Communications, where the accused, a printer, and the two men he knifed in a drunken argument were employed. Court was to be held in a large hall that smelled like an old high-school auditorium; it was the factory and trade-union club, which in one form or another is an essential part of every Soviet organization. It is there that meetings are held, agitation is organized, elections are conducted, lectures are given, dances are held, and entertainment is presented—that the collective life is lived.

The auditorium was full when we arrived: about seven hundred employees in denim and work shoes (they were ready to start the evening shift at 4 P.M.) jammed the seats and aisles. The court occupied an improvised bench on the stage under the familiar red banner, "FORWARD TO THE VICTORY OF COMMUNISM!"; chairs and tables were arranged for procurator, defense counsel and defendant in the space directly in front of the stage; and defendant and complainants sat in the first row of benches. It looked as if a school play, rather than a trial, was about to take place.

The crime itself was an "ordinary" one of drink and violence; the most unusual circumstance was the saving of a victim's slashed arm by a new English medical technique. How the trial was going to be conducted under those makeshift, gladiatorial conditions was what interested me most.

It seemed, when it was over, to have been conducted pretty much as it would have been in a regular courtroom, except that the speakers had sometimes to shout over the din of the crowd and the judge had to rush a bit to free the auditorium by 5 P.M. Sometimes I had the uncomfortable impression that judge and procurator were at least as interested in making points to the audience as in picking the bones of the case, but the facts seemed open-and-shut in any event—no doubt just such cases are chosen for *obshchestvennii* consumption. Naturally, the dignity of the court was considerably compromised in the course of the noisy proceedings. As the afternoon wore on, the audience grew restless. There were sarcastic comments from the rear, then shouts, *"Nu,* enough!"; "Get to the sentence!"; "Finish with it, already!" The judge repeatedly pleaded and warned about the need for quiet. She was ignored. "Oh," a man yelled back at her, "I thought this was a general meeting where we can all talk. I didn't know it was a *court."*

Recollections of mob justice kept running through my thoughts, but this trial never deteriorated to that. And in the end, I felt that the concept of the traveling session was not without some appeal. Obvious unfairness by the court would have been resented by the public and would have defeated the purpose of the session. (The sentence *was* severe, but probably not much more so than it would have been in the courts.) The people around me on the benches knew the accused and his victims—although they knew nothing about the educative role of the court—and felt it a good idea that the trial was held in the factory, because it was a "community affair."

Toward the accused, the sentiment of the audience was mixed. The assemblage groaned when it heard at the outset that he had been convicted before ("He's simply a criminal!"), booed when he testified that he remembered nothing about the stabbings, and roared in approval when the procurator shouted that the man was dangerous and demanded six years' detention. (For five minutes after the procurator's speech, order could not be restored; some of the spectators were shouting, "Six years is too little!") On the other hand, the audience gushed with sympathy when it heard about the hard times of his childhood, applauded lengthily when fellow workers testified that he was a highly regarded toiler, cheered when counsel said that two years' confinement would be enough, and remained respectfully silent when the defendant,

THE PEOPLE'S COURTS

in a final statement, said that he knew he must be punished, but begged for indulgence. It was the typical reaction of a Russian theater audience: emotional, naïve, uninhibited, and wildly fluctuating to the action of the moment.

A stunning roar followed the reading of the sentence—five years—but it seemed to be both approving and disapproving: "Yes!"; "No!"; "Ridiculous!"; "Correct!"; "Too little!"; "Too much!" I tried to get closer for a final word with the judge but was carried out the door and to the street by the throng, which started its surge at the word "five."

Later there were more traveling sessions in factory clubs. Four women at a perfumery (the scent in this club was literally intoxicating) charged with sneaking "Red Moscow," "Evening" and "Stone Flower" out of the plant in wet sponges, squeezing them into bottles, and selling the latter to friends. A husband and wife at a textile mill accused of systematically taking remnants from the finishing department. Several Malicious Hooliganisms. Lord knows what the educative value of these on-the-scene trials turned out to be. They too were well attended—the perfume case drew over a thousand spectators from the plant and neighborhood—by workers who knew the parties more or less intimately. But, booing and cheering lustily on both sides, growing noisy and restless whenever the action on stage slowed down, they seemed to take it more as entertainment than as a trial, to say nothing of a lesson.

Something about this design—leaving the detachment of the courthouse to try a man, and especially holding the trial at the scene of the crime—went against my legal grain. And something too about encouraging the lay public, especially the public least likely to be unprejudiced, to be "drawn into" the trial. And about making a lesson out of a man's fate! The law at these traveling sessions seemed to have traveled a step away from the house-in-good-order which the West holds essential for the protection of due process against the tempests of outside influence.

On the other hand, Russians have different legal and historical traditions and this kind of community justice seemed to be much less abhorrent to them. No one, not even the lawyers, complained much about the traveling sessions. And I myself came away with the feeling that in actuality they are less pernicious than they seem in the imagination.

The great bulk of *obshchestvennost's* work is done on the fringes of the judicial system, not at its innards. An ever-growing system of quasi-judicial innovations in method and means is being engineered in order to free Soviet society of all those violations of ethics, morality and clean living which, although not serious enough to be called crimes, must be eliminated before Communism is reached. In this noble undertaking, the brunt of the job is assigned to *obshchestvennost,* for it is a job to which *obshchestvennost,* with its virtues of flexibility and freedom from the formal and traditional procedures demanded of state agencies, is well suited.

Of all of *obshchestvennost's* quasi-legal, peripheral operations, an invention called the Comradely Court interested me most. This is an authentic Soviet invention; more than anything else judicial it seemed to suggest revolutionary ideology.* Its function is to transform bourgeois decadence into

* "In the battle against survivals of the past, against manifestations of individualism and egoism, a great role belongs to *obshchestvennost,* to the influence of social opinion, to the development of criticism and self-criticism. Comradely censure of antisocial actions will gradually become the principal means of eradication of manifestations of bourgeois views, customs and habits." (Program of the Communist Party of the Soviet Union, 1961.)

"Comradely courts are elected *obshchestvenniye* organs summoned to actively promote the upbringing and education of citizens in the spirit of socialist virtue. The very name, *Tovarishcheskii Sud*, suggested Bolshevism. As soon as I unpacked in Moscow I set out to watch a session.

To find a session, however, turned out to be a difficult job, and the fact that I searched for months before finding one and then found three in five days speaks of their nature. For there are hundreds, perhaps thousands, of Comradely Courts in the city but they convene only when a comrade goes astray—which no one can predict. In large factories sessions seemed to be held regularly, but I was not permitted to watch any. My only chance was to discover one in a residential area, which meant spotting in time a little hand-penned public announcement posted on a wall or bulletin board about a week before the event.

I hunted for these announcements during the winter months, tramping the snowy back streets for hours, shuffling in and out of courtyards, scanning bulletin boards. Up and back, region to region, street to dreary street, I became a connoisseur of the Moscow apartment-house bulletin board, which is an institution of some importance. Among the posters of propaganda and agitation (this is a world all its own: "Surpass America in Meat and Milk!" "Lenin—More Alive than Anyone Living!" "Glory to the Communist Party, Conqueror of Space!" "Doing More Today Means Having More Tomorrow.") there are semiofficial notices of all sorts informing of lectures, community events and job offers in town and in Siberia; and also private announcements by the hundreds:

Communist attitudes toward work and socialist society, development among the Soviet people of feelings of collectivism and comradely mutual help, respect for the dignity and honor of citizens. Most important is the work of comradely courts in the prevention of violations of the law and actions which harm the community, education of the people by means of persuasion and social influence, creation of an atmosphere of intolerance toward any sort of antisocial action." (Decree of the Praesidium of the R.S.F.S.R. Supreme Soviet, 1961.)

offers to buy and sell furniture, clothes, lessons, books. By far the most common subject is apartments:

Announcement No. 64531 (30 kopeks)

WILL TRADE A ROOM—18 square meters, first floor in a sparsely populated apartment. Plenty of storage room. No telephone or bathroom, but the former may be installed if desired—we are already on line. Trade for a smaller room with all comforts. Address . . .

These were not unpleasant hours. The winter was endurably frozen and while there was never a thaw, waterproof shoes and a heavy scarf kept the cold under control except for a fortnight in February. The thrill of watching Moscow and Muscovites in winter never quite wore off. Nor the thrill of finding out how things Soviet work. Buying a can of herring and a half loaf of black bread in a back-street grocery sometimes led to adventures.

After a time, however, it was frustrating. Often I came upon announcements of sessions scheduled for *yesterday*. Friends at the university told of cases they had watched the week before. Afraid that the Comradely Courts were going to elude me entirely, I asked my adviser, the dean, for help. He promised six or seven times at our biweekly meetings to locate one for me. Each time he "forgot" and finally said that it could not be done. More eager than ever, surer than ever that the Comradely Courts held some special clues to the secrets of socialist society, I resumed the hunt on the streets.

I ought to mention, meanwhile, something about the judicial characteristics of the Comradely Court. For—as I have been suggesting—it is not a court at all; not, at least, a court in the normal sense. It stands apart from the hierarchy of the regular court system, apart from the criminal and procedural codes of the Russian Republic and all they encompass. In fact, it stands apart from crime itself, dealing instead with "survivals of capitalism," "bourgeois views and morals," "anti-social attitudes," "violations of the socialist order," and "instances of misbehavior." And it stands apart from criminal punishment—applying only "measures of public influence."

A miniature town meeting; a group of neighbors or fellow workers, comrades; *obshchestvennost;* an attempt to set the deviant straight without recourse to the law; one of the Party's myriad methods of mobilizing public opinion, shaping the New Soviet Man, implementing the Moral Code of the Builders of Communism; an attempt to diminish drinking, squabbling and truancy from work; an organ of *socialist discipline*—the Comradely Court is all these things. "Comradely Courts promote Communist education and upbringing of the masses, strengthen work discipline, increase the productivity of labor . . ." They operate in factories, institutions, organizations, universities, collective farms, villages, apartment houses, et cetera; members of the court are chosen at general meetings of the collective and serve one year.

Their jurisdiction is limited: violation of labor discipline (truancy and lateness, sloppy work, spoilage); drunkenness and undignified behavior in public places or at work; undignified attitudes toward women or parents, and neglect of children; insults and swearing; damage to trees, greenery, and public property; violation of rules in shared apartments and dormitories, property squabbles involving less than fifty rubles; administrative and petty violations of the law if police, procurator or court consider transfer of the case to a Comradely Court advisable; other antisocial actions, and so on.

Nothing major, in a word. I suppose for this reason the Comradely Court should be thought of as lower than the People's Court (to which it may turn for advice), although in another sense it is higher than the Supreme Court of the U.S.S.R. For, we are told, it is a prototype of the court of the future: under Communism something like the Comradely

Court will settle—simply, in an *obshchestvennoye* way—any minor social disputes that still exist.

Comradely Courts too are an old idea: in the 1920s they were established on collective farms, in housing developments and especially in factories to deal with minor violations of labor discipline. But the concept was implemented with enthusiasm only in the late 1950s when Chairman Khrushchev announced the final march on Communism.

At last I saw it. "ON TUESDAY, APRIL 10, 1962, AT 1900, THERE WILL BE A SESSION OF THE COMRADELY COURT OF HOUSING BUREAU NUMBER 5 OF LENINSKII DISTRICT TO HEAR THE CASE OF CITIZENESS KLIUCHKOVA IN THE *KRASNII UGOLOK* IN THE COURTYARD OF 2b LENINSKII PROSPEKT. ALL COMRADES ARE INVITED."

By then I knew all too well from my wanderings that a Housing Bureau is the next-to-lowest link in city administration, the organ of five or so adjacent apartment houses (the lowest link is the office in individual apartment houses, where every inhabitant is registered and his vital statistics are kept up-to-date) and that *krasnii ugolok* (literally "little red nook") is the common room of the Housing Bureau, used for local government and Party business, for sewing lessons, administration of pensions, agitation and lectures, a children's library, social functions . . . I had been in a hundred of them.

In the seedy little *krasnii ugolok* at 2b Leninskii Prospekt, the tables were covered with flaming red cloths and the walls were strewn with typical banners: "Glory to the Communist Party!" "Brotherly Greetings to All Peoples Fighting for the Complete Eradication of Colonialism!" "The People and the Party Are Indivisible!" "Glory to Our Cosmonauts!" "Glory to Communism, Shining Future of All Mankind!" In one corner hung a wall newspaper devoted to apartment-house matters and sermons by the local Party organization. Lenin was everywhere—on posters, in photographs, water colors and reproductions, and in two fading-yellow plaster busts.

Four rows of benches were squeezed into the rear of the room, and squeezed upon them were about seventy-five spectators, almost all shabby, aged *babas*, grandmothers with nothing better to do that evening.

Sometime after seven o'clock the session began. Court was convened by an elderly woman who sat behind one of the tables. (It turned out that she was a former People's Court judge, retired on pension and filling her time with socially useful work.) To her left was another elderly woman, to her right, an elderly man. Nearby sat an ancient secretary. I was the youngest person there, by perhaps a score of years.

"Will you make it up?" the chairman asked the parties, not yet identified.

"Let's hear the case!" shouted a woman from the rear. "Read the complaint! Get on with it!"

"All right," said the chairman, and she began by reading a tattered letter from one Sobeleva, the complainant.

Sobeleva had written (in her own rules of grammar) roughly this: "Members of our Comradely Court, I ask you to examine the case of Federovna, the woman living with me in our apartment. Last February I was in the hospital recuperating. As soon as I returned, Federovna came to me and demanded money for the electricity and gas bill. [Her share came to twenty-eight kopeks.] When I said, 'No, I was in the hospital that month,' she started insulting me in the filthiest language. It was frightful. This is not the first time she behaved like an animal; you can expect only all sorts of unpleasantness from her mouth. Once she was about to beat me with her fists. Her son stopped her just in time. She constantly swears and insults me vilely, as well as all the others in our apartment. To live with her is to live in filth. I ask that the Comradely Court stop her from making my life miserable."

"What else can you add to your complaint, Sobeleva?" asked the chairman when she had finished reading the note.

"Just what I wrote," answered a hurt voice. Sobeleva, a heavy-set housewife, stood up.

"On what day did this last incident take place?"

"I can't remember—sometime in March. I know it was my day of *dezhurstvo* [duty day]." (In shared apartments as in dormitories and at work, everyone takes a turn cleaning the common bathroom, kitchen and halls.)

At the word *dezhurstvo*, there was an explosion. Federovna, the defendant, who could have been Sobeleva's twin, began shrieking from the other side of the room. "*Dezhurstvo!* Why don't you say anything about your refusing to clean up, you obscenity? How many times did you skip *dezhurstvo?* How many times did I have to clean up for you? You slanderer!" She shot a look of amazon fury at Sobeleva and advanced a step.

Sobeleva moved back a pace. "I never skipped my *dezhurstvo*. Once, just after I left the hospital. What are you trying to invent, you liar and hussy?"

"*You're* the liar. What about before? What about this winter? You worm, you sneaked out of your turn."

"I washed the floors for three weeks this winter . . ."

"Shut up. You never washed. Never. We had to do it for you whenever it was your turn."

"I washed in February, I did my—"

"You did not, you refused. And *you* have the gall to complain about *me!*"

After floors, the screams shifted to cleaning rags and cooking smells, while the chairman followed from side to side as if at a tennis match. At last she broke in: "All right comrades, please calm down. *Dezhurstvo* is not the point now; we have gathered to discuss the matter of insults. Federovna, what do you say about that?"

Federovna had a great deal to say. About her son, whom, she screeched, Sobeleva did all in her power to prevent from studying; about her wash, which Sobeleva took from the line while still wet; about the kitchen, which Sobeleva forbade to be used after 11 P.M., although the rules said it should be open until midnight. ("You lie, you lie," Sobeleva now was chanting.) About how that old spinster Sobeleva was impossible to live with because she had no respect for working people and constantly ignored or insulted everyone around her.

The chairman begged her to come to the issue of the gas and electricity bill.

"I simply asked her to pay her share. Twenty-eight kopeks —that's the big deal. She makes a scandal for a kopek, her stinginess is unbelievable. I never said an insulting word to that woman. She insulted *me*. She called me a—excuse the word— prostitute . . ."

"Tell them what you called *me*, you liar."

"I never called you anything, you shameless slanderer. Why don't you tell them about the filthy language you use? I won't repeat it. You are an impossible egotist—you, an *obshchet- vennitsa* [a community worker], who is supposed to set an example . . ."

By this time they were drowned out by the cackling of the spectators, who took sides hotly, defending one, attacking the other. The grandmother-neighbors, almost as aroused as Sobeleva and Federovna themselves (they were all cut from the same homespun cloth), made a deafening din. Later, when something like order had been restored, a few witnesses tried to be heard: Federovna's husband ("Sobeleva is unendurable, she squabbles about everything, every petty little thing") and Mikhailovskaya, a youngish woman who shared the apartment ("I've quarreled with the Fedorovs too, that's unavoidable, unfortunately, in one apartment; but Sobeleva fights with *everyone* about *everything*"). The chairman studiously ignored the cat-call interruptions from the floor.

"You forget *my* witness," whined Sobeleva.

"Oh yes, the other witness."

The other witness was the apartment house chairman. He took Sobeleva's side. "The Federovs are hotheaded, and I heard that Federovna has been reprimanded at work. Once she swore at me."

One of the peculiarities of the Comradely Court is open testimony: anyone present is entitled to stand and speak to the issue or around it. When the chairman opened the floor to the neighbors—"Does anyone want to express himself?"— the friends of one side and the other used this rare chance to show their loyalty and pettiness. "Sobeleva keeps a dirty room." "Federovna pushes her son too hard." "I've lived here since 1933. Sobeleva is the best neighbor of all." "I worked in a hospital, I know people. Federovna is an honest person." "Sobeleva swears." "Federovna spits." While the old women were having their say, the protagonists continued to shake fists at one another.

Pity the poor chairman—she was nonplused. "It's hard to say who is lying here and who is not, I don't know *whom* to believe . . ."

After about an hour she said she thought that the court had better retire for deliberation. The three went behind a flimsy curtain in a corner of the room, and soon their perplexed voices could be heard, since by that time the spectators and partisans had calmed down somewhat.

Everyone seemed to have lost interest by the time (after 9 P.M.) the verdict was read. The court concluded that the women were equally at fault and that their arguments could be easily, amicably resolved. It encouraged them to face their problems gracefully, in a socialist, comradely spirit, and

warned that further scandals would be punished strictly.
There was no punishment and no censure; the twenty-eight-
kopek debt was divided in half. A cackle of comments followed the decision—"Correct!" "Very good!" "Sensible!"—
and Sobeleva and Federovna looked at each other with shy,
tentative smiles.

I felt sadly swindled as I pushed my way out of the airless
krasnii ugolok. Was *that* a Comradely Court? Were those
petty quibblings typical of an institution about which I had
read so many indignant articles containing so many sinister ad-
jectives in Western journals? They seemed to be, for later I
saw four more Comradely Courts and none was more exciting, more politically significant or more ideologically directed
than the Sobeleva-Fedorovna squabble. All involved petty
personal conflicts, the kind that might have been heard in
Family Court in New York and disposed of similarly, if less
speedily.

The second case was similar to the first, except that the
principal scene of action had been the bathroom rather than
the kitchen and that two bulky women had come to face-
scratching and hair-pulling as well as insults. Before the chairman could read the complaint, the "accused," a peppery,
painted hussy in her forties, screamed that the court had no
right to hear the case because the same judges had tried her a
year before on a similar matter. Then she stormed out of the
room to everyone's amazement; but the hearing went on in
her absence, the court deciding to send the record to the local
People's Court for a possible criminal charge of minor bodily
injury.

I never found out what was involved in the third case, because the complainant, a timid young woman, and the "accused," an old man with a full beard, agreed to reconciliation
at the start. The fourth case concerned a slight, meek, ap-

parently respectable accountant who had gone on a four-day binge, starting on May Day, terrorizing his tremendous wife and the neighbors. He admitted his guilt "fully and completely before everyone present" and begged his wife to forgive him. She did, and the court limited itself to a social reprimand.

The last session I found promised to be more inspiring. So great, in fact, was its potential social significance that the hearing was widely publicized in advance and was held in the club of a local bindery, the largest auditorium in the neighborhood, instead of in the apartment's *krasnii ugolok*. About seven hundred local citizens, with grim *élan*, came to watch. And because the educational content promised to be sensational, a team of cameramen was on hand, with ponderous, clanking cameras and searing lights, to film the event for the Soviet newsreel "News of the Day."

The "defendants" were five teen-age boys—wise guys they seemed, but not quite toughs—charged with behaving disrespectfully to the elderly social worker in charge of youth activities in the courtyard of their huge apartment house. That they had made her life miserable was certain from the outset: they had insulted, sworn at, threatened, and ridiculed her. They had made her chase soccer balls around the yard, had returned borrowed money only after weeks of pleading, had thrown lighted cigarettes in her direction (she said they had set her hat afire, too), and out of exuberant adolescent spite, had ruined her attempts to organize activities for the younger children. The boys and the social worker seemed to have had a natural, grandmother-spoiled brat affection for each other, but the more she had pleaded with them to be decent the more they had taken advantage of her.

It was a classic case of "antisocial behavior," perfect raw material for a Comradely Court. It could put an end to an intolerable, though not criminal, human situation and preach the lessons of "socialist morality," "Communist upbringing," and "comradely, communal living"—all at the same time. The camera director had a fabulous script.

But his cameras hardly clacked. For this session in the bindery accomplished nothing besides entertaining the spectators with slapstick and discrediting the institution of Comradely Courts. The naïveté of the dear, misused social worker, the incredible bungling of the chairman (a senior Tory backbencher type whom I had overheard three days before in Moskvoretskii District Party Headquarters admonishing other officials pompously about the importance of making a good showing in the case), and the instinctive, malicious wit of the boys ruined this shining opportunity.

It was a fiasco from the start: the auditorium lights went out for ten-minute intervals, and the audience, restless in utter darkness, shouted every kind of mocking comment forward. ("A Court of Madmen"—the title of a current film discrediting American justice—was the favorite phrase.) When the lights worked, the microphone did not, and the chairman, though bellowing at full voice, could not be heard beyond the tenth row. No one seemed interested in hearing him anyway. The social worker was a sweet old do-gooder. She brought a list of sixty "wonderful" boys lest anyone think *all* her young ones were bad ("some of the youngest ones are simply beautiful toilers, future heroes of labor"). But she was so obviously unsuited to working with teen-age boys, so perfectly "square," that the audience mocked her in spite of her woeful tales. "Put her in a kindergarten where she belongs!" "It's her own fault for babying the boys." "What is this, the fairy-tale hour?" Paroxysms of laughter followed these comments.

The boys refused to "admit their guilt," and the chairman, who had no idea of how to produce evidence or conduct questioning (or how to defend himself against their repartee), ended simply and unashamedly by pleading with them to say that they had behaved badly, felt sorry and would change their ways.

"You heard what she [the social worker] said. Why did you chase the younger boys away from their own little play area?"

"That's what *she* says. I say different."

"You must tell the truth."

"You don't want to hear it."

"Are you a Young Communist? You know what's required of Young Communists. Tell us the truth as a Young Communist."

"And *you* know what's required of *old* Communists."

The gang finally went through the motions of repentance, through mocking grins, but not before bringing the audience again and again to laughter at the expense of their slow-witted questioner. They so clearly had the upper hand that even when mouthing the magic words of remorse, repentance or apology which are *de rigueur* at every self-respecting Soviet trial, they made the chairman look foolish.

The witnesses added nothing to the educational value of the afternoon. In desperation, the chairman called the boys' mothers to promise to reform their sons. But they rebelled. "Really," said one, "can it be true that grown men like you [the judges] have nothing better to do than this foolishness? What a ridiculous waste of time, your big-deal Comradely Court. Just get rid of that incompetent social worker and my boy will be fine." The audience cheered. Another mother insisted that her son learned his bad habits from the *druzhiniki*, which his Young Communist group had pressed him to join. The audience sympathized. A social worker from a neighboring apartment said that the boys were handled incompetently. The audience applauded. Then followed a parade of speakers, who could not be called witnesses, because they knew nothing about the case at hand and marched off the stage before they could be questioned about it. A woman talked about the universal need to love children, an excited sportsman proposed to sponsor a soccer team, the chairman of another Comradely Court described the tough row he had had to hoe as a youth and told how he had become a success in the socialist world. He exploded in anger when one of the boys asked how this was related to the hearing. The chairman of the apartment house appealed for a cleaner courtyard and stairways. The policeman on the beat quoted Lenin on the need to respect the People's Police. The Party secretary of the apartment-house group (16,000 persons) held forth on the origins of crime ("it festered in the filth of capitalist society") and its obvious incompatibility with socialist society, and he ended with the most stirring fifteen minutes of agitation—perfect for a revival meeting—that I had ever heard. The audience became noisier and noisier. The boys went on wisecracking marvelously. The chairman kept trying to get someone to condemn the defendants' behavior—"What do you think of the way they acted?" "I can't say; I don't know them at all." "But from what you heard today . . . ?"—but the speakers were concerned with loftier themes.

It lasted three hours, the audience had dwindled by half toward the end, and that half booed wildly when the chairman shouted that it would take at least a half hour to write the decision. He wrote it, therefore, in five minutes; although the court found that the boys had indeed behaved poorly, it "limited itself to a public examination of the case," and it prescribed no punishment, since the boys "saw the danger of their ways and promised to reform." *Sic!*

The cameramen packed their gear angrily. If a few coherent minutes of film could be pieced together to demonstrate the Comradely Court in action, it would do great credit to the editing ability of the Moscow studios. Uncut, it could only make a comedy—"A farce," my neighbor on the bench said disgustedly. The chairman looked beaten; he knew that the session had weakened local discipline and had destroyed the image of the Comradely Courts and *obshchestvennost* as a force to be taken seriously.

Outside the factory, the most gentlemanly of the youths, a well-spoken lad in a crew cut and a tasteful suit, approached me. "I guess you don't have anything like this in America, do you?" he said. "Well, it was our own fault; it's time to stop this kid stuff with our poor lady. Say, do you mind if I call you? I'd like you to meet some of my older friends. We've got our own little *obshchestvennost*—you'll have some fun."

The workings of official *obshchestvennost* still puzzle me in many ways.

How is it run? On paper, members of Comradely Courts and *obshchestvenniye* accusers and defendants are the people next door; they are elected at open general meetings of their respective collectives—the apartment-house group or the trade-union local. But in practice? I never attended any of their election meetings (the dean would not arrange it, and I was unable to do it on my own), but from what I learned from firsthand sources they do *not* follow the ordinary Soviet pattern of predetermined "elections." On the lowest level of public affairs in Moscow—trade-union and Young Communist committees, local boards, factory and apartment-house meetings—genuinely democratic procedures seem to be followed: more than one candidate is nominated, opinions and proposals are offered, and the voting is free and not unanimous. The Young Communist group of the Juridical Faculty provided a vivid example of this democracy while I was there. At one of its general meetings, the committee—that is, the activist, official leadership—recommended the expulsion of a nonconformist student for poor studies and wild behavior, and in the course of an hour's discussion it furiously assailed him.

Yet the rank and file voted almost unanimously not to expel him.

"Do you understand how *obshchestvennost* works?" an old woman, a member of the Comradely Court, asked me. "The people decide. That's democracy. It's the drawing of the people into the administration of public affairs. It's truly people's justice." And indeed, everyone I knew who attended these meetings assured me that at this level the rank and file *does* decide. It is not a rubber stamp.

On the other hand, the one thing most clear from a year's stay in Moscow is the utter absence of "public" or "community" apart from the Party. In Russia, "public opinion" in the professional sense means Party opinion writ into appropriate forms. Nothing can be openly done or expressed against the Party's will. It is the single cohesive element within society. The Party's part in introducing *obshchestvennost* into the law could not have been more prominent: the very concept was a Party invention.

The "opinion makers," the organizers, the chairmen, the leaders of *obshchestvenniye* organizations are almost always Party members specifically designated by the Party to conduct that kind of work; and even those who are not Party members are responsible to the Party apparatus. One trip to a district Party headquarters is enough to discover that: Party headquarters is the general staff. The Party's direction and co-ordination is above-board, since in Soviet public life the Party, as the "leading core of all organizations of the working people, both public and state" (according to the Constitution), is *supposed* to co-ordinate. And so, it would be very easy for the Party to rig the elections, predetermine the decisions of the meetings, and dictate the sentences in the Comradely Courts. The Party's wish to punish or censure a man is a command to the leadership of the local group. Thus, the great campaign to draw *obshchestvennost* into the administration of the law, far from being democratization of public life, may be the very opposite—a gimmick, a cynical and flexible, because so informal, instrument of Party dictatorship.

But I do not believe that that is the practice now in most individual cases. No one ever mentioned to me an instance of direct Party interference, and from what I saw, there was too much confusion and uncertainty behind the desk, too much genuine debate in the auditoriums, and too little preparation on paper to suggest prearrangement. And too little importance in the cases. I saw no *overt* signs of rigging. My free-speaking acquaintances thought it made better sense for the Party to let matters take their own course in these minor affairs—and thus engage the interest of the "broad masses"—than to decide the issues beforehand. And so, the Party actually seems to be encouraging the rudiments of grass-roots democracy in *obshchestvennost*. There may be pressure by higher-ups in some cases to make an example of some poor devil, but on the whole the refreshing experience of a general meeting run by majority rule no doubt stimulates healthy thoughts in the Soviet body politic.

There is, too, a legal question. The cardinal principle of all civilized legal theory—that no one be subjected to criminal penalty except by a duly constituted court after an impartial investigation conducted according to established procedure—is embodied in the Soviet Fundamentals of Criminal Procedure; but here, in violation of that canon, are the Comradely Courts, imposing fines and publishing censures (no matter that these are called "social measures" rather than "punishment") on the basis of some lesser procedure. No doubt this is potentially dangerous to socialist legality (I will return to this in connection with administrative punishments) but again, the practice seemed to me much less sinister than the theories about it. A warning, a reprimand, a fine of ten rubles; at most the Comradely Courts refer a serious case to the People's

Courts, where regular criminal laws apply. The sanctions at the disposal of the Comradely Courts are simply too insignificant to warrant indignation over their departure from traditional procedure.

Besides, what ought to be done with the women who fight in bathrooms and kitchens? Should they be sent to the regular courts under criminal charge? To a domestic-relations counselor? Left alone to pull each other's hair and scream away the neighbors' sleep? The Comradely Court does not seem an absurd alternative. Though probably less effective than Soviet legislators had hoped it would be, it is not really an objectionable way—except to legal purists—to try to smooth out these petty squabbles and disorders.

Finally, there is the question of what the activation of *obshchestvennost* is going to do to Soviet society. Some Western specialists consider institutions like the Comradely Courts the nth degree of totalitarianism, since *everyone* becomes Big Brother—the neighbors, the fellow workers, the comrades; all brother's keepers. A society is truly tyrannized, say these experts, when the citizen has been trained to do the job of the police, keeping a sharp lookout for breaches of discipline and hints of nonconformity. Such a society is like a monstrous "honor system" where honor is superfluous because everyone is watching everyone else, and everything is regulated.

Yes, but— That is not the way it works; that is not the way Russians act. "There is a trace of anarchy in the Russian man," an old Soviet ex-diplomat, who had seen the world, explained to me. "In this respect, we are rather different from the Chinese." The House and Street Committees and the Committees for Public Order in the Chinese Republic *do* appear to be functioning the way political scientists predicted they would, but the "Russian character" does not lend itself easily to restrictive regulation of personal life. (Long before the split, Chinese industriousness and asceticism provided material for humorous anecdotes all over Moscow, especially among university students, who are most repelled by Chinese conformity and lack of individuality.) The deep sense of community and of *belonging*—to the Russian earth, to the Russian people, to *Rossiya*, and to smaller divisions like the "collective" and the family—that Russians enjoy does not bring with it eagerness to spy on others or intolerance of individual habits. In the daily things, Muscovites seemed to me less conformist than New Yorkers; less concerned with the appearance they make and what strangers think of them; less self-conscious when they make a scene, bawl out the waiter, slurp over the soup, make a misstep on the dance floor; less reticent about expressing their pleasure or displeasure; less preoccupied with smiling and smelling sweetly. In that land of political dictatorship, there is in many ways less private tyranny than in the Free World, less subtle and not-so-subtle pressure to conform. *Obshchestvennost* has far to go to "catch up with and surpass" American advertising in this respect.

Western jurists say that a man ought not to be judged by fellows who live in such intimate contact with him. I think that depends partly upon the fellows. If the Party leadership, moved by its deep-seated yearning for control and orthodoxy, did in fact plan the Comradely Courts as a totalitarian instrument, the plans have run afoul of human stuff. In any case, from the few sessions I saw, it seemed that Americans who become angry over the ideological menace of the Comradely Courts are more doctrinaire than the Russians who take part in them. I found not much to admire in this whole massive movement involving *obshchestvennost*, but not much, so far, about which to be self-righteously indignant.

V

Comrade Procurator

THE PROCURATOR is the "commissar" of the Soviet judicial system. Think of the average one as a thickset, squarish, officious man (or woman) whose briefcase is stuffed with lunch and who forgets to hold the door open for the person behind him. He is a heavy-footed plodder, a grim self-righteous censor. Everything about him brings to mind the words "Old Style," which are used with dates in the tsarist calendar.

About a third of the time he appears in uniform: darkish blue with faint gold striping, insignia on the lapels, and a white shirt; a tasteful uniform—when it is pressed—roughly in naval style. (Women wear the same.) It is no accident, as Soviet writers love to say, that he alone in the courtroom is not in mufti.

If by "procurator" I have suggested in earlier pages a close counterpart of the American district attorney or state prosecutor, I have been misleading. The Soviet procurator is much more than a prosecutor. He has a unique conglomeration of duties and powers; he is responsible for "legality" everywhere, in all of its aspects, throughout Soviet life. He is more like the procurator of prereform (1864) Russia than the *avocat général* of the Continent. "We consider our procuracy to be another form of a court," said my adviser, the Dean of the Judicial Faculty at the university. And while some of his own colleagues would think that a bit strong, they all agree (as do

Western jurists) that one of the principal procedural differences between Soviet and Western law is the nature of the procuracy.

"Supreme supervisory power to ensure strict observance of the law by all ministries and institutions subordinate to them, as well as by officials and citizens of the U.S.S.R. generally, is vested in the Procurator General in the U.S.S.R." (Constitution of the U.S.S.R., Article 113.) What this enormously broad authority means in practice is difficult to describe, because the scope of activities too is enormously broad. There is, for one thing, a general supervisory power: the procurator looks (is required to look) everywhere and at everyone to see that there are no violations of any law; and everyone, on his part, is encouraged to report all violations to the procurator. For another thing, the procurator is charged with overseeing all directives issued by local government and economic establishments, to make certain that executive and administrative authority remain within legal limits. Then, too, he very closely supervises all legal and quasi-legal institutions. The functions of Federal Commission, Standing Committee, Mayor's Office, Congressional Committee, Attorney General, City Editor, and sometimes Royal Commission, are combined here with something else: a special, official monopoly of law enforcement.

The organization of the procuracy is special too, and it is considered so important that it is outlined by the Federal Constitution. The Procurator General is appointed for seven years, the longest term of any Soviet official; his subordinate procurators serve five years. The procuracy is one of the few entirely centralized Soviet institutions which have not been affected by the post-Stalin tendency to decentralize authority. "The organs of the procurator's office perform their functions independently of any local organs whatsoever, being subordinate solely to the Procurator General of the U.S.S.R."

The theory is that the procurator must be entirely free of local influences so as to be able to root out aberrations wherever they occur.

Dealing with the judicial organs, the procurator's functions are manifold. He sanctions arrest, supervises the investigation, must be heard by every appellate court, may open a case through *nadzor* (a form of higher court review) at any time, is responsible for the execution of sentences and supervises the places of detention. He may enter a civil suit at any time. And in all of this activity his holy grail is *zakonnost* ("legality") and *obosnovannost* ("validity," or "groundedness").

One might imagine that all these extraordinary powers and prerogatives make the procurator's status at the trial itself ambiguous. It is. On the one hand, he is the state accuser, the prosecutor, a "side" with no greater rights and powers than the other side. On the other hand, he continues to be the Protector of the Laws and to discharge his general duty to ensure legality everywhere. "The Procurator General of the U.S.S.R. and the procurators subordinate to him are required to exercise supervision over the legality and validity of sentences, decisions, determinations and enactments promulgated by court organs." How, exactly, these two disparate functions of the procurator ought to be discharged by one man I cannot say, for Soviet jurists themselves are not of one mind about it. The question of whether the procurator exercises any kind of *control* over the court is a hot one in legal circles.

In any case, the procurator at the trial is a special player, and he shows his special hand in a thousand ways. He speaks in the name of the guardian of the state, a state concerned with every aspect of the lives of its people and institutions. When a theft has been committed, he may take almost as much time in criticizing the security arrangements of the factory as in analyzing the character of the accused. When a man is knifed, he may castigate the victim for drinking with the accused

132

more than commiserate with him for his wounds. When youngsters are involved as malefactors, he is as likely to tweak the noses of their teachers, fellow workers, Young Communist and local Party officials as those of the culprits themselves for their shortcomings. When a pretty girl is married to a good-for-nothing shyster and has suffered at his hands, he may take time to preach to her about socialist marriage, scold her for making the wrong choice and make her promise not to take love so lightly, instead of offering her sympathy. One and all —sometimes even the judge—are lectured for their deviations from the written norms. And more than the written norms, the moral imperatives too are preached. For the procurator is not so much interested in settling accounts for a crime already committed as in taking measures to eliminate all potential violations.

Nevertheless, a specially aggrieved tone is reserved for the defendant. Oh, you scoundrel! Why did you do it? How, as a Young Communist, could you face yourself? How *could* you steal from your own collective, your own people? Why? *Why?* When women defendants are brought to tears, the procurator will leave off, mollified.

There is another side to this exalted role: intervention in the cause of the accused when required by justice, dismissing unfounded charges, mitigating the indictment, requalifying, speaking up for the accused, protesting sentences which are too harsh as well as those which are too lenient. The same procurator who prosecuted a case in his capacity as public prosecutor may protest the decision as unfair to the defendant in his capacity as supervisor of legality.

Predictably, justice requires the procurator at a trial to speak out against the accused far more frequently than in his behalf. But instances of the latter can be found. I saw several cases in which the procurator one way or another departed from the role of accuser.

There was a trial in City Court in which the procurator, his head glisteningly shaved in the Russian manner, asked that the charge be reclassified from intentional murder with aggravating circumstances, which carries the death penalty, to ordinary intentional murder, which does not. The defendants were a pair of skinny deaf-mute boys who had killed a counselor in their institution. There had been evidence, the procurator argued, that one of the boys had been cruelly tormented by the counselor; there were mitigating circumstances; the boys deserved another chance.

A woman on the dais interpreted furiously into sign language for the boys, gesturing frantically and grimacing soundless syllables. It was a macabre scene. When she came to the procurator's recommendation that the boys be saved, the hall burst into a flurry of fingers and jerky nods, for most of the spectators were deaf-mutes too.

The court spared the boys' lives.

And a case in a People's Court concerning an accidental electrocution in a local metalwork factory on the night shift of December 27–28. The last days of the month in most Soviet factories are a frenzied lunge to meet monthly quotas. "You know how it is," explained one of the accused, a master electrician in the plant, "we had *shtormovshchina* [storming] at that time like in every factory. We were all working furiously; in those days, hours, even minutes, count."

The second accused was a foreman of the shop where the electrocution occurred. What had happened was that a vital electroplating machine had broken down when it was most urgently needed; in the rush to repair it insufficient caution was exercised, and a man who was working on it was killed.

The electrician and the foreman were charged with "violation by responsible persons of the rules of industrial safety, resulting in death." The expert witness, an electrical engineer, said that an examination of the plant had convinced him that safety provisions in the factory were a sham and that the director and chief engineer were the *real* culprits, but there was no comment from the bench about this.

During the course of the trial the soft-spoken procurator, who wore a loud civilian tie with his uniform, helped the defense establish that the defendants, both of whom had been apprenticed at the factory as boys, had returned to it after the war, had accumulated together forty-two years on the job, and, with hardly any formal education, had worked up to positions of responsibility, were dedicated workers who labored under great pressure to meet production quotas. Their records were exemplary. In fact they were working on their own time to repair the electroplating machine when the accident occurred. The death drew attention to the need for drastic reforms in the factory, including the need to relieve the defendants' jobs of some of their too-diverse responsibilities.

The procurator emphasized all this, encouraged the defendants when the going was difficult for them, took pains at every opportunity to say that these were men of whom Soviet society could be proud, and contributed a general feeling of camaraderie to the trial. Summing up, he asked the court to dismiss some parts of the charge as "purely formal," and then he said:

The court must remember that for them the factory was their whole life. They entered it as apprentices and developed their qualifications to the point where they became administrators. They are skilled, motivated, dedicated workers whose first concern is production.

Of course, neither desired the death of a fellow worker. They represent, therefore—considering their character and all the circumstances of the case—a very slight social danger. They have already experienced what Soviet society requires of punishment: reform and re-education. [In addition to any spiritual suffering, both were transferred to lower-paying jobs.]

How should they be punished? The law provides for deprivation of freedom for up to five years. This is very severe. On the other hand, our courts must ensure that the Soviet people live in complete safety and health. The Soviet people, creators of the world's first Sputnik and leading warriors in the fight for peace, are our strength and joy, and anyone who permits their safety to be threatened is a criminal. Every violation of safety rules must be punished.

On the one hand, then, there is a dead man, a good, honest Soviet man; on the other hand we have two Soviet workers, excellent toilers who bend all their efforts to increased production, vital to the operation of the plant. . . .

Finally he recommended that they be returned to the production line and sentenced only to corrective labor. Counsel for the defense thanked him for his fair and objective summary, and agreed. The court concurred: both were given a year's corrective labor at their old jobs in the plant.

But the case that illustrates most clearly the curious dual, "higher" role of the procurator was one with an unusual pretrial history that I came upon in May. The charge again was murder. (There were two or three murder trials a week in the Moscow courts.) A man had killed his father in a fit of rage after years of feuding which had split the entire family into two irreconcilable camps.

The investigator classified the killing as intentional murder with aggravating circumstances (punishable by death), and the district procurator agreed. At this point a procurator from the city office entered the case, because under that charge the trial had to be held in a higher court, and he did not agree. Nor did he agree with the accused's counsel, who petitioned that the charge be reclassified as intentional murder committed in a state of great emotional excitement (punishable by up to five years' detention). The city procurator viewed it as *ordinary* intentional murder (punishable by up to ten years' detention) and with that qualification sent the case to the district People's Court.

The judge who was to hear the case, however, disagreed with the city procurator—in a preliminary stage of trial procedure called "transfer to court"—and ordered the original qualification, intentional murder with aggravating circumstances, reassigned. That was the charge under which the trial was finally held.

The facts were sordid, as they always are in a case of this kind, and the bereaved family, still spitting insults at each other in court, made a repulsive scene. The "victims" (special figures in Soviet law; I shall say more about them on page 275) were the dead man's wife, two daughters and a second son; and a more disreputable lot I never saw outside the dock. They screamed and swore, made threatening gestures with their hands, and showed the court little more respect than each other.

JUDGE: That's enough! You cannot use such language in court.
A SISTER: That's *not* enough, I'll say what I want to. My brother is a little bastard, the murderer.
JUDGE: Sit down, sit still, stop disturbing the trial.
THE OTHER SISTER: Stop talking like a big shot yourself. It's easy for *you* to sit down, you have a comfortable chair. Though I don't see how you rate it.

The scene of the crime and immediate source of friction was the family cottage in a village recently incorporated into Moscow's limits. The defendant lived there with his family in —he testified—harmony and peace. ("You must listen to me, I beg you to listen to me. You must understand what made me do a thing like kill my father when I loved him dearly.")

137

In 1959 the defendant married and brought his wife home to the cottage. A son was born shortly afterward, and from that time hatred racked the household. The two sisters became violently hostile to their brother, the defendant, and to his wife and the baby ("the new heir"), and in time they won the father to their side. There were violent arguments, some of which became physical set-tos, about dwelling space in the one-room cottage and about the inheritance. The father began to drink heavily and spend his time with prostitutes, but he dedicated his business hours to a holy war of meters and centimeters, rights of access and of use, against his son. Battles were fought at home, in the village cafeteria, in the Comradely Court, in the local housing office and in the Party headquarters. And more than once the battleground shifted to the People's Court, where the living arrangements of the cottage were pondered by the bench.

The greatest of the issues was an extension which the defendant had built onto the cottage to separate his part of the family and to give them entrance and exit independent of the father's section of the room. The addition projected some 35 centimeters (about fourteen inches) into the father's portion of the land (earlier, a court decision had divided the cottage plot down to the centimeter, as in old peasant Russia), and this enraged the old man. Egged on by the daughters, he vowed to have the terrace destroyed, and a later court decision did direct the son to remove the offending section of the terrace. The son refused, protesting that it would mean ruin of the entire extension, which he had built only with great effort and after great difficulty in obtaining materials, and a return to the impossible life in one common room.

This was the state of things when, early one October morning, he saw his wife returning from what had sounded like a physical struggle with his father and sisters. Blood was streaming from her face. "Your father—" she began to say. He flew into the courtyard, where he saw his father with a stick in his hand; losing control of himself, he hit his father on the head with a rock.

In the course of a day and a half, the trial established, more than anything else, that the sisters were a foul pair. One was known by the villagers as "the drunkard," the other as "the whore." They had done everything they could to inflame the father against his son. Witness after witness said that they were constantly, unendurably drunk, and I think they were oiled at the trial. The judge could not conceal his disgust with them; he constantly ordered them to be silent, and at one point he threatened to throw them out permanently in spite of their procedural status as "victims."

As to who was "right" in the feud, there was testimony on both sides, but the weight of it lay with the son. The chairman of the local Comradely Court and the deputy to the local soviet said that the defendant was a peaceful family man who had tried hard to settle the arguments, but that the *starik* ("old man") was a stubborn crank who refused every rational suggestion and seemed bent on fighting. The neighbors testified that the sisters were filthy and spiteful. A third sister, who lived elsewhere, took her brother's part, saying that the trouble was entirely the fault of the sisters. The most dramatic scene of the trial was the mother's testimony. For a moment, while the wrinkled old woman, shaking with grief and age, walked to the witness box, the hostility in the courtroom gave way to compassion. Did she consider herself a "victim," asked the defendant's counsel? She did. Of whose actions? "Of my daughters', of course. Oh, it will be terrible living with them now, without my son. Only he cared about me. My girls only beat me."

When the procurator summed up, he ignored all of this evidence and attributed full fault to the son. However, he urged again, like his colleague before the trial, that the killing be reclassified to ordinary murder.

His argument was this: The circumstances in aggravation were alleged to be (1) killing for mercenary motives, and (2) with special cruelty. Neither, he said, had been shown at the trial. Mercenary motives were impossible, because the son knew that killing his father would mean living in jail, not in the cottage. Moreover, he had approached his father empty-handed and had picked up a rock only at the last minute, when he saw the stick used on his wife. As for killing with special cruelty, the medical report determined that death was caused by a single blow, and one blow cannot be especially cruel.

Taking into consideration the especially abhorrent nature of patricide, he recommended ten years' deprivation of freedom.

Counsel for the defense argued that, taking into consideration that the crime was described precisely by a different article—"Intentional murder, committed in a state of great emotional excitement which develops suddenly as a result of . . . illegal acts by the victim if these acts caused or could cause serious consequences for the guilty person or his close ones"—the punishment ought to be no more than five years. This seemed to me an irrefutable argument.

The court agreed with the procurator and reclassified the crime. The punishment was ten years.

This case was reported ten days *before* the trial in a local newspaper under the headline "Spiders Behind the Fence." Here is that story in full, except for the deletion of some repetitions:

Once upon a time, Peter Yakovlevich Kasuanov [the murdered father] worked as a joiner on the railroad. Many years ago he was given a plot of land in Biryulev. Peter Yakovlevich, together with his wife, Olga Romanovna, built a house on this plot and planted a garden. The Kasuanovs began to live in style.

But something gave way from that time in the heart of the workingman Peter Yakovlevich. True, outward changes were not noticeable. Just as he had before, he went to work each morning at 7 o'clock. But work now did not occupy his thoughts. The house. The garden. A stick, a nail, a piece of iron found on the road—these he carried home. He had become a *khozyain* [a "homeowner," or "proprietor"]. And his neighbors pronounced this word in the way one talks of *kulaks* [rich farmers who were "eliminated as a class" by Stalin in 1930] in old times. Soon the Kasuanov family lived not only on working wages. Apples and flowers from Biryulev were sold at high prices at Moscow markets.

The children were taught the same. And when Alex [the son], who worked as an inspector on the railroad, took bribes for illegal transport of hitchhikers and was sent up the river, his behavior was not condemned by the family. Why, he helped furnish the house . . . he was the father's heir, a young *khozyain*. . . .

What had led to this tragedy? Why did the son kill his father? Why did the whole family fight, just like spiders in a can?

Some consider that Peter Yakovlevich's trouble-making character is the source of guilt; others, Alex's hot temper. But of course this is not the answer. . . . Raised in an atmosphere of love of property, the children no longer built a *common* home or garden. Each wanted *his* share. An epidemic of partitioning seized them all. . . .

Blinded by stinginess, the Kasuanovs stopped thinking of anything but amounts of apples, centimeters of land, rubles of income. . . . Although *obshchestvennost* and officialdom understood that the dissension of the Kasuanovs was a birthmark of the past, they tolerantly investigated the incessant disputes. . . . People saw what was going on. Often after fights at the Kasuanovs', neighbors went to court, to the police, and testified who was right, who was guilty.

But they didn't understand that all were guilty: father, mother and children. That they all should have been placed before a court of the people, once and for all, and stopped from making a home on a Soviet street into a *kulak's* private farmstead. In proper time, this would have saved the family from being engulfed by a quagmire of private property.

But as it turned out, they *helped* the Kasuanovs partition, instead of *putting an end to* the quibbling litigation.

A man who plants a fruit tree hopes that it will become a good memory of him. But Peter Yakovlevich did not desire this, and therefore the house and the garden did not bring happiness to his family. A natural desire to improve his life developed into senseless grabbing—into a fatal disease. The tree planted by Peter Yakovlevich bore poisoned fruit.

The life of the old man Kasuanov cost little—in all, 35 centimeters of farmstead—less than needed for a grave.

It is a horrible story; many shudder when they hear it. But it taught the Kasuanov family nothing. Once more they are suing, this time for the living space "vacated" by the father.

But this article is not written for them; they do not understand and, most likely, will not understand, that love of money is responsible for all this horror. And this article is not designed to demand strict punishment for the killer: in this case, he is not much worse than his victim, and he will be judged without our interference.

We want the neighbors to think about this story. And not only the Kasuanovs' neighbors, but neighbors in general. When rust begins to corrode metal, it can be worked away. But if it is unattended, the iron will be eaten through and will corrode away.

We want the tragedy in Biryulev to serve as a warning to those who have chosen private property as their idol. Let them know: greed makes them into beasts and deprives them of all human joys, bereaves their families, makes them renegades. Like the Kasuanovs.

Comrade Procurator warmly praised the article throughout the trial, bemoaning the love of proprietorship which still plagued the family forty years after private ownership of land had been abolished,* castigating the son, daughters and almost everyone else who took the stand, lecturing the spectators in the article's phrases ("Blinded by stinginess") and shaking his fist at the world about greed, evil, and private property. Only the "Soviet mother" escaped his righteous wrath.

But when it came to cases, he interceded for the defendant, carrying on the tradition of impartiality of the Soviet procuracy.

* Like every land-user in the Soviet Union, including collective farms and factories, the Kasuanovs were given the *use* of land (in the case of collective farms, "in perpetuity"), not its ownership.

VI

Settling Disputes:
Petrov v. *Kaminskii*

LIKE MOST lower courts, the People's Courts have more to do than to hear criminal cases, and although it was these that interested me most, I tried to get the flavor of their other functions on quiet days.

Civil cases are heard in the same rooms as criminal cases, and with the same arrangements: a judge and two assessors, and almost identical procedure. Until 1957, court districts were divided geographically into wards, one judge handling all affairs of the ward to which he was assigned. Under the present system all judges of one district are assigned to the district as a whole, thereby encouraging specialization. A judge now may hear only civil cases for six months, and afterwards only criminal.

Civil litigation is remarkably easy to follow. Court is convened, the parties are identified and examined, witnesses are sworn in and questioned, closing statements are made—by lawyers when present—and the decision is made in the "deciding room." Without policemen or the threat of criminal sanctions, informality runs almost to nonchalance. Witnesses are likely to interject opinions from their seats, and the judge is likely to listen to them. Sometimes the parties, lawyers, or spectators are allowed to have a go at each other without interference from the bench. Once a matronly judge rushed into the corridor to fetch water for a young girl witness who had begun to cry, and her gesture seemed so natural that no one took notice. Tempers, oratory, urgency and harshness are rare in these proceedings; a family-council atmosphere prevails.

The cases all seem to be petty, and one wonders why, in this land of industrial giants and economic trusts. It is because disputes between state enterprises, large and small, are heard not in the People's Courts but by an independent quasi-judicial tribunal called *Gosarbitrazh* ("State Arbitration"). If, say, Moscow Construction Company Number Four has a claim against the Hammer and Sickle Plant for faulty steel beams (there are hundreds of thousands of such cases involving industrial enterprises each year), it is heard by the arbitration machinery of the Moscow Economic Council, which has no direct relationship with the regular court system.

What is left, then, are the daily personal claims.

A medical student hung his raincoat in the cloakroom of the hospital where he was training; in the evening, it was gone. He is suing for eighty rubles. The hospital's lawyer says that on that day the cloakroom attendant was sick; that the student ought to have given his coat to an attendant in a cloakroom adjoining, instead of hanging it himself in an unwatched section; that the hospital is not responsible for articles not checked in the proper manner. Four jolly fellow students testify to the disappearance, and the court, ignoring the hospital's argument, awards seventy rubles. (But the student is disappointed nevertheless. It was an Italian nylon coat, the height of current fashion, bought on the black market, and now irreplaceable. He eyes my coat as he walks out.)

A toothless old woman, wrinkled to ripples, in felt boots, versus the Moscow–Yaroslavl Division of the Moscow Railroad Trust. She mumbles so unintelligibly that the judge asks her often to repeat. "Please, Comrade Judges, I don't know laws, I don't understand anything, I just know my son is dead and my life is hard and please help me." Her son was run over at a grade crossing a year ago, and she asks forty-eight rubles a month, half his salary, in compensation. The case had been in the courts before and was returned to the procuracy for investigation because no one—trainman, brakeman, conductor, gatekeeper, passerby—saw the accident. "This case ought to have been heard long ago," the judge says; and when the old woman fumbles for an apology he says, "Oh no, it's not *your* fault." The woman now lives alone on a pension of thirty-five rubles a month. Her remaining sons are invalids: one lost a leg in a mine, the second an eye in a factory, the third the use of his lower body during the war. The representative of the trust does not appear, but has sent a statement asking that the case be heard in his absence and arguing that since the circumstances of death are not known, and since the victim might have been drunk, the railroad is not responsible. The suit is rejected because guilt by the respondent has not been established, and the old woman turns away without a sound, to while away the rest of the afternoon with her fellow *pensionerkas* watching other cases.

A blond man in his thirties, with a stutter, wants his wife to give back his winter coat, topcoat and a suit, which she was keeping to "punish him" for leaving home and living with another woman. The court orders her to return the clothes. (Afterward he tells me that he spent the first months of 1945 in Portland, Oregon, while his ship was being overhauled in drydock. "I'll never forget it. Coming from Murmansk in those days, it was like going from night to day, from hell to heaven. You couldn't even tell there was a war going on. What a paradise! I hope my kid will live like that.")

A construction engineer is suing his "company" for 174

rubles awarded him as a *progressivka* ("bonus")—40 per cent of his wages for the second quarter of 1962, when his department exceeded its production quotas in building apartment houses. The State Bank refused to make payment, however, on the ground that in 1960 the "company" had been discovered 64,000 rubles short, and that bonuses are prohibited to officials involved in overexpenditure. The engineer, who has spent months with his claim in offices of the municipal government and the procuracy and of his trade union's Commission of Labor Disputes (which hears all labor cases in the first instance), protests that he joined the enterprise only in 1961; that all of the administrators involved in the "violation of financial discipline" have since been fired; that he had no connection whatsoever with the overexpenditure. The representative of the construction enterprise, also an engineer, supports the claim against his organization, and when, after three minutes of deliberation, the suit is won, both engineers shake the judge's hand.

A nondescript man in his forties asks the court to reinstate him at work. In September ulcers kept him in a hospital for three weeks, and when he was released he was told not to work the night shift. He showed the certificate to his superior —a foreman at a suburban post office depot—but just before the holidays commemorating the October Revolution the depot was heavily overworked, and he was scheduled, as before, for both days and nights. He began to feel ill again, stayed home on the night of November 5, and was fired for truancy. A procurator participates in the trial, and she, the judge, and a lawyer scream shrilly, sometimes simultaneously, at the respondent, represented by the depot's inspector of cadres and the chairman of the trade-union committee. "This is fantastic. You know the law; you know that a sick man must not be made to work where his health is endangered.

Even a murderer in prison is treated according to a doctor's orders. And you force a first-rate worker to sacrifice his health. It's not only illegal, but inhuman, *cruel.* You know that firing is an extreme measure, a last resort. You had no right to fire him even if he *had* been at fault; under the circumstances it was your *duty* to relieve him of night work *immediately.*" The trade-union and administration officials, neither less proletarian in appearance than the complainant, try to defend themselves: "But we were worried about operations; we are a Brigade of Communist Labor. In the interests of production—"

"In the interests of production," the procurator cuts in, "you do not ruin a man's health. You do not permit slogans to mean callousness to toilers. You're supposed to be a Brigade of Communist Labor? What do your actions have to do with Communism? Communism means, first of all, decency in human relations; and you spit on a man, a sterling worker. This is an outrage. I'm going to take it up at the Party meeting. You administrators too often forget the law and forget the toilers in the name of the state and of production. Well, we'll have to teach you that it can't continue."

When the women have exhausted themselves, the postal worker is reinstated with full retroactive pay, and the judge announces that the court will issue a "private opinion" in the case. This will be a scathing critique of the depot's administration for permitting the firing.

A mousy young girl is sued by Clothes Factory Number 3, where she worked as an examiner of material; shortages of material worth 81 rubles and 18 kopeks were discovered in her department in the course of a periodic check. She has no idea where the missing material went; people came in and out of her storeroom taking things, for which she couldn't get them to sign. Besides, she was sometimes sick, sometimes at other work.

The principal witness, her boss, is not called because he is in jail for undisclosed matters. The girl, who is legally responsible because she signed a contract making her so before she took the job, says timidly that thirty rubles might be a fair amount for her to pay; the representative of the factory, an ancient lawyer, fumbling and trembling with age, produces invoices totaling 81.18. The judge is a kindly man who takes time to talk about it soberly. The room is empty except for the participants, who almost whisper. They have to strain to hear the girl. When finally the court rules that she must pay forty rubles, everyone feels that it is the only fair decision.

A tough cooky of a woman seeks alimony of 15 rubles per month from her former man. Both are truck drivers. They met when assigned to the same dormitory on a construction site in 1954; a private room was obtained in 1956; a son was born in 1957; the relationship, never registered as marriage, was dissolved in 1957. Afterward, he voluntarily supported the child, but stopped when he married into another family. "*He* wanted the child so he could stop drinking and make his life meaningful. A woman shouldn't have to raise a child alone." While the figures are aired (she earns 120 rubles—"Because I work like a slave, fourteen hours a day and holidays" —and he 55), there are rumblings from the public benches, the families on both sides hissing at each other. Suddenly the defendant's current wife shouts "you slut" at the complainant, and the courtroom becomes a battleground. When peace is restored, the judge is sympathetic to the woman; but he cannot satisfy her suit, because the code states that a mother is not entitled even to apply to a court for alimony for a child born out of wedlock. "There is nothing I can do to help you," the judge says afterward. She asks about an article she read in a popular magazine stating that she was entitled to alimony. "It was an improper interpretation of the law. We've had dozens of such cases lately because of that article. Sorry. We really oughtn't to have heard your case, you've no right . . ."

STATEMENT OF CLAIM

I, Citizeness Vedenskaya, Tatyana Romanovna, entered registered marriage with Citizen Vedenskii, Pyotr Ivanovich, on 8 July 1960.

From the marriage with him, I have a daughter, Elena Vedenskaya, born 29 May 1961.

For a long time Citizen Vedenskii has not given me material help in the bringing up of our daughter, therefore I ask the PEOPLE'S COURT to DEMAND alimony from Citizen Vedenskii, Pyotr Ivanovich, in a compulsory manner.

City of Moscow, Nineteen Hundred Sixty Two, Month of October, Sixteenth Day.   [signed] VEDENSKAYA

In the record also were a copy of the Vedenskiis' marriage chit, a copy of the daughter's birth certificate, and certificates showing that the daughter lived with the mother and that the father had been notified of the suit.

Vedenskii and Vedenskaya enter together, both plain factory workers in their thirties. The judge asks why she seeks alimony. "Because I've asked for divorce. I don't want to live with him, I will definitely get a divorce." The judge asks whether he is willing to pay. "I am willing. But I've already been giving her twenty-five per cent of my pay. What she writes is not true—it's just this last month I couldn't." Then, to Vedenskaya: "There's no need to lie about it, you know, you've got to tell the court the truth." "Why do *you* lie? I have to beg you for money. You stuff your mother with caviar and don't care what your daughter eats. That's not decent."

In a few minutes the court orders Vedenskii to pay Vedenskaya 25 per cent of his salary (a standard figure established by the code) until the maturity of the daughter. The couple, now tranquil, leave together—with the daughter and mother-in-law.

A used, frighteningly Neanderthal woman—huge crevassed mouth, beady, sunken eyes above massive cheekbones, tiny forehead—is suing to establish a judicial fact. She has spent seventeen years in jail. In 1937 she was convicted under a subsequently repealed Article 58(10), "Propaganda or agitation containing an appeal . . . to weaken Soviet rule." She had been charged simply with "swearing at Stalin." She was released in 1941, but was arrested again almost immediately afterward for having no job (during the war), and spent the years until the 1953 amnesty in labor camps. Now she is on pension and also works as a gatekeeper. She wants the court to certify that a labor book issued at one of the camps in her married name—she subsequently resumed her maiden name—is in fact hers. While the court is out, she leans, bent, on her cane, coughs horribly, mutters to herself about her arrest ("I was a young maiden then") and her decade in a Siberian labor camp, which sapped her strength and made her a hag. Not a trace of resentment enters her voice; all she wants is to straighten out the labor book for her pension's sake. The court certifies that the book in question is in fact hers.

A well-tailored older woman, a rare touch of Soviet swank, is waiting in the corridor during a recess in a dragged-out hearing concerning thousands of rubles in royalties, an eight-room *dacha* and a new car—the legacy of her husband, a writer of popular novels. The will is contested by the dead man's brothers. The pace is slow; this is the second day; three smooth-looking lawyers are having a field day. The whole case reeks, all the more because of its uncommonness, of bourgeois legalism and self-interest.

A peasant collective in the person of six or seven miserably bedraggled country folk in muddy boots and jackets smelling of manure is trying to recover some part of the value of last fall's crop of apples. They loaded them on the truck of a city swindler who was to have delivered them to market but whom they never saw again until his trial. He was convicted of theft; now the peasants are asking the court for a civil judgment providing compensation. (The convicted man's wages in labor camp can be attached.) The judge awards half the amount requested, explaining that the convicted man is already being punished sternly and that the collective knew quite well that the truck belonged to a construction enterprise and was being used illegally for private gain.

Usinov, Yurii Aleksandrovich, seeks damages of 1,273 rubles and 18 kopeks to repair his 1949 Pobeda automobile. On a September evening it was almost totally demolished when hit head-on by a truck belonging to Autobase Number 51 of Omsk region on the Irtis-Omsk road, near the village of Pokrovka. (It would hardly have paid to repair the car if Usinov would not have had to wait years on line to buy a new one.) The local (Omsk) People's Court found the truck driver guilty of reckless driving—he had been drunk—and sentenced him to two years' deprivation of freedom. Now plaintiff requests damages in full. But the case is not heard; Usinov does not appear and has informed no one why.

A shy young woman asks for alimony for her child.
"How much alimony?" the judge wants to know.
"Oh I don't know. Whatever you think is fair."

"You must make a claim," says the judge; "we cannot make it for you."

"I don't know what is fair," the girl answers. "Please help me."

They settle on the standard amount: 25 per cent of her estranged husband's wages.

An angry, disheveled woman has brought a claim for reinstatement in her job at Moscow Bread Factory Number 8. She worked there from 1944 and eventually became the dispatcher of trucks, in which job she was responsible for every loaf that left the bakery. Two months ago, dozens of extra loaves were found on a truck whose driver did a humble private business alongside his regular deliveries. The woman was immediately transferred (in spite of a doctor's orders prohibiting it because of her weak heart and high blood pressure) to unskilled labor in a warehouse; and after the driver was convicted, she was fired altogether.

"The director called me a swindler and a thief," cries the woman, now in tears. "How dare he say that? How can they ruin me this way just because someone else was thieving?"

The judge asks her to calm herself, and he points out that, according to the system, finished bread could leave the factory only through her. How could the extra bread be loaded onto a truck without her knowledge? Wasn't it her job to check just that? He then refers to her conviction for petty theft in 1941, and to several minor reprimands and reproofs in her record at the factory.

"That's unfair. I knew nothing about any extra loaves. It's all untrue. How can they kick me out of a job without the slightest proof or even indication that I am guilty? Is this what you call justice?"

The judge postpones decision so that he can study the

record of the driver's trial and confer with the woman's trade-union representatives.

On a fresh piece of cardboard was drawn unevenly:

PEOPLE'S COURT, MOSKVORETSKII DISTRICT
HOURS OF CONSULTATION

C.	1. EVICTION	
	2. LODGING	
	3. THE RIGHT TO DWELL-ING AREA	People's Judges Zhalkunov and Morozov.
	4. DIVISION OF DWELLING AREA	Tues. and Thurs. 10–12
	5. DISPUTES ABOUT RENT	

I know no parallel in Western law for about half of the civil cases in the People's Courts, those that concern *Zhilploshchad* ("dwelling area"). *Zhilploshchad* is one of the most valuable possessions in Moscow, and one of the most litigated.

Karaleva v. Karalev: division of dwelling space. A man and his former woman—they were divorced a year ago but still had to share their single room—re-enact the petty conflicts of two people who no longer can endure living together. "He does . . ." "She does . . ." "That swine . . ." "That witch . . ." Bitterness of this kind is rarely expressed in divorce cases, for Muscovites seem to consider physical separation more significant than legal parting. The judge has just heard two of these cases, one in which a new wife joined the divorced but still-rooming-together couple, and makes an effort to display his boredom rather than conceal it. He plays with the words of the woman's lawyer, a startlingly young girl with pink cheeks and a canary-yellow hat; then he divides the room —six square meters for Karaleva and five for Karalev.

Uderevskaya v. Uderevskii: eviction. A woman lives with her son and daughter-in-law in a room of twenty-seven square meters. Two years ago her husband left to go to another woman, and she wants him officially evicted. (The law provides that a person loses his right to *zhilploshchad* if he does not make use of it for six consecutive months.) But she has opposed divorce. The man's problem is that if he is expelled from the apartment and prevented from marrying the other woman, he will lose his right to reside in Moscow. At the same time the son, who is twenty-three, requests permission to divide the twenty-seven square meters into two parts so that his wife can be registered there officially. The court tries to reconcile the senior couple because that would be the easiest solution to the dwelling-space problem; they refuse. The third woman agrees to register the man at her room. The court grants the eviction and orders the room divided, giving the son and his wife twelve square meters.

Paramanova v. Vlassova, Kurilkina, and Sidorenko: division of living space. This is a friendly suit; the four women, with their families, live in three rooms (eight people in 32.94 square meters) and have agreed among themselves to divide one of the rooms and rearrange themselves in the others. They have resorted to the courts because the municipal housing officer refused permission on the grounds that one of the families would have less than the legally established minimum area per person. The women entreat the court. "We cannot go on any longer. Eleven years! We are all respectable people; we try to respect each other's feelings, but we simply cannot live a decent life under the existing arrangements." When the suit is rejected, they charge upon the judge, while he tries to calm them by explaining the procedure for appeal.

There is a dispute about a door, about a stove, curtains, a bed, square meters, square centimeters . . . Russians of the wide and generous nature can be petty too, and petty bourgeois. "Rights" of *zhilploshchad* are selfishly squabbled over. But how would Anglo-Saxons behave in their place, where square centimeters *do* make a difference? Probably with greater use of schedules and self-made regulations, with more order. But probably with far more litigation too.

Certain things stand out in these cases. One is that everyone, even a child, knows the amount of space he occupies, to the nearest square centimeter. A second is that socialist mothers-in-law cause as much friction as capitalist ones, but are better tolerated because they are needed to mind the younger children and to cook.

Another is the amount of paper that is required. A good part of a judge's week is spent at the *priyem*—that is, the consultation period, usually held on alternate mornings. Citizens come to petition him and seek advice about the whole range of judicial matters. Almost all civil cases are preceded by a meeting during the *priyem*, sometimes with both parties participating. The judge listens to problems and he advises—none too graciously, from what I observed—as to procedure in dealing with them: what to do, whom to see, how to proceed, what documents are needed. And what documents *are* needed! The records of the most petty cases are thick with *spravkas* ("certificates," or "chits"), that omnipresent Soviet phenomenon. From the housing office, the procurator's office, the health office, the repair office, the city Soviet, the Comradely Courts. . . . Of course, the judges are never able to read them through during the trial, or even before rendering a decision, but the party that lacks a *spravka* or two is out of luck.

In these cases, one is struck also by the seemingly great incidence of marital infidelity and the restraint and maturity with which it is handled. On the part of the court, there is no lingering on details, and no delicate avoidance of them. On the part of the parties and witnesses, even adolescents, there are no snickers and sneers. Sex and all of the problems it creates are treated like other facts of life; adultery, loss of desire, children out of wedlock are spoken of here—if not in criminal trials—as natural, if unfortunate, realities. When a man says, as one often does, "I simply prefer the other woman," the court accepts it as a valid argument.

Common-law relationships seem to be widespread, among older people as well as younger. This is evidence not of promiscuity—although that too is fashionable with certain strata of Moscow youth—but of a nonchalant attitude toward legal formalities. When people live together they are considered, by themselves and their friends, married; and when they make arrangements that suit them better, no one, except the old *babushkas*, talks much about it. In fact, no one talks much about sex in general. It is enjoyed in a rough sort of way, without the refinements of playing at long range. This healthy naturalness, I have been told, is a Russian quality that has nothing to do with Bolshevism or the Kremlin. Undoubtedly. But Bolsheviks are Russians too, and I think that there has been too much made of the Soviet regime's supposed prudishness. The enlightened abortion, birth-control and marriage arrangements belie this, and so does the liberal treatment of infidelity in the civil courts. When vodka is mentioned, judges respond as if Pavlov's bell had been rung, but there is little of this bearing down to change old habits and attitudes in the realm of sexual relationships.

I am tempted to summarize a dozen eviction cases, because more than the others they give the flavor of Muscovites' private lives. But I'll take only one more—one with more than just an observer's interest for me.

A poor mushroom season means no war, a Russian folk saying goes, and because the 1962 season was very poor, Muscovites lived through the Cuban crisis with extraordinary *sang froid.* My colleagues in the dormitory would not interrupt their dominoes to watch television news broadcasts down the corridor. No one seemed excited; rather few were even interested.

I was very much interested, however, and in late October I hurried to the American Embassy frequently for news. On the way there one day, I ducked into a ramshackle, two-story wooden house set back in a courtyard about two hundred yards from the Embassy building, the People's Court of Krasnopresnenskii District. I intended to stay only a minute to scan the list of cases, but circumstances held me there two full days.

Just as I pushed my way through the loiterers at the entrance, someone shouted my name. It was Vitya, a young photographer, and Natasha, his black-eyed wife, a chemical engineer. I had spent several delightful, warm evenings in their home, a single, dank basement room where three people were crowded, but which somehow even enriched their Russian hospitality. Vitya and Natasha had been called as witnesses in a civil case of eviction which had become a minor *cause célèbre* in the jazz world of Moscow, and they insisted that I stay to hear it because, they assured me, it would be a "fascinating" case. And indeed, I never got to the Embassy.

It was a case of young love turned to hate. The history of domestic misery which led to the trial was typically bitter, and it involved a mother-in-law, a lover, and visits by the police. Passionate antagonism smothered the marriage. In the end, Valya Yatsenko, a coolly handsome blond engineer, sued for the eviction of her husband, Evgenii Timofeyev, a slight, dimpled jazz trumpeter, the long-standing friend of Vitya and Natasha, on the grounds of hooliganistic behavior.

What made the case unusual was the attention given it in the press. Soviet trials are not "covered" in the Western sense; one sees no exploitation of courtroom sensations or lurid background articles. When newspapers do report criminal affairs and expose antisocial behavior, the copy is heavily weighted with moral exhortation: crime does not pay; every citizen must battle with every violation of the law; *this* could have been prevented; little violations grow into big ones; where were *you* when this happened?; the people must constantly be on guard for legality; live as a Communist. Typical headlines are: "The Hooligan Is Punished"; "A Just Reward"; "The Sentence Was Deserved"; "The Cheaters Were Gotten Rid Of"; "Stop the Bribers." Civil cases are reported even more rarely. But this was an exception. The Yatsenko-Timofeyev dispute was written up with a splash in *Moskovskaya Pravda*, the organ of the Communist Party of Moscow, three months before the trial. It was entitled "A Rotten Soul," and it exposed the social danger of that scoundrel Evgenii Timofeyev. Timofeyev, it said, was an ogre, a vicious hooligan who ruined the marriage, behaved bestially to Yatsenko, and lived a self-seeking, anti-Soviet way of life. "Timofeyev's puny soul is rotten through and through. He is a man capable of outright forgery and deceit. . . . He must be made to pay in full."

It was a three-column article, written in *Time*-cum-sermon style—"The general opinion of all teachers: Timofeyev is a mediocre student"—and it naturally became the focal point of the trial because it set out the facts and circumstances of the case and of the Timofeyevs' domestic history in great detail. "If we are going to listen to testimony which tries to contradict *Moskovskaya Pravda*," said Valya's lawyer, "I must protest. Our press deals in facts. We have it in black and white that Timofeyev is a hooligan."

Luckily for Timofeyev, the court did not sustain this reasoning, and one after another, the witnesses made a shambles of the article's "facts." It turned out that *she*, not he, had suggested legal marriage, as a way of getting an extra room in a new apartment; that she, not he, had obtained the new apartment in a building constructed for workers of the procuracy through her afternoon acquaintance with one Lev from the district housing office; that she, not he, began dividing the household's property after they quarreled; that she, not he, created angry scenes and was thought by all the neighbors to be the source of their domestic troubles; that she had changed the locks and refused to admit him, threatening to have him exiled from Moscow for hooliganism if he continued to come home; that she had had him sentenced to ten days in jail for petty hooliganism, charging that he beat her on an evening when he was in fact at rehearsal (he was released when his friends proved this to the procurator and showed that her subsequent recollection that it happened on August 7 and not August 6 was impossible since her complaint had been signed on August 6); that he had been treated at a local clinic for face scratches, and that she had tried to induce the doctor to destroy the files; that Timofeyev (who also studied conducting at a musical institute) was not a poor student (although he was expelled from the school after the publication of the article); that he *had* paid his Young Communist League dues regularly; that his character and record were *not* filthy; et cetera, et cetera.

The article had distorted or falsified outright every circumstance in the wildest possible way, and this was understandable, since (it was finally revealed) it had been written by a friend of Valya's. It had been submitted in the form of a letter to the editor, had been rewritten only for style, and had been published over the signature of one of the paper's staff men. "How can our central press publish such things?" witnesses moaned.

Valya's witnesses, speaking in her defense and in defense of the article, lied obviously, stuttering and stammering, confusing dates and contradicting one another, sometimes snarling from the public benches. Evgenii's witness, by contrast,

brought stacks of documents and tape-recorded interviews
(which the judge declined to hear) to support his cause.

In a word, the article was pure invention. The City Editor
must have sensed trouble, because he came to the trial and
sat in the stifling room the two full days, a gray-haired,
distinguished-looking gentleman who frequently looked at
his nails. Perturbation never so much as flickered across his
handsome face, even when the most damning proof of the
article's fallaciousness came out; but he must have been worried, because during recesses he tried feverishly to find out
who I was—he suspected a foreign correspondent—and the
people he queried told me afterward that he was very upset by
"the stranger's" presence. After one of these breaks when
he went into the chambers, the judge instructed me to stop
taking notes.

The procurator participated in this trial, as she is entitled
to do in any civil case which she feels affects the public interest, and appealed for moderation. "I must say emphatically
that the question is not of jazz. Soviet society has nothing
against the proper kinds of jazz, and it is wrong of complainant's counsel to imply that jazz musicians are *ipso facto*
suspect." Both lawyers then made impassioned speeches for
their clients, and in five minutes the court returned with the
decision not to evict Timofeyev. The judge said nothing
about the newspaper article.

The decision, of course, solved little, because the doors were
still locked to Timofeyev, the family was still in shambles, and
Valya still vengeful. When I visited Vitya and Natasha again
in their room, they mentioned that Timofeyev was again fighting eviction. Yatsenko had appealed the decision to the City
Court, and in his brief her lawyer referred again to "facts
proved" in the article in *Moskovskaya Pravda*.

The fact that the case was still shuttling around in the

courts showed that the article's principle lesson had been lost on Moscow judiciary:

"It was clear to everyone what kind of bird Timofeyev is. But for some reason he is sentimentalized over to this day. The Soviet court is humane. Its main task is to educate people. Everywhere Timofeyev was spoken to politely, with restraint. The usual hot air which he produced in self-justification was listened to attentively each time; there was even sympathy for his tears. And Timofeyev made use of this. . . .

"Formally, the people in whose power it lay to put this faking petty-bourgeois in his place 'took measures,' in the words of protocol. The police, the courts, the procuracy will show you proof of that. But none of the comrades handling Timofeyev's case set himself the task to probe more deeply into this man. Each of them 'reacted' exactly as much as was needed in order to be able to say, if necessary, What do you want of me? I took action according to the instructions. Oi these instructions! How often they still become a shield behind which hooligans hide from fair retribution, how often we are unwarrantably good to people who spit on our goodness!"

Evidently a zealous press sometimes diminishes the chances of an impartial hearing even in Moscow. Nevertheless, most of the civil cases I watched were handled with dispatch and a kind of rough reason, and without the complicated legal maneuvering that sours good citizens on the value of the courts as an arbiter of their private conflicts.

VII

Divorce: *Ivanova* v. *Ivanov*

ONE EVENING in late March a friend who knew of my interest
in courts suggested that I come along the next morning to his
divorce. Sasha (Aleksandr), an undergraduate in Russian literature at the university and an occasional contributor, on
literary themes, to Moscow Radio, was a sensitive, widely read
young man of twenty-seven, the most likable among those I
knew in the dormitory. He could have transferred to Harvard
—and back—with only minor adjustments, and there are few
outstanding students in humanities about which this can be
said. Sasha preserved an intellectual honesty while winning
steady "excellents" in his courses, which is probably harder to
do in Moscow than elsewhere. He was a passionate socialist,
a humanist and a liberal, and it was in our endless talks that I
first began to sense that some of the best of Russia's youth, for
all their disgust with the restrictions and crudities of Soviet
society, believe deeply in its fundamental rightness because
only socialism offers hope for societal decency, individual dignity and the perfectability of man from a psychology of
greed to one of generosity.

Sasha's wife, Lena, was a chemist, quiet, well-groomed, self-
possessed, the New Soviet Young Woman—which means she
looked almost West European. She had finished her course in
the university in December and soon thereafter, when it

became clear that the marriage was not to be continued—I never knew exactly why; it apparently was an intimate matter—left their room in the dormitory to move in with a friend in town. Their child, a girl of two, continued as before to live with her grandmother.

About divorce, I knew at that time only that it was a multistage procedure heard first in the People's Courts and then in the Provincial Courts, one level higher. Lena told me that their proceedings started with a short advisory talk with a lawyer, after which she applied to a local People's Judge for a hearing in his court. The judge tried briefly to dissuade her, but after a few routine questions and payment of ten rubles, set a date some weeks ahead for the preliminary hearing. It was at this stage that Sasha invited me.

Their session was held in an ordinary People's Court. We waited in the corridor and the courtroom while the cases preceding theirs were heard in an atmosphere conspicuous for its lack of tension.

In time it was their turn. The judge checked their *personalia* quickly and glanced at the application.

"Frankly, I think your reasons are very flimsy. Have you thought seriously about it?"

After a pause Sasha said, "Yes, I think we've thought enough."

Lena was asked to stand.

"You initiated the action?"

Lena said she did.

"Why?"

"We . . . decided to. It has to be."

"Why? Is he a bad man? Does he drink? Insult you?"

Lena shook her head.

"Then why?"

"It's just no good."

"That's hardly a reason for an educated girl, is it?"

Lena said nothing.

"And you [Sasha] are not opposed?"

"No, I am not opposed. We no longer have a marriage."

"It all seems pretty weak to me. Are you *sure?*"

Both said they were.

"What a shame. Such a nice couple. *Nu*, all right, then, we will not engage in useless talk. Come on Wednesday [five days later] and you can pick up your application. There's nothing I can do for you."

In ten minutes Sasha and Lena and I went off together sadly to watch a mutual friend defend his *diplom* (undergraduate thesis) at the university. Sasha and Lena treated each other like long-standing library-friends.

The purpose of this first hearing in the People's Court was to try to effect reconciliation. Everyone regarded it as sheer formality. None of the later divorce cases, when I got around to watching a few on my own, attained the level of dignity of Sasha's, but none was more elaborate. Couples, sometimes close, even touching, sometimes kidding each other good-naturedly, sometimes the woman crying softly, stood before the judge at the start. Sometimes there were smirks, sometimes scowls, but rarely scenes; the lack of trauma and animosity surprised me.

"You will not make up?"

"No."

To the woman: "What is your reason?"

"I don't know. It's a bad marriage. It doesn't work."

"That's all?"

"He carries on. Drinks."

"Didn't you know that before you were married?"

"Not really. Can I get the papers today? It's hard for me to get here."

"You will get the papers in the normal order. Five days. We have rules."

To the man: "You don't object?"

"It's all the same to me."

"What do you mean?"

"I don't object, of course."

"*I* object to your lightheaded attitude to marriage. But I suppose it's too late for that."

The next pair came on after five minutes.

"Will you not make it up?"

"Oh, *nyet, nyet.*"

"Why do you want a divorce?"

The woman had been alternately crying and laughing with her husband while waiting their turn.

"It was impossible. Nothing worked. Impossible."

"What was impossible?"

"Our family life."

"Why?"

"Because he doesn't love me."

"He told you that?"

"Yes."

The judge scanned the dossier. "But you were married to and divorced from the same man once before. Didn't you *know* whether he loved you after all that?"

"This is the last time I'll divorce him."

"Did you leave him, or he you?"

"I left him. I had enough. He doesn't love me."

"When?"

"Last spring."

"And that's your reason for wanting divorce? Because he doesn't love you?"

"Yes."

"Sit down."

The partner was nonchalant.

"Is it true?"

"What?"

"That you told her you didn't love her?"

"Maybe. It's very possible."

"Is that the proper thing to say to a wife?"

"If you don't love her, it is."

"Then why did you marry her?"

"It was a mistake. She's a good girl, but I'm not made for marriage. She makes me too tense."

"Then you have no objections?"

"You might say not. I'll be very happy."

Publication of intention to divorce in *Vechernaya Moskva*, Moscow's evening newspaper, is the next step in the divorce procedure. It costs about forty rubles, and at least a two months' wait, for the list of applicants who have had their preliminary hearings is long.

The final hearing is held in Moscow City Court. Old and young, respectable and frowsy, makers of a dozen children and children themselves, the motley procession, timed to half-hour intervals, is continuous from 10 A.M. to 6 P.M.

One day at 3 P.M. it is a very pretty couple married two years, Egorov and Egorova. He is twenty-two, a fourth-year student at a physics institute, a big, dark charmer, dressed as a *stilyag* ("zoot-suiter," or "teddy boy"). He makes known to the spectators that he is highly successful with girls.

"Then you insist on divorce? Perhaps you are making a mistake. Perhaps, at your age, you should think it over. You should think of your child."

"We were as good as divorced long ago, in fact. Before our son was born. There's nothing to think over."

"Why? What's the trouble? Why are you so insistent?"

"Because we can't live together."

"Why can't you live together?"

"Because I don't love her."

"And how long did you love her?"

"That's hard to say. Not very long."

"What will happen to her now?"

"What?"

"I asked, What will happen to her later?"

"Nothing. She'll live by herself. She's a healthy girl. My mother will bring up the kid."

"And who decided this?"

"I did—together with her."

"But perhaps you are making a mistake? Think."

"No. No mistake whatsoever."

"Maybe you want to make up?"

"No. Not on your life. I cannot live with her."

"How do you know, really? You're still a child."

The girl is a fragilely beautiful young blonde, entirely without make-up. Earlier she had worked as a cook in a hospital; now she is busy with the two-month-old child.

"Are you agreed to divorce?"

"Yes." Quiet sobs.

"Why?"

A long pause. "All the same, we've no home left."

"And how could this have happened so soon?"

No answer.

"Hmmmm?"

"I . . . don't know."

"What do you *think?*"

"I can't think."

Gently: "Then maybe you are hurrying here? Maybe you should take some time to think? In the People's Court you were against divorce."

"Yes."

"There was still no baby then?"

"No."

"And now?"

"Now there is nothing to talk about."

Very kindly: "Why? It is your life—to talk now is important for you."

Sobs. She looks away.

"*Nu*, tell us. Why did you come to the conclusion that you must be divorced. Earlier you thought differently."

"Because we just can't live together. We lost our love."

"And you agreed that his mother will raise the child?"

"No."

"Then he was not telling the truth?"

"She will help out. It's *my* baby."

"Did you talk seriously with your mother-in-law?"

"No."

"Why? She's older; she might be able to help."

"She said that she wouldn't interfere in this."

"You should talk with her. As a woman, she must understand. A baby is born, and . . . you should not be alone . . . now tell us this: before marriage, did you love him?"

"Yes."

"Or was the marriage just a whim?"

"For me, no; for him, yes."

"Did you talk about everything before you were married?"

"We knew each other very little."

"How long?"

"A month."

"You were living where?"

"In the Urals, near Sverdlovsk."

"And you saw each other there?"

"We corresponded, mostly."

"You liked him?"

"Yes."

"And you were married there?"

"Yes."

"Did you have relations together before marriage?"

"Yes."

"Were you pregnant when you went to register?"

"No."

"And now, you are agreed to separate forever? Take your time and think."

Sobs. "I'm agreed."

"How will you live?"

"By myself, in a room."

"Why do you say the marriage was just a whim for him?"

"He . . . had a girl."

"A girl whom he saw? While you were married?"

"Not at the beginning. After about two months he began. She's prettier than I am. She attracts him more." Choking sobs.

"Then what happened? How did your marriage end?"

"He left—to go to her, I suppose. Then he asked for a divorce."

"Why, is he going to be married to her? Is she pregnant?"

"I don't know."

"Now, how do you consider him as a person? Good? Or bad?"

"He's a good man."

"*A good man?* After all this, you say he's good?"

"He's good. Only it's too bad that he likes another girl."

To the boy, sharply: "Stand up. We want you to tell us more. Exactly why do you want a divorce? From the beginning."

"From the beginning? We met in Sverdlovsk, saw each other for about two weeks. Then we corresponded, and I came back, as I'd promised. Then she told me she was pregnant, we had to be married. That was the method she used."

The judge asks the girl if this is true; she nods shamefully, yes.

The boy goes on, without being asked.

"I knew immediately it was a mistake. I came back to Moscow and sent for her soon afterward, and we started to live

170

together. She traveled badly, if you know what I mean: she was a different person in Moscow than in the country. It was no good from the beginning. We quarreled constantly. I would come home dead tired from the institute, and all she wanted was to make love. She would never go out or see my friends, or anything. She kept saying, 'I'm too ignorant. *You* go.' It was a terribly monotonous life with her; she bored me. Then, by the time the baby was coming—"

"And the other girl—is it true that you had one?"

"She sat home and dreamed that up. I meet lots of girls—"

"And *that* one? Did you *keep company* with another girl?"

"All right, let's say I met her. Big deal!"

"Don't you think that is insulting to a pregnant wife? That it is *wrong* to be seeing another girl?"

"No."

"No? Explain."

"I just don't think it's wrong. I wasn't meeting with her until the marriage bored me to death. She's much smarter than my wife. Much. My wife bores all my friends."

"How do you evaluate that kind of behavior now?—Seeing another girl?"

"Evaluate?"

"Yes, evaluate—what do you think now of the way you acted? Are you a Young Communist?"

"Yes."

"Well . . . ?"

"What can I say? And what difference does it make? *You* have to decide."

"We want to hear from you. How did you treat your young wife?"

"I might say I acted normally; *you* might say badly. I think I acted normally."

"Badly? That's hardly the word; I'd say much worse than

'badly,' after the way you behaved. I'd say disgustingly. And now a baby is left . . ."

"The baby will be O.K. I won't abandon the baby. My mother will bring it up. The point is that if I found I made a mistake with a girl there's no need to prolong it and ruin my life."

"You made more than a mistake. You acted like a scoundrel."

"I don't think so. She's so limited. She has a difficult character—"

"And your character is not difficult?"

"I consider that a wife must obey her husband."

"Just as the husband must obey his wife." Then, to the girl: "Have you irrevocably decided to be divorced? Are you *sure* you can't make up and make a family?"

In due course the divorce is granted, because when both parties have agreed, there is little else the court can do. Egorov is assessed fifty rubles in costs; Egorova, nothing. "We are going to inform the institute about your behavior," the judge announces angrily to him. "We'll have to teach you how to behave if you don't know. Come in here [to his chambers] with me, I want to talk to you, you wise guy." The girl has stopped crying and wears the look of a country girl lost in the big city.

Next comes Gurasov and Gurasova, an older couple.

"At first we lived in my room with my mother, that was O.K. Then we got a separate room, and he started drinking— inviting his friends, having drunken parties, creating scenes. I'm a Soviet woman, after all. We're building a decent society for women. I can't put up with that."

"You were blameless?"

"I treated him very well. Nursed him when he was sick,

cleaned up after his friends. I even had an abortion for him."

"That's your responsibility too. Or did he force you to have an abortion?"

"I wanted the baby. His mother talked me out of it."

"How long did you know him before you were married?"

"Four months."

"Don't you think you were hurrying things?"

"I guess I was. His own father warned me about him, told me that he drinks and fools around."

"You are a grown person; you ought to have thought about such things earlier. Is this your first marriage?"

"No."

"All the more reason. You acted frivolously. Why did you, a Soviet woman, as you say, rush into a marriage not knowing where you were going?"

Gurasov, Ivan Ivanovich, is a hail-fellow-well-met who works at a metal lathe.

"You agree to the divorce?"

"Yes."

"Everything she says is correct?"

"Not everything. We don't get along; that's not all my fault. She doesn't like my friends. A jealous woman, Lord knows why."

"But when you were married, didn't you agree to love her? Why don't you fulfill your human obligations, the first of which is to your wife, not your friends."

"I don't drink every day like she claims. What's wrong with a drink now and then?"

"Obviously you haven't given her a good life. A woman doesn't sue for divorce if she is treated decently."

"That's her business. She pulled the same thing with her other marriage too. Ask her first husband if you don't believe me."

"That's not fair. After all, you knew her after her first mar-

173

riage, you knew what kind of person she was."

"I knew her only two months, not four like she says."

"But you asked her to marry you. You assumed the responsibility."

"No, she asked me." Laughter. The judge laughs too.

"But you agreed."

"I didn't want to. She insisted it would be O.K. 'Let's go to the registration bureau and try it out' is what she said."

At this the judge gives up and approves the divorce.

At 4:15 P.M., Plekhanov and Plekhanova stood before the desk. Nikolai Petrovich Plekhanov, a prosperous-looking engineer, had gone to the Siberian north in 1956 to work on construction projects which pay almost double wages. There were plans to send for Plekhanova when he was settled but they were never realized, and in six years, although they had seen each other once or twice on his trips to Moscow, there had been no conjugal relations. In the meantime Svetlana Vasilievna Plekhanova—who contested the divorce—worked as a waitress (55 rubles a month) in the Hotel Moskva. "He is my husband and I am not going to let him go under any circumstances. He's gotten rich while I slaved away waiting on tables. He tricked me. Why should another woman get the rewards now after what I did for him?"

The judge tried perfunctorily to make Plekhanov change his mind. "Is there nothing of your family life that you can salvage? Have you nothing in common?" But Plekhanov, highly paid (220 rubles a month plus 180 for a northern bonus) and established with a new woman and children, was adamant. "This is no marriage and it is foolish to pretend legally that it is. She never wanted to come north with me—only later, when I made good."

Divorce was granted on the grounds that the marriage had

factually ceased to exist after six years' separation. Plekhanova chose to resume her maiden name, Stepanova.

The next-to-last pair of the day was the Garbunovs. When Garbunov was a student at the Moscow Aviation Institute, Garbunova had to remain in Dnepropetrovsk because he was unable to obtain quarters for her. His course of study was five years. Their love did not survive them. Now they had nothing in common.

"I'm going to give you one more chance to change your minds," said the judge earnestly. "There is no reason whatsoever here to give up your lives together. Why, you are just starting. And you say yourselves that you are fond of each other."

The Garbunovs declined. "It would be worse than starting from scratch," she said. "At least if we are not married, we can stay friends. I like him very much; it's just one of those things: we both made new lives."

The judge did not argue with her.

Finally it was Lazerev and Lazereva, washed-out working people in the most ordinary dress, indistinguishable from millions of others on the Moscow streets. Both had found mates who pleased them more, from this same proletarian mass. They were married in 1957, while he was in the army. Unable to find a room together in Moscow, he extended his term. She was to have joined him in October of that year, but waited until after the November holidays, then New Year's, then May First. By the time she went to join him, in June 1958, she found him living with another woman. At the same time, she had taken a lover in Moscow.

The judge went through the motions of discouraging the Lazerevs from separating; but he soon gave up. He had nothing apropos to say; the sting was out of his questions. He pronounced the divorce in deliberate haste and pulled the pants from the backs of his legs as he left the courtroom. The young secretary remained in her chair a minute after everyone else had left, to dot some final *i*'s, then stretched and yawned loudly. *"Nakonets!"* she complained to herself disgustedly— "At last!"—and hurried home.

In 1926, Soviet divorce—and marriage—was performed entirely by the parties involved, without so much as registration at the housing office. The divorced party was informed by post card. Those were the days when some Bolshevik thinkers were still writing that the family had outlived its usefulness. This "leftism" was abandoned in the 1930s, when divorce policy was reconstructed, leaning to the opposite side of strict orthodoxy. Stalin ordered society stabilized by stabilizing the family. By 1944, divorce law had become prohibitively severe.

Now the pendulum is swinging back.

Rumor had it in Moscow that divorce procedure would soon be modified again, almost certainly in the direction of simplification. A new Code of Marriage, the Family and Guardianship was being prepared by the Supreme Soviet, and I was assured that it would eliminate one of the stages, probably the preliminary hearing in the People's Courts. Some thought that divorce would be taken from the courts altogether and given over to *obshchestvenniye* organizations of some kind. Everyone felt that form does not now correspond to content: the present procedure is long and rather complex because it originally intended to discourage, but on the other hand it is generally known that if both parties really want divorce, it is almost certainly obtained. Once a derelict-looking husband snarled in a People's Court: "What's this divorce business—all this bureaucratic nonsense, this game with paper, this waste of time and money?" The judge reprimanded him for his attitude, but afterward in private agreed that some of the forms have become formalities. In five years of practice he had reconciled only one couple in his court.

Probably courts will go on in their *pro forma* way to encourage respect for the Soviet family and Soviet marriage, but the criterion for divorce will continue to be sensible and practical: a broken marriage which cannot reasonably be restored.

After its initial violent shifts left toward free love and right toward rigidity, Soviet family law seems to be feeling its way to a dignified, adult and humane Golden Mean, encouraging marital and familial constancy when it can, but not by means of hypocrisy or puritanism.

Western courts still follow a medieval standard: they establish whether a matrimonial *offense* has been committed, and, if it has, whether it is legal grounds for divorce. Soviet courts have adopted a much more simple and rational standard: does the marriage work?

VIII

Summary Justice

I MENTIONED that there is no summary procedure in Soviet law for this is the way the law is worded: every criminal charge, however minor, must be tried according to the standard procedures, with full guarantees, the hearing of witnesses, the participation of lay assessors, the right to representation and appeal—the works.

The simplest misdemeanors too? Disturbing the peace, drunk and disorderly, swearing and insulting, "violation of social order," "disrespect for society"—does every piddling infraction entail the complication, the effort, the expense of a trial? Reasonably not. "Summary justice" is a disreputable term among Soviet jurists, but the People's Courts do dispense "administrative measures" according to a procedure which is called summary in other countries. Petty speculation, petty disobedience to the police and *druzhiniki*, and petty hooliganism fall within the jurisdiction of this administrative authority. A judge sitting alone may order a fine of up to fifty rubles or detention of up to fifteen days, neither of which go into the offender's record as *criminal* convictions. Until 1956 all petty hooliganism was treated as criminal and was dealt with under the code to the extent of two to five years' confinement. "The bums of Moscow welcomed the new law," remarked a Western jurist. Criminal petty hooliganism now may be charged only when the accused has twice before during the year been subjected to administrative measures.

On a March Monday morning at 10:30 A.M., the room of the duty judge of Krasnopresnenskii district is thick with unshaven men, mostly over thirty-five, mostly down-at-the-heels, mostly played out on this morning after. (Monday is the busiest day in this court, because vodka has been flowing freely all over town since the final factory whistle on Saturday afternoon.) A scattering of sympathetic wives and bored policemen look on. The judge, an overripe cherub in scarlet lipstick, is examining the passport of a dirty and inattentive man slouching before her, and she is scratching rapidly into the record.

"Kalchenko?"

"Right."

"How are you called?"

"Pyotr Romanovich."

"How old?"

"Thirty-seven."

"You work where?"

"Third Auto Base, Moscow Construction Trust."

"As what?"

"Mechanic second class."

"Education?"

"Four classes."

"*Partiinost?*"

"*Bezpartiinii.*"

"Convicted before?"

"Uh . . . once."

"For what?"

"Uh . . . theft."

"When?"

"In 1959."

"For theft of tools. Shameful, simply shameful. You live where?"

"Great Serpukhovskaya Street, Number twelve, Apartment forty-six."

"Married?"

"Yes, two children; two little girls."

The judge reads a brief police report: On Sunday afternoon Kalchenko had been stopped from entering the metro by the attendants at the turnstiles because he was demonstrably drunk. He then swore at the girls and made a disturbance. The policeman on duty in the vestibule seized him.

"Is it true?"

"Afraid so."

"Shameful, simply shameful. And why did you behave like a hooligan?"

"I don't know; I was drunk. My father visited me, we had some vodka, then decided to visit my brother by metro. I guess I got angry when they stopped me, but I meant no harm."

"Was it a pretty way to behave?"

"No."

"Certainly not. It was scandalous. You know better than that. You know you can't behave that way in a public place. Have you been in trouble since 1959?"

"This is the first time."

"Make it the last. You have got to learn to respect society and the sensibilities of others. I am going to give you ten days."

The next man looks very much the same.

"Married?"

"Seven years."

"It was your wife that you struck?"

A sigh. "My wife."

"Aren't you ashamed of yourself? Goodness! All right, how did it happen?"

"I unfortunately had too much to drink."

"How ugly!"

The wife is called four paces to the desk. A careless gauze wrapping hangs over her left eye.

"What happened to you?"

"I don't know myself. He came home drunk from work; we quarreled, he slapped me."

"How many times?"

"Just the once."

"Once? Then why do you write that he beats you systematically?"

"I was angry when I put that down. It's not really true. He never hit me before. Comrade Judge, I ask you please not to send him to jail. It never happened before; he treats me very well. He begged my pardon afterward. Fine him instead, please!"

"Let me see your face."

She lifts the bandage, revealing an indigo eye, swollen shut.

"I hurt it falling down. It was an accident."

"Then you say now that he does *not* beat you systematically? Often?"

"No, not at all often. Never. Rarely."

To the man: "And how often do you drink on the job?"

"Never. I'm a driver, I can't have vodka during the day. This happened after the shift."

Very quickly: "I'm going to fine you thirty rubles. This is a disgrace. I don't want to see you here again."

The next man is shabbier than average. Filthy overcoat, wild hair. He does not remember why he was arrested. Fifteen days.

The fourth was in a cafeteria.

"The cloakroom attendants were drunk too, I swear they were. They had been drinking all afternoon. They started with me."

"That is no reason to hit a man. Shameful. You will get eight days."

"Please, Comrade Judge, I have young children. Fine me instead. I'm sorry."

"Eight days!"

He turns away, shaking his head.

It was discovered that number five had had administrative sentences twice before during the year. This time he lost control in the waiting room of a railway station. He was unmanageably drunk and swore to the skies in front of children. His record is sent to the local police precinct so that a criminal charge can be instituted.

"Hello." Number six.

"Come up here. What is your name? Take off your cap."

"Federenko." He is a tough but gentle man, embarrassed, at his grandfatherly age, to be reprimanded by the teacher again.

"Ever convicted before?"

"Never had anything to do with the police before, never in my life."

"How did this thing happen?"

"I don't know myself; it just happened."

"*How?*"

"I honestly don't know. I was feeling strange. I . . . came home drunk—" A pause.

"And hit your wife and carried on and insulted the neighbors. How about it? Is it all written correctly here?"

"I suppose so."

"Aren't you ashamed?"

"Terribly ashamed. This is the first time. I'm truly sorry."

"Shameful, just plain disgraceful. You see what vodka leads

to, don't you? You can do very well without it. Hmmm . . .
Nu, I don't think this incident calls for strict punishment.
I'm going to inform your trade union about it; they can dis-
cuss your behavior at the factory and decide."

The next man is on mismatched, splintery crutches.

"You may sit down. Name? Date of birth? Address? Employment? Education? Convictions? *Partiinost?*"

"You have it all down right in front of you."

"I want to hear it from *you*. Now tell me exactly what you
did on Saturday."

On Saturday he drank heavily, together with his wife, and
then made a *skandal* with whoever passed by in the courtyard of their apartment house. They had done the same before.

"Ten days."

"Please, Comrade Judge, can't you fine me? Give me a fine,
better."

"No."

"*Please.*"

"I say no. You need some time to think about your behavior.
How dare you disturb your neighbors, who want only to
rest after an honest week's work."

"But . . ."

"*Next!*" Three policemen have come to life and roar it
together.

Suddenly a clean-shaven young man with narrow cuffs, a
white shirt and tie and a briefcase appears. A university graduate working as a chemist in a testing laboratory, he looks even
more out of place among the ragged men than the judge. The
police reported that he swore at and hit a man on Saturday
evening in the park.

"Do you concur?"

"I most certainly do not. I never hit him or swore at him.
I just pushed him away from my girl, whom he was annoying."

"So you deny the *protokol?*"

"Absolutely."

"Well, that is your right—if you are sure you are not making up a story. We must hear the girl if that's the case; come back with her tomorrow."

The next man is another ruffian, whose words are something less than intelligible. When the police arrived he was taking on all comers outside a movie house.

"Why?"

No answer; a disinterested shrug.

"Why, I'm asking you. Look at me."

"Drunk, I was."

"On whose money? You haven't been working for two months. This is disgusting. Why don't you work? Disgusting, this riffraff, sousing on money from God-knows-where. I am going to suggest that your record be reviewed—maybe it's time you were banished from Moscow as a parasite."

Number ten was drunk in his communal apartment, number eleven in a café, number twelve on the sidewalk of Collective Farm Square. It goes without saying that the incidence of drunkenness in these cases is not representative of society generally, but vodka does play a role in Moscow life which I never expected. "A Russian man drinks," I was often told. "He drinks vodka." It was usually said proudly. Even the Ukrainian forewoman of ninety-six workers in a dairy plant who told me that her biggest problem was to keep the men sober during the week spoke of their drinking powers in a tone of respect.

Russians drink seriously; they drink to get drunk; nothing remains in the bottle. Vodka is that kind of liquid. But it's the same with brandy, wine or any other liquor; they all go down *zalpom*—"at a gulp." Vodka is vital to peasant Russia, and there are not many who are long removed from it, even in Moscow. (And four million transients pass through the capital every day.) My roommates at the university, for example, were country boys. Often they went for weeks without a sip, but when they found occasion for a party they somehow managed out of the meager stipends (of course, tuition, books, rent, medical care and much of their entertainment were free) to purchase several bottles of *vodichka*. They drank it from water glasses, filled to the brim. Every one of those affairs ended in stupefaction.

Criminologists are beginning to mount a serious attack on vodka; it was revealed recently that 90 per cent of cases of hooliganism and 70 per cent of intentional murders are committed under its influence.

Number thirteen has a slight nervous wince. He is in a long, thick black overcoat, like almost everyone else.

"What's the idea of all this, Denisov? Creating a scandal at home, arguing with the police, making a nuisance of yourself."

"I just make a little noise, that's all, and my wife runs to the police to complain. Typical. It's my second wife, you know."

"What difference does that make? It gives you no right to hit her."

"Pfou, what a joke! I never laid a hand on a hair of hers in my life. I hit the wall."

"She says it was her face and arms, and not any wall."

"What she says is her business. She's always saying things. I know what I did."

"And I know what you're going to do—think it over under guard. Ten days."

Another somewhat-less-than-average-looking workingman shuffles up.

"Are you guilty?"

"Of course I'm guilty."

"Guilty, of course." A pronounced *tsk*. "Simply shameful and disgraceful for a Soviet worker. You will not do it again, I hope."

"No, I won't do it again."

"Do you promise you won't do it again?"

"I promise you that I won't do it again."

"You promise that you will never do it again. Good. You know yourself that the people who use the metro are honest toilers just like you, with the same rights and feelings as you have. You have got to respect your comrades. However, I think a fine will do in this case. Twenty rubles."

A disproportionate number of the incidents have happened in the metro. Drunks are not allowed to use it, and although in theory they are not allowed in any public place, the metro rule is sometimes carefully observed. Perhaps this is because the metro itself is disproportionate. Whatever it is that moves the owners of New York to rip down elegant lower Park Avenue, leaving slummy upper Park Avenue untouched, also moves the planners of Moscow to sink money into the metro rather than into construction on the surface. The magnificent metro is so much better than almost anything else. And better kept up: teams of biddies ride the long escalators polishing woodwork—at the same time that labor cannot be found to restore the bricks fallen from the façades of new buildings. And more efficient: a sparkling train appears about every ninety seconds—while there can be an annoying wait in line for almost everything else. And so the cult of the metro makes it sacrilegious to enter the temple inebriated. And the docket on Mondays is crowded.

The session in Krasnopresnenskii district was a longer one than usual. When I left, there were two men yet to be heard, but the judge, as duty judge, had been given a criminal case transferred from the calendar of a colleague taken ill, and she now, in turn, transferred the two remaining administrative cases to the judge next door.

In Moskvoretskii district the following Monday the judge was a shiny-bald inquisitor who took the questioning much more seriously. He gave stern sermons and seldom less than twelve days. In Dzerzhinskii district the judge had his secretary fill in the biographical data beforehand and was able thereby to run through eight cases in the time he chain-smoked two and a half cigarettes. In Oktyabrskii district the judge was interrupted by a telephone call, and four rough men waited while she gossiped with her niece—she sounded like Aunt Rosie from the Bronx—about school work, shopping and summer plans. In every district, although there were standard questions—Why? Aren't you ashamed? Must you drink?—the most important one depended upon the judge's personality, because the word of the police, as in summary procedure anywhere, is almost always taken as fact. The rare protest—"I *wasn't* drunk. . . ." "The other fellow pushed *me*. . . ." "That policeman swore at *me*. . . ."—is almost certain to be brushed aside.

"It depends on what side of the bed she got up on," said a man waiting next to me in Kirovskii district. He had gone to sleep in the snow, bottle in hand. "I'll be happy if she gives me thirty rubles and lets it go at that." He was subdued but unfrightened. None of them looked afraid. The newcomers appeared embarrassed, the old-timers blasé; but no one was excited. Most waited their turns joking, reminiscing about the night before, or breathing deeply to clear their heads. They all hoped to be fined rather than jailed, because the latter means loss of pay as well as deprivation of freedom, "and they make life so tough that after you've had it for ten days you don't ever want to come back." But most of them do.

IX

He Who Does Not Work, Neither Shall He Eat

THE HANDLING of petty-hooliganism infractions has its counterparts in most countries—in the Chambres Correctionelles, the Magistrates' Courts, Night Courts, Police Courts, the Magistratgerichte. Despite Soviet sensitivity about references to summary justice, there is nothing in the way it is administered (except, perhaps, the length of confinement that is usually imposed) that offends Western sensibilities. But the People's Courts discharge other "administrative" functions as well as this ordinary one, and one of these has no counterpart that I know of on this side of the Curtain. I am referring to their implementation of the notorious Parasite Law.

The Parasite Law is famous for its legislative history as well as for its extraordinary substance. When it was introduced, in 1959, to several of the lesser, outlying Soviet republics, prominent jurists predicted that it would never be adopted in the major ones. I remember an internationally known scholar giving assurances, when he visited Columbia University in 1960, that it was a temporary measure for certain localities and never was meant to be applied in Russia proper. Jurists, including many that I met in Moscow, considered it reprobate. But in May 1961, the Praesidium of the Supreme Soviet of the Russian Republic did issue a parasite decree, and its application since that time has steadily widened.

The intention of the Russian decree, in its own language, is that

adult, able-bodied citizens who do not wish to fulfill their most important constitutional obligation* to toil honestly according to their abilities, who shun socially useful work, wringing unearned income from exploitation of garden plots, automobiles, or dwelling space, or committing other antisocial actions which allow them to lead a parasitic way of life, are subject to banishment . . .

Banishment from Moscow is meant in this text; either one is gainfully, usefully employed or he may be sent out of the city. Accusations under this law are reviewed either by a court, which will employ summary procedure, or by the "collective" —again, a general meeting of the accused's co-workers or neighbors.

The one hearing that I came across under the Parasite Law was in a People's Court. The accused was a filthy, unshaven, fiendish-looking little man, a hunchback, with a strident feminine voice.

"It's not true, damn it. I worked part time, I have the chits at home. No, I did not, absolutely not, booze it up all the time. And I never created any wild scenes, damn it, why do you listen to liars?"

"Were you arrested for petty hooliganism?"

"Just twice."

"And you consider that little?"

* Constitution of the U.S.S.R., Article 12: "Work in the U.S.S.R. is a duty and a matter of honor for every able-bodied citizen in accordance with the principle 'He who does not work, neither shall he eat.'" This is an old Bolshevik precept; but its force, except in times of rationing, when food was distributed on the basis of work, has been mostly moral. The Parasite Law is one attempt to make it enforceable.

"Of course I consider it too much."

"Were you warned by the police?"

"About what?"

"About your debauchery. About drinking incessantly and never working, about the way you spit on society and lead a depraved life. Have you been warned at least ten times?"

"I've been warned. Those bullies called policemen."

"Is that good?"

"Very bad."

"How do you permit yourself to live like that? Why don't you work like a normal man—oh no, stop interrupting, we have proof that you don't work. And why do you make an ugly, depraved place out of your home?"

"That's not true, so help me."

"You create disgusting scandals with your wife and mother-in-law."

"I never fought with my wife, damn it."

"You consistently behaved disgracefully. You lived only to cheat, to avoid work, and to drown yourself in drink and scandals and filth."

"No. Why are you bullying me?"

"We'll hear the witnesses, your neighbors. They all say that you are nothing but a parasite, a worthless fungus. Or are we supposed to believe that only you are telling the truth and that everyone else is lying? Your selfishness is inexcusable. Do you think we don't have laws to deal with good-for-nothings like you? Of course we do."

Afterward the witnesses substantiated the judge's comments. The policeman on the beat, the chief of the local *druzhiniki*, the chairman of the apartment-house committee, a few neighbors, and the resident mother-in-law put together a frightful portrait of the man: insensibly drunk—on lacquer or sleeping pills when there was no money for vodka—day and night with his wife; naked in a buggy bed all day; refusing even to empty his garbage, let alone take a job; taunting his blind mother-in-law; insulting, loathsome, scandalous; the quintessence of debauchery. Police records and other written evidence were introduced which proved his inconstancy at work.

"That's not true. Oh you, that's mostly made up. You are purposely making it all worse than it really is. The whole trouble started a couple of years ago when my mother-in-law came out of the hospital to live with us. She is impossible; she always had a grudge against me; of course she tells you I'm bad. I pleaded with her a thousand times to move. I even offered to buy her a separate room so that we could live in peace. She refused. To torment us. Then she stirred up the neighbors against us."

"Now don't you be disrespectful. Your mother-in-law does not tell lies. She is a Party member since 1924 and she would have been dismissed long ago if she were the kind of person who told lies."

The little man's wife was present, shouting profane encouragement to her husband, although she was refused permission to testify officially in his behalf. She was a shrew of a woman, hardly cleaner than he; and all of the testimony suggested that she was rarely more sober. When the judge left to write his decision, the couple gave a hint in the courtroom of what their life at home must have been. Alternately they hugged each other in theatrical tears ("But it is cold in Krasnoyarskii Krai and you are a sick man. They will make you do heavy work. The police will beat you." "*Nichevo*, they'll give me light work and I'll earn some money at last. I'll come back to Moscow on leave after a year"), laughed themselves sick over their own ridiculousness and a new limerick she sang crudely mocking the Party, and tossed a piece of butter from her shredded pocketbook at one another

and at the blind mother-in-law. Their language was obscene.
The verdict came quickly.

On 17 September 1962 the People's Court of Oktyabrskii District, city of Moscow, in the composition of People's Judge Firsov and lay assessors Budadov and Maslovskaya with secretary Prokopova, having examined in open court the case of administrative expulsion of Zbarskii, Aleksandr Aleksandrovich, born 5 May 1919 in the city of Moscow, Russian, *bezpartiinii*, 6 years of education, living in the city of Moscow at Kazanskii Pereulok Number 5, Apartment 14, charged under Article I of the Decree of the Praesidium of the Supreme Soviet of the R.S.F.S.R. of 4 May 1961, "Concerning the Intensification of the Fight with Persons Shunning Socially Useful Work and Leading an Antisocial, Parasitical Way of Life." The court established: Zbarskii systematically gets drunk, frequently changes his place of work and secures himself work only for purposes of show. On 13 May 1961 he was fired from store No. 12 of Moskvoretskii District Food Trust and secured a job at store No. 18 of Oktyabrskii District Food Trust, where he worked from 15 May 1961 to 5 June 1961. From that date until 22 October 1961 he worked nowhere. Having worked three months in a phonograph factory, he quit on 1 February 1962 and in the course of a month until 1 March 1962 again worked nowhere. From 1 March 1962 to 22 July 1962 he again changed jobs twice and at the present time is not employed anywhere but is constantly drunk and creates scandals in his home. Zbarskii has been repeatedly warned by organs of the police; however this made no impression on him and he continues to lead an openly parasitic way of life.

On the basis of the aforesaid and in accordance with Article I of the Decree of the Praesidium . . . RESOLVED:

To expel Zbarskii, Aleksandr Aleksandrovich, to a specially designated place for three years without confiscation of property and with obligatory designation of work at the place of expulsion.

The enactment is final, and is not subject to appeal.

Of all the cases I saw in my year in Moscow, this was the worst. Not because Zbarskii and his wife were mistreated respectable citizens, not because the judge refused to allow Zbarskii's mother—he made her leave the room when she protested this refusal—and his wife to tell the other side of the story, not even because there was no defense and no procedural guarantees and the whole spirit of the trial was so blatantly one-sided that one of Zbarskii's neighbors, who had testified against him, shouted angrily, "You're making a joke out of this trial. Arrest me if you want to, but I can't sit here and watch this unfairness." The judge grew livid, but he did nothing about it.

What was terribly wrong in the Zbarskii case was that no crime was involved! True, none was charged: it was a mere "administrative" matter. But to say, as Soviet texts do, that these are not *criminal* cases and that the court is not here meting out criminal punishment but is only applying administrative measures is purest sophistry. I cannot understand how a man's exile of two to five years from his home and the possible confiscation of his property represent anything but punishment. (Americans too, unfortunately, are familiar with this reasoning. Basic rights of defense are brushed aside in security hearings, and repugnant methods are used in deportation proceedings, because these are "only" administrative matters not involving criminal punishment.)

All of this runs roughshod over both letter and spirit of the Fundamental Principles of Soviet Criminal Law, according to which a crime is only that which is described in one of the articles of the criminal code, and no person may be subject to criminal punishment except when found guilty of a crime by a court which conducts a hearing according to established procedures.

This principle was hailed as a triumph when it was affirmed in 1958, as a victory over the evils of extralegal punishment which had caused so much misery in the Soviet Union—and in tsarist Russia too. For Stalin's abuses were to some extent prepared in the past. Centuries before 1917 a legal tradition was developing in Russia that differed markedly from those developing further west. Geography, economics, climate, philosophy, religion—all these together make history—made the Russian people far less concerned with formal principles and abstract theory than West Europeans. Muscovites long scorned the "excessive legalism" of the West. An American observer has noted that "they have looked to spontaneous personal and administrative relationships rather than the formalism of the law, with its time-consuming emphasis on due process and its rationalism." They relied more on custom (peasant custom still has a place in Soviet civil law) than on documents; they hated the idea of brother making contracts with brother.

During the second half of the nineteenth century, after the Crimean disaster, great legal reforms carried feudal Russia toward the legal protection of the West. And while Law never established its Rule—and probably never would have done so as long as the tsar remained supreme autocrat and Russians remained Russians—some aspects of a modern society based on law appeared. Soviet rule both speeded and slowed this movement toward legalism: speeded it in that, even in the years of the greatest lawlessness in the Soviet Union, the years of purges, disappearances and terror, law was more and more relied upon under Stalin as an economic regulator and an instrument of social change for his maturing industrial society; weakened it in that any revolution is antithetical to legalism, and the Bolshevik one all the more. And so both the legal and the nonlegal and extralegal traditions of old Russia were nourished. Codes were written, courts were staffed, procedures were established and enforced; and at the same time expediency and direct action were sometimes allowed to brush aside the law, extralegal methods were resorted to, and the most horrible perversions of the court were practiced by those responsible for legality.

Scholars of the Soviet Union devote their lives to explaining what all of this has bequeathed to contemporary Russia and to discussing the extent to which contemporary institutions, attitudes and characteristics are *Russian* and to what extent they are Soviet. To what extent, no one can say with any certainty. But the tradition of extralegalism lives on in the Parasite Law, even though by comparison with the Stalin years it is almost extinguished. In the spring of my year in Moscow Premier Khrushchev talked about parasites and thieves and the law at the Fourteenth Congress of the Young Communist League:

The law of life of our society is that he who does not work shall not eat. This is a good, a correct principle of our life. But there still exist spongers who do not work themselves, and sometimes eat better than those who do work. We must intensify the battle against parasites, against all sorts of cheats, hooligans, against all antisocial elements . . . The main force in this battle must be *obshchestvennost* . . . We must organize the work of *obshchestvenniye* organizations to rule out the possibility that people who do not contribute their labor to the creation of material and culture for society can spoon out from the bowl to which all toilers have contributed their labor. [Prolonged applause.]

You probably know this rather malicious joke: A man goes to the police and says, "A certain citizen is threatening me, attempting to kill me." He is answered, "But he hasn't killed you. When he does, write a complaint; then we'll take him to court." [Commotion in the hall.]

It turns out that a parasite may poison the life of those surrounding him, but he cannot be punished. The same can be said of thieves and swindlers who haven't been caught. Some people reason that even if a man has stolen but hasn't been caught, you cannot call him a thief, even though many know he's a thief. But that concept is characteristic of bourgeois society; there it is said, "If he's not caught, he's not a thief." No, we must have other principles . . .

The Soviet people are entitled to make accountable people who do not work but live at the expense of society, to make a thief answerable not only when he's caught with his hand in another's pocket but also when he prospers without working. Why, he is stealing from socialist society, he is robbing you, because he is living off your labor. We don't have to wait until he is caught red-handed to take him to court. Society can and must present its demands to parasites: you live in the house we built and the suit and shoes made by our hands. What did you do to help build this house, to heat it; what did you do to improve the lives of the people among whom you live? Thousands, millions of people worked in order to build a house—poured metal, mixed cement, baked bricks, toiled to build a house out of these materials—and you, having done nothing, live in that house. The Soviet people have a right to say that spongers must not be in our ranks.

Can we cope with this task? Yes, we can. You, comrades, have only to revise your conception of a plunderer, a thief: Is it only one who has stolen something or also one who lives at others' expense as a parasite. It must be clear to all that both are thieves. . . . [Stir in the hall.]

Our task is to rid society of such people, to do everything possible to return all capable of leading an honest working life to socially useful labor and to prevent the fall of others.

We might ask why we must wait until such a man steals something before we imprison him . . . I repeat: Must we wait until such a man, contemptuous of society, steals something or commits some other crime and only then bring him to justice? Wouldn't it be better for us to establish some kind of institution which, according to the decision of society, would force parasites to work under compulsion? [Shouts of approval. Prolonged applause.]

Two thousand persons were expelled from Moscow in 1961 as parasites, under these administrative procedures. The records of ten thousand were examined; eight thousand were sent to work in Moscow. Most of those expelled seemed to be of Zbarskii's type, mature idlers. Only fifteen had their property confiscated; these probably were the speculators and the operators. But young *stilyagi* and good-time girls who keep conspicuous company with foreigners and have neither visible means of support nor registration in an educational institute are sometimes sent away, too. Full-time prostitutes, pimps and profligates are the likeliest candidates. From the talk of the town, the present place of settlement is Krasnoyarskii Krai, the site, in Central Siberia, of the famous Brotherly Hydroelectric Station, soon to be the world's largest dam. "To the salt mines" is not used in Moscow jargon; "to Krasnoyarskii Krai" is the hip way of saying it. "Careful," someone will joke when the champagne cork pops, "if they hear us, we're on the way to the *krai*."

Banishment to Siberia is perhaps not so calamitous a punishment for Russian ne'er-do-wells as it seems to the Western imagination. I once bumped into a young man who was on his holiday from three years of compulsory work at the Brotherly Dam. He was a coarse fellow, a natural ruffian who, he admitted proudly, had done nothing but drink, gamble, steal and pester girls before he was sent away. If anything, banishment had done him good. He still drank, gambled, stole and pestered girls ("What great girls out there!") in Krasnoyarskii Krai, but he was earning a salary, learning how to operate construction machines and even, he now admitted sheepishly, taking an interest in the work. Complain as he did about the primitive living conditions—barracks, mud, potatoes, boredom —his final comment was, "It's not so bad as all that. We survive. Maybe I'll fool around with construction work when I leave." Maybe he was finding himself in that half-forced labor.

Most of the people I knew felt as Khrushchev did, though

much less strongly, about people who do not work. There is, apparently, slight but genuine popular indignation about parasites. This is one of the facets of capitalism which disturb Soviet people. "Why doesn't it make you angry," asked my closest friend on the Juridical Faculty, "that many Americans who don't work live at the expense of society—and ten or twenty times as well as those who do work? We want none of that here." The woman who cleaned our corridor said, "I just don't see how you can justify people living off capital instead of sweat. Who wants that—except the thieves and exploiters?" A gregarious taxi driver told me that "when I read of rich American *dami* spending more for their French poodles than families do for food, I know where parasites can lead to, and I know we are right to stop it."

The antiparasite campaign has not, therefore, met the resistance it would have met in other countries. And (I harp on this because I think it important to keep in mind) it is not to be equated with the extralegality—the midnight raids and false confessions—of Stalin's era. For eliminating all that, Khrushchev and Company can hardly be praised enough—from the juridical point of view alone, to say nothing of the human. No parasite is sent to a labor camp of the type described in *One Day in the Life of Ivan Denisovich*, and none is "tried" without previous warnings, sometimes tens of them, from police, Party, trade union, local government and Comradely Courts.

Still, this is extralegalism once again, and the cure strikes one as no more healthy than the ailment. It is probably especially dangerous in a country like the Soviet Union, with its strong "administrative" traditions. I heard rumors that not only drunks and loafers, but other kinds of "undesirables," such as avant-garde painters and writers, were being banished. It is the kind of thing that *can* happen (I have no reliable evidence that it did) under these informal arrangements. No crime is charged, no conviction is made; an abstract painter is simply sent off to a construction site, after some easily arranged hearing.

Jurists do not like the Parasite Law. Almost unanimously, they look upon it as a step backward. If socialist legality is ever to mean the Rule of Law, the step will have to be made up. But Premier Khrushchev is not a jurist, and it sometimes seems that in his eagerness to do good and get the job done he lacks the patience to follow their precept—to wait until the thief is caught.

[Since this chapter was written, the Supreme Court of the Russian Republic has directed that accused parasites must have the benefit of counsel. That is a measure of the jurists' fight for procedural safeguards and their success in eliminating one of the most obnoxious elements of the Parasite Law.]

X

Behind Closed Doors

SOVIET TRIALS are open. The doors may be closed only when state security is involved, when juveniles must be protected, or when sexual and other intimate details of the participants' lives are to be considered.

The open trials are indeed open. At most official institutions in Moscow—institutes of higher education, factories, newspapers, commercial offices—soldiers, policemen or old women stand watch at the door demanding documents or explanations; but none of this is needed at the courts. That first time in a People's Court I walked in without a word, dashed through the nearest brown door and sank down on the last bench as quickly as I could in the middle of a lawyer's summation, waiting for a reaction. There was none, and I had a delicious feeling of accomplishment, as if I had swung something difficult.

I had not. After that there was never any trouble at all about seeing an ordinary trial. I walked in and sat down. (That, incidentally, is the best way to do almost anything in Moscow; official channels must be avoided whenever possible. An appointment through the Juridical Faculty usually took months to arrange, but a direct knock on the desired door often succeeded immediately.) Even when a courtroom was so crowded that regular spectators were turned away, my coat and tie and briefcase, and in rare cases of need my university pass, got me inside.

Not that I passed unnoticed; a foreigner still stands out in a Russian crowd. When I took notes, I sometimes received dark stares from the judge or the procurator. Three judges directed me—illegally, I believe—to stop writing. It was usually assumed that I was a journalist, but even when it was a *Soviet* journalist that I was taken for, I was treated with suspicion.

Still, in spite of the accessibility of the trial court, I had the annoying feeling that the most exciting and probably most enlightening cases were escaping me. There was, for example, the trial of twelve *valiuchiki* ("currency speculators"—from *valiuta*, "currency") in a higher court in May. This was one of the sensational trials that were connected with the recent campaign against economic crimes that has been given considerable prominence in the Western press. Seven of the defendants here were sentenced to be shot, but I had to find that out secondhand, for no outsider was allowed to watch. I tried several times to argue my way past the snarling, rifle-carrying soldier at the door, but gave it up after some lawyers told me that not even they were admitted unless they were professionally involved. When I peeped inside, before the door was slammed, to see the twelve shaved, glum *valiuchiki*, I noticed that the room was indeed empty of outsiders.

Then there was a case of ordinary speculation which, I was told after arriving at the People's Court to watch it, was to be tried in jail, because most of the witnesses, as well as the defendants, were under custody, and it was inconvenient to transfer them all to the courthouse.

And there was persistent talk about a series of *in-camera* trials of former investigators, procurators and judges, charged with complicity in organized swindling. They were alleged to have taken bribes from cliques of embezzlers in return for looking the other way. I was told that many of the judges of

Kirovskii district were under arrest and that personnel from other districts had recently been convicted.

None of these cases seemed to involve state security, juveniles or sexual matters. They were closed, I assume, only for the authorities' convenience.

I spent the morning of May 11 wandering about in the People's Court of Leninskii district. In one of the larger rooms, a case was being heard behind closed doors. I joined a dozen or so intrigued time-wasters who were waiting to find out what it was about. When the court retired to deliberate, the doors were opened to us, and they remained open, for the verdict in closed cases is delivered publicly.

The charge was rape. I shall not bother with the details, spicy as they were in this case (the more so because the defendant was a dark, body-building type who would have been primitively handsome had he hair on his head, and the girl was very pretty—fair, slightly plump, and fresh, as if she had just left the farm). From the verdict alone what had happened between them was not entirely clear. Had she been willing or afraid? Had she tempted him or had he forced her? Had she undressed herself while he was drinking or had he stripped her? Had she been virginal or experienced? Had she told him she was fifteen, or had she lied and said eighteen? Had she pleaded to make love again in the morning or demanded to go home? Had the mothers reached an agreement? Had there been a promise of marriage?

Whatever really happened, the court found him guilty of raping a minor and sentenced him to seven years in a colony under strict regime. When the decision was read, the girl wailed hysterically and threw herself past her bulky mother and a bulky policeman, upon the young man's neck as he was led away.

But what attracted my attention more than this was something peculiar in the verdict: references to a "first trial." And in fact there had been one. There was more to the case than one night of violent love. I was told the rest of the story by the judge, whom I disturbed at lunch after the verdict (she brought hard-boiled eggs and black bread and butter from home and ate in the chambers with one of the assessors), and the chairman of the court, who permitted me to skim the *protokol.*

The first trial had been held in the same court, with a different judge, four months before. The charge then too was rape of a minor; but on the witness stand the girl changed her testimony, saying that she had in fact succumbed voluntarily to the boy and had invented the story of rape out of fear of her mother. The procurator was dubious; he suspected that the law was being tampered with—an agreement, perhaps, between the mothers to "make the girl honest" by marriage, and suitable compensation—but with mother and daughter now denying rape, he had no choice but to requalify the charge to a lesser crime: sexual relations with a person not having achieved sexual maturity. The boy was sentenced to three years, the maximum penalty under this article.

Within the seven-day limit, the boy's lawyer appealed, claiming that since the girl was in fact sexually mature and had said she was eighteen—and looked eighteen—the elements of a crime were missing. (That the girl had since fallen in love with the boy had no bearing on the case; once charges are pressed, only the procurator can drop them.) So far, nothing here was unusual; in Soviet law, every verdict by a court of first instance in the regular hierarchy may be appealed in a court of cassation. Appeal must be made within a week, before the decision "comes into legal force"; if it *is* made, execution of the sentence is postponed. (An accused who has been taken under custody awaiting trial, of course, invariably remains under custody while awaiting appeal.) The percentage of decisions appealed appears quite high, though no figures are released; in cases handled by lawyers appeals are almost automatic.

The prohibition against *reformatio in pejus* on appeal is as complete in Soviet as in other European systems: an appeals court may not directly increase the severity of punishment awarded by the trial court or apply another law involving a heavier crime; and only on appeal by the procurator or by a victim may the appeal court upset a verdict on the grounds of inadequate punishment—in which event it is empowered only to send the case back for retrial. (This kind of reversal is common in England, but is not the practice in the United States.) In other words, appeal *by a convicted man* cannot cause his punishment to be increased. Without this protection, not many would risk appeal.

Therefore, the appeals court in this rape case, although it would have liked to increase the punishment—it was convinced that the girl's sudden change of testimony was dishonest—was limited to denying the appeal and leaving the sentence in force. The boy (he was twenty-two) began his stay in a labor colony. At the same time, however, the appeals court issued a "private opinion" to the effect that the trial court had erred in requalifying the crime and that the sentence had been too mild. The "private opinion" had no force of law, for reasons which I have just explained, but it did bear heavily on the boy's fate.

To understand how this happened, one must be acquainted with one of the peculiarities of Soviet criminal procedure. In that procedure there are *two* systems of review by higher courts of the work of lower ones: *kassatsiya* ("cassation"); and *nadzor* ("inspection," or "supervision"). Cassation corresponds, with some minor differences, to what is generally known as appeal. The victim, as well as the defendant, is entitled to appeal. The procurator is *obliged* to appeal all unlawful or ungrounded decisions. It was under this system that the boy's appeal was rejected.

Nadzor is something different and special, and is known, I believe, only to Norway and Austria as well as to the Soviet Union. It too is an examination of the trial from above. "The same task," a Soviet commentator explains, "in the final analysis, stands before a court examining a case in *nadzor* as in *kassatsiya:* to check the legality and groundedness of all decisions made." But—to repeat—this is not appeal, but an entirely separate instance, because it takes place *after* the sentence has come into legal force. (Up to a year later, if it is unfavorable to the accused; at any time, if it is favorable to him.) Besides, *nadzor* is initiated not by the participants of a given case, but by the chairman of a higher court or by a higher-ranking procurator. It is, in short, a method of self-supervision, the courts checking on the courts for the sake of the courts, although the procurator's right to bring protest in *nadzor* underlines his special position in Soviet procedure. Certain of the protections guaranteed in *kassatsiya*—the right of a lawyer to participate, for example—are absent in *nadzor* because, the reasoning goes, it is a "company" process designed for the courts to rectify their own mistakes and not for the parties, who have already had the right of appeal, to challenge them.

In the case in Leninskii court, the "private opinion" of the appeal court was sent to the chairman of Moscow City Court, where the appeal was heard, and he protested the original (three-year) sentence in *nadzor*. His protest was approved by the praesidium of Moscow City Court; the trial and appeal decisions were overruled; and the case sent back for retrial, with indication that the girl's story ought to be thoroughly checked and that three years' deprivation of freedom was too little.

I doubt that the muscular boy really understood the procedure which led to his second trial and the more-than-doubling of his punishment. When the judge asked him if he understood the sentence, he was too stunned to reply.

Later, I came across other retrials brought about by *nadzor*. It was always the same: on a procurator's or chairman's protest, a higher court had remanded the case to the trial court for "mildness of punishment." In every case the lower court followed the recommendation from above, awarding more severe penalties: two railroad workers who had killed a third in a drunken fight got death instead of fifteen years; a driver of a milk truck who had been sneaking extra yoghurt from his plant and selling it to stores not on his route was given seven years instead of four; a group of textile-plant officials who had been profiteering in various ways had their sentences doubled.

The most violent outburst of grief I have ever seen took place at one of these retrials. A twenty-year-old boy was being tried again for having beaten a stranger to death in a streetcar two stops from the university. It was a stupid, senseless killing caused by vodka and arrogance, and the defendant aroused only the minimum sympathy due a shaved, ashen-faced criminal in the dock. The procurator had protested the first sentence, fifteen years in a labor colony ("He even said himself that he simply didn't go to work on the day of the killing because he felt like drinking. Have such people the right to life in Soviet society?"). This second verdict was read on the defendant's twenty-first birthday; he was sentenced to be shot.

When the words were spoken the boy's mother, who appeared to be about sixty years old, seemed to go mad. Weeping, wailing, clawing, she charged toward her son, as if determined to free him from the guards. The soldiers led her outside as gently as they could, and there she threw herself on the ground and gave herself up to frenzy. When I left the room I had to step over her, for she was still writhing prostrate on the threshold moaning hysterically. "My son, my blood, my only son." She could not be coaxed from the floor. The wives of the accused and the murdered man joined her anguished wailing. The sounds were horrifying. The condemned boy himself seemed dumb-struck by his change of fate; a soldier gave him a cigarette, but it fell from his shaking hands to the floor.

In the midst of this, the lawyer in the case tried to reassure me. Lest I get the wrong impression, he said, the court does not automatically follow the procurator's protest and the higher court's suggestion in *nadzor*. Recently he defended a woman who was sentenced to five years. Twice, on the procurator's protest the case was retried; and twice the trial court left the five-year sentence in force. At that point the procurator gave up.

The lawyer, a small, soft-spoken young man was unnerved by the outcome of this last case and the mother's reaction, but he wanted to set the record straight. "In three years of practice, I've had seven murder trials . . . this is only the second that brought the death penalty."

To return to the cases behind closed doors: There is an article in the code that I would have thought unnecessary; it deals with homosexuality.* Muscovites are so strongly heterosexual—so little titillating talk, so much real activity. One never sees obvious homosexuals in public places, and I had assumed

---

* *Article 121: Homosexuality.*

Sexual relations of a man with a man (homosexuality) is punishable by deprivation of freedom for a period of up to five years.

Homosexuality committed by means of application of physical force, threat, or in relation to a minor, or by taking advantage of a dependent position of the victim, is punishable by deprivation of freedom for a period of up to eight years.

that I would never see them in court. Russians seemed too healthy for that.

The exception proved the rule. Late one afternoon I came across it in a wretchedly damp, low-ceilinged basement room in the form of two elderly men, fifty-five and sixty-one, the first with a full eighteenth-century peasant beard, the other in high boots and a tunic. Insensibly drunk, they had exposed themselves on a bitter November day in a park and made some sort of contact with each other. They listened in deep embarrassment while the court found them guilty; but "considering their ages, their families, their honest confessions, and their promises of future good behavior," it decided not to deprive them of freedom but merely to fine them 20 per cent of their salaries for a year.

The men sputtered thanks to the judge and left separately without exchanging a glance. A once-very-pretty, fortyish woman who heard the sentence with me shook her head incredulously. "I just don't believe it. You mean they . . . ? The two of them? Good God, what *for?*"

At last I see a trial behind closed doors from beginning to end. The furniture is dark with use, the portrait of Lenin faded, and the smell is from the toilet next door. Judge, procurator and lawyer look like brothers in the moving business: beefy men in baggy suits, without ties. In the dock, a skinny, gangling Georgian lad twitches spasmodically. He suffers from a mild form of Saint Vitus's dance, enough to cause his rejection by the Red Army. Until his arrest two months before, he worked as a research assistant in the Union of Writers and studied evenings in Moscow's Archival Institute. He wanted to become a librarian. A few feet away, in the second row of public benches, the girl he is charged with attempting to rape sits primly. She is pretty in a Western way, a graceful, long-legged brunette with bangs and a black sweater.

The Georgian's twitching never lets up and is still more pronounced when he must talk. His speech is irritatingly slow: each word is a separate unit, set off before and after by a breath and a twitch. "I . . . admit . . . my . . . guilt . . . in . . . the sense . . . that . . . I . . . er . . . well . . . because . . . I . . . desired . . . her . . . that . . . night . . . and . . . I . . . scratched . . . her . . . and . . . er . . . behaved . . . very . . . badly . . ."

"How did you meet the girl?"

The Georgian, eyes bulging and Adam's apple vibrating, answers each question painstakingly, but he cannot put together a story of his own. The judge must draw it out with questions.

"Had you ever seen her before?"

In April, his mother had departed for a sanatorium in Riga to recover from a long-standing illness. When word got around that there was an "empty" room, an acquaintance from the Institute asked him for permission to use it one Saturday evening for a party.

"He said it was his birthday but it wasn't."

At first the accused refused—he was wary of that crude fellow—and told the neighbors in the apartment not to admit the company. But they kept returning, the acquaintance, another young man, and two girls. At 8 P.M. the party began, with three bottles of vodka and two of red wine.

"What happened at the party? Tell us particularly about your relationship to the girl."

They danced and talked and sang and drank. The girl appealed to him very much, and they danced together when he had the courage to ask her, but he made no advances because his friend had told him that he had been seeing her steadily for three weeks. They all drank steadily.

Suddenly the halting speech halts completely. The Georgian looks over his shoulder toward the rear of the room, where his mother is crying softly. "Mother, maybe you ought to leave." She begs to stay, but the judge agrees with the son and sends her out.

"How much did you drink?"

Rather much; the bottles were almost empty. Everyone was high. Then, sometime later, the girl undressed and made love to her boy friend on the divan in view of the others. He was angry, and ashamed of his friend for this behavior, but excited by what he saw. She was lovely and passionate. Afterward, the lovers fell asleep on the divan and the other couple left.

At 3 A.M. the girl awoke. Her man was too drunk to stand, and she asked the defendant to take her home instead.

"How did you respond to her suggestion?"

"I was happy to accompany her. I liked her and wanted to know her better."

They set out on foot toward a taxi stand and on the way he suggested a short cut through an apartment building under construction. It was a trick. On a second-floor landing, he asked her to stop a minute and talk. She was so much better than he, so much more attractive and self-assured. He said, "I like you very much, you are lovely." Something made him hope she would find him not awkward. She seemed kind. Then, in the darkness, a feeling of desire overcame him.

"I wanted to take her in my arms and kiss her. If she kissed me I would have been so proud."

She resisted. Suddenly she became terrified of him. But why? *He* was frightened of *her*. He only wanted to kiss her. It was not easy for him to kiss girls. Most didn't want to. He felt so small and stupid when they refused. He thought this girl would let him kiss her— After all, on the divan . . . But she pulled away, and he felt more awkward than ever. In the movements that followed in the dark he accidentally scratched her cheek and pulled her to him by the neck.

"And did you threaten her? Did you say, 'Stop struggling or I will choke you or rape you'?"

"Yes, I did. I said exactly that."

"You used those words? 'I will choke you or rape you.' *Why?*"

"I don't know why. It was a joke, a stupid threat, one of those big-shot things I sometimes say when I feel skinny and ugly. I didn't mean it—oh no, you must understand I never dreamed of choking or raping her. I only wanted to get acquainted; it is so hard for me to meet girls. If she let me kiss her lips, I would feel good. So I used this joke."

"This *joke?* What kind of a joke is that? Grabbing someone by the throat and saying, 'I will choke you or rape you.' Who jokes like that?"

"It was a bad joke . . . a . . . mistake . . . forgive me."

"Why did you use those words—*choke or rape?* Don't you know what that means to a girl? What did you have in mind at that moment?"

"The goal of those words was to kiss her. I didn't even kiss her. She was disgusted."

"What happened then? After you scratched her and threatened to kill her and seized her by the throat?"

Not by the throat, by the back of the neck. She fell and cried out, "Help! Rape!" Very frightened, he ran home. That man was still drunk on his couch. He couldn't fall asleep. After about an hour the police came, told him to dress, and took him to the station. He told them what had happened.

"How do you feel now about it—about the way you behaved?"

"Of course I behaved terribly. I feel terrible. I would like to erase my guilt. I am so sorry."

The procurator asks: "If in fact you planned only to kiss her, why did you manhandle her and make such threats? Your explanation sounds mighty flimsy, you know."

"To kiss to get acquainted."

"What is that, a new method of getting acquainted? Did you try to undress her?"

"No."

The defense counsel asks: "And were you sexually excited at any time on the landing?"

"No, not sexually."

"In fact you attempted only to put your arms around her and kiss her?"

"That's all I did . . . I think."

The judge asks: "But you waited until you reached the landing—alone, in the dark—to do this. Why? Why not earlier? Do you trap a girl like an animal just for a kiss?"

The defendant shrugs his shaved head and continues to twitch. Back and forth the questions go between judge, procurator and lawyer, and it is a strange performance. The Georgian tries to answer as objectively as he can and at the same time to convey his sense of grief and repentance.

The girl (she is twenty-one, two years younger than the accused) remembers nothing about the party. They danced and it was gay, but she cannot say whether or not she made love on the divan. She remembers waking at three o'clock, and the blackness on the landing. He grabbed her by the throat and said, "Stop struggling; I'll choke you or rape you," and tried to . . .

"Defendant, stand. You heard the testimony. Did you take her by the throat or by the neck, as you say?"

"I think . . . by the neck."

He tried to kiss her and God knows what else. She fell—her coat was smeared with rubbish—and screamed. A passer-by stopped a patrol car and arrived with the police.

"With whom do you live?" It is one of the lay assessors, her spreading breast resting on the desk, come to life.

"With my mother."

"She gives you permission to stay out until three in the morning?"

"No."

"Well, what do you think about such behavior now? About the way you treated your mother—is that the way to treat a Soviet mother?"

"No, I behaved very badly, of course."

The defense counsel asks: "Was he excited on the stairs? Could you feel sexual excitement in him?"

"I cannot say. No. I don't think he was excited."

"Did he try to remove your clothes?"

"No."

"His own clothes?"

"No."

"How do you feel toward him now?"

"I don't know what to feel. At first I was terribly disturbed by the thought of him. But all that has gone now. I have no feelings about him any longer. Pity, I suppose, just pity."

The judge then deals quickly and competently with the rest, with the witnesses—the passer-by and the policeman, both of whom the girl had told that a man had tried to rape her—with the documents, and the supplementary questions. The Georgian twitches in silence and the girl, her primness giving way to discomposure, looks at her shoes as the story of the evening is told again and again. "Has anyone else something to add? Nothing? Comrade Procurator, your conclusions, please."

"Comrade Judges! The facts in this case are not complicated. On April 17, the accused attempted to rape a girl whose acquaintance he had made that evening. His actions represent a serious danger to the community. They threaten the honor and dignity of Soviet women. He must be punished in accordance with the law."

It is a brief talk, standard and uninspired. The story told again, the testimony distilled to support the accusation, the qualification (attempted rape accompanied by threat of murder) justified. The facts leave no room for doubt: the accused prepared to commit a sexual act without the girl's permission and was stopped only by circumstances—the scream for help—beyond his control. His own explanation deserves no credence; a naïve and obvious attempt to mitigate his guilt. Who grabs a girl's throat and threatens death or rape when he wants to kiss her?

"As for measures of punishment, it must be remembered that although the accused has certain positive characteristics, he has a negative side too. His behavior on that landing is proof enough of this. Considering, therefore, the social danger of the crime, the impermissibility of such behavior in today's Soviet society, and all of the circumstances involved, I ask the court to sentence the defendant to five years' deprivation of freedom." This is the minimum penalty under the article that was invoked.

Defense counsel's speech is longer and more subtle.

"No one denies the danger of the acts described in Article 117, but the question is: Did they take place in the present case? I think that Comrade Procurator is mistaken about the facts.

"The girl says she was taken by the throat. The boy says by the back of the neck—the usual technique for trying to force a kiss. Whom to believe? You, Comrade Judges, must decide, but the girl's accusation ought to be believed only if supported by other evidence, and no facts in the case—not even the medical report—do this.

"Secondly, the crime has been misqualified. There was no threat on the girl's life, for a threat must be *real*, there must be some reason to believe it is serious, to have juridical significance. Here there was no substance to the words—no possibility that the accused would or could have carried out the threat.

"Moreover, there was no attempt at rape. Rape was physiologically impossible. Even the girl testified that the defendant was not excited—and she knows what sexual excitement means. There was an attempt to kiss, to hug, but not to force intercourse. Rape presupposes a series of acts necessary for its accomplishment, all of which were missing here. Nothing smacked of sexual intimacy; no intimate clothing, his or hers, was even touched. This you must contrast with the simple declarations of the procurator.

"What did happen on the landing? Of course, the accused acted in a manner unbefitting a Soviet citizen. Of course, what he did was wrong and must be punished. His were foul and vile acts, and they ought not to be ignored. But we are jurists; it is our task to give the acts their *proper* juridical qualification. This is not attempted rape, but a classic case of hooliganism. This is Article 206, nothing more. He must be punished for what he did, not for what the procurator imagined he did.

"Our law requires that in awarding punishment, the defendant's personality must be considered. I have submitted documents from his job supervisors showing that he was a highly valued, reliable worker; and from his Institute, showing that he was a capable student; and depositions from people testifying that they never heard an improper word from him from birth. They were amazed at this charge, and request that he be given another chance. The procurator has dismissed these documents as 'superficial,' but this is unfair—they tell the story of his life. It has been an exemplary life; he both worked and studied hard; he gave his maximum to the building of Communism.

"Yes, he knows he must be punished. But it would be senseless to deal harshly with this young man. There is no need to send him away for five years. It is enough to look at him—to hear how he talked today—to know this. We have every reason to believe that he will never err again.

"Comrade Judges! Marxism-Leninism teaches that inevitability of punishment, not severity, is the key to its effectiveness. I beg you to keep this in mind. . . ."

The Georgian's last words are a jumble of tears and twitches; he uses his sleeves as a handkerchief.

". . . tried to improve myself . . . to work . . . my sick mother . . . sorry . . . so sorry . . . beg for indulgence . . . return to society . . . useful member . . . studied . . . my mother . . . I promise . . . promise . . . please . . ."

"Is that all?"

"I believe in the . . . humanity of the Soviet . . . court."

For the first time during the trial, the girl looks directly at her attacker, making no attempt to conceal that she too is weeping freely.

I am not a competent observer of criminal trials. I find myself siding always with the accused, believing his story, understanding the mitigating circumstances, appreciating the arguments of his lawyer, questioning the narrowness of the law, the insensitivity of the prosecution, the relentless workmanship of the judge. Punish the man? No, give him another chance! The sad face and sad story of a captive already humbled in the dock, defending himself futilely against the punitive power of an awesome, invulnerable state always wins out easily in my psyche over the logical understanding that society (if only society too had a face) has a duty to protect itself against repeated harm. From the moment the ordeal begins— "Defendant, stand!"—my professional judgment is undermined by undiscriminating sympathy for the underdog. In Moscow, as elsewhere, I *wanted* to believe that little man in danger. I found myself inwardly straining for the defense.

So, too, for the skinny, shaved Georgian. Of course I was

not hoping he would be acquitted; acquittals in the People's Courts are preciously rare. They do occur; lawyers boasted to me of cases they had won, and I have read of others in the journals. But I never saw one myself, and I became accustomed to taking a guilty verdict for granted. Certainly there was no encouragement to hope for it in this case; the defendant had, after all, sinned and confessed.

So had the vast majority of defendants I saw. Almost everyone "admitted my guilt," and there were strong cases against the others. It was rare too, therefore, that I felt a *blameless* man was being convicted, however sure I was that he was innocent of the particular crime as it was described in the legal qualification of his acts, or that he did not deserve the punishment awarded. All of the sad faces had done *something* wrong, *something* which justified the state's intervention and punitive action.

The question was always: Wrong to what extent? What measure of protection was justified? Had the Georgian attempted rape—the real thing? I was sure he had not. His lawyer's argument convinced me entirely. No intimate clothes had been touched, no real preparations had been made, not even the lips had been involved; and had it come to a serious struggle I think the girl would easily have overcome the puny spastic. He seemed incapable of physical violence and in any case so horrified and contrite over what he had done (have many men not done something similar in their youth?) that token punishment seemed enough. Here was the place for a conditional sentence, for a second chance, for separating the accidental, one-time offender from the hardened recidivist, as Soviet texts and journals constantly exhort. Here was a chance for the most humane court in the world to show its heart.

But this too was rare in Moscow.

The court found the facts fully proved: there was no doubt that the accused had grabbed the girl by the throat and tried to rape her under threat of murder. The sentence was five years in a labor colony under strict regime. A gasp of amazement sounded when this was coolly announced—the room had filled with dozens of friends, relatives, neighbors, co-workers, and fellow students, who too believed *this* defendant, because they knew him as honest and harmless—and anguished groans followed as he was led, twitching, away.

"Yes . . . Comrade . . . Judge . . . the . . . sentence . . . is . . . clear."

XI

In a Russian Village

Spring in Moscow was steadily, dismally wet. The snow melted slowly and although the city proper was kept scrupulously clean and dry, outlying areas—the university is in one of them—where landscaping and drainage do not keep pace with the frantic construction were seeped in slush and soggy clay. During one weary stretch in April it rained for seven consecutive days, and there were seven or eight days more in which the sun did not once appear. It was damp and cold, gray and oppressive.

Early one raw, cold morning in the middle of this period, a busy, ebullient lawyer whom I had followed to several cases in the People's Courts and around town on his errands—he spent a quarter of his time keeping his rattletrap car in repair, a frantic job that reminded me of America during the war—drove me to a trial in a small village just outside of Moscow. He was a portly, jolly fellow, who seemed to know everyone everywhere, and after a few weeks he was greeting me with the same easy familiarity that he used with procurators, mechanics and traffic cops. When speaking in court, however, he became thoroughly professional, intensely serious and eloquent. He was one of the best folksy orators I ever heard.

On the way out of Moscow he—I shall call him Aleksandr Solomonovich—told me the background of the case at hand.

It concerned pickles and a coat. Like so many of those I was encountering, it combined a number of charges.

The coat was involved indirectly. Sometime during the autumn of the previous year a saleswoman in the food store of the little village got wind of a shipment of winter coats that had arrived in the local clothing store down the street. She ran there directly, saw a coat that struck her fancy and rushed back to her own store to ask the manager—her friend of four years' standing—to lend her the money to buy it. She had her own money at home, a twenty-minute walk away, and promised to fetch it after the purchase and return within the hour. The manager handed her two hundred rubles from the store's cash drawer without a thought.

(By the time Aleksandr Solomonovich told me this story, there was no need for him to explain to me the sense of urgency about buying the coat. The first rule of shopping in Russia is that purchases of this kind are not put off, for there is much more money in circulation than attractive goods, and the latter are snapped up instantaneously. Buy now if you see something tolerable—tomorrow it will be gone.)

The saleswoman bought the coat in time and returned to work gaily with her own two hundred rubles in forty-five minutes—but too late: in the meantime an auditing team had arrived on a surprise visit. The manager explained the two-hundred ruble deficit and promised its return forthwith, but when the money came, the inspectors would not allow it to be replaced into the cash drawer. They reported the shortage to the procuracy and the manager was charged with criminal misuse of her official position by illegally dispensing state funds.

During the investigation, other irregularities in the operation of the little food store came to light. Most important was the matter of the pickles. When questioned about the manager's character and competence, the local citizens angrily held forth about her pickles. Pickles—sharp, delicious dills—are a staple of the Russian diet, in winter often the only greens. Pickles, it turned out, were sold at the store for 30 kopeks a kilo, and there were no cheaper ones, even though according to the vegetable plan there were supposed to be two varieties, one at 30 and one at 10 kopeks. The investigator was sure he had stumbled onto the kind of shenanigans he was looking for. Further investigation revealed that the manager had indeed received a two-ton shipment of 10-kopek pickles just prior to the coat incident, but that pickles were never sold in the store for less than 30 kopeks. With this, both manager and saleswoman, the very ones, of course, who made light of the two hundred rubles, were charged with selling two tons of 10-kopek pickles at 30 kopeks: Deception of Customers Involving Large Amounts.

The store was then subjected to a series of test purchases (these are normally carried out in every store as a matter of routine at regular intervals) by volunteer workers called *obshchestvenniye* controllers. Careful weighing on test scales indicated that the same saleswoman had short-weighted and overcharged on several purchases from her department: potatoes, onions, cabbages and, of course, pickles. The amount in each case was in grams, or tens of grams, and kopeks, the sum of the discrepancies amounting to 1 ruble and 81 kopeks. The saleswoman was charged with Deception of Customers Involving Small Amounts.

It was, Aleksandr Solomonovich explained while clutching his wheel fondly and waving to traffic cops, on these four charges—misuse of official position and large-scale deception of customers by the manager, and large-scale and petty deception of customers by the saleswoman—that the case first came to trial in February, two months before, in the village court.

During the course of that trial, the manager casually mentioned to Aleksandr Solomonovich that she once trucked some pickles to a nearby collective farm ("The Way of Stalin") as swill for the pigs, because they were rotten when they were delivered. Who can say why *these* pickles had never been noticed before? For reasons unclear to everyone, revelations like this one sometimes popped up at trials, even after the most thorough-seeming investigations. Aleksandr Solomonovich was startled into action: couldn't these be the 10-kopek pickles allegedly palmed off at 30 kopeks? He petitioned the court for a postponement and supplementary investigation, which indeed uncovered documents showing that exactly two tons of rotten dill pickles had been dumped at the farm. The large-scale-deception charge against both women was dropped.

That left the charge of misuse of an official position (the coat) against the manager and that of petty cheating (short-weighting and overcharging) against the saleswoman—the charges we were on our way to hear.

Aleksandr Solomonovich drove proudly and self-consciously through the morning truck-and-taxi traffic, and out of the city. Suddenly we were in the countryside, slightly hilly, slightly eroded, slightly untidy and muddy, with clumps of birches looking as if they would never bloom. It was that unmistakably Russian countryside, which manages to look more like luckless virginal Nature than any other countryside. But an unfortunate rash of new industrial projects along the way looks very much like sooty northern New Jersey along the Turnpike.

The village was about fifteen miles north of Moscow on the road to Leningrad. It was an ordinary one-street hamlet, distinguished by nothing in particular. Those charming, ramshackle Russian cottages which never show their age, because after the first winter they are already cozily out of kilter, made up most of it. But in the center was a development of brick buildings recently thrown up in the standard, square, graceless style called socialist realism which sprouts everywhere in Russia. All the villagers, including women, wore *sapogi*, the traditional high black boots which are fast disappearing from metropolitan Moscow, and there was a simple reason for their addiction to that footgear: mud. The mud was astonishing; was thick; was everywhere. It made me remember, out of the depths of my schoolboy accumulation of facts, that some colonial or constitutional convention in eighteenth-century America was canceled or postponed because the members could not get their wagons through the spring mud. Such was the feel of things in that roughhewn, backwoods *mestechko* ("hick town in the sticks"). Many of the men wore full beards, and with their unfinished branches for walking sticks, they looked like the Bolshoi Theater's stereotype of the legendary *muzhik*. It was old peasant Russia, forty minutes from downtown Gorky Street. (And this juxtaposition is one of the delights of Moscow. On Sundays, hordes of families travel quickly to the country by bus, subway and *elektrichka*, to ski, swim and pick mushrooms, or simply to "breathe the fresh air" and "retire" for a day.)

Our courtroom—there was just one for the village, and a single judge—was on the ground floor of one of the typical brick apartments, a stark, cold room of moderate size. Organizationally, this was not a Moscow court but one branch of a rural court district of the *province* of Moscow. It is the difference, in a smaller way, between New York City and New York State. Dry mud caked the concrete floor. Although the building was new, the courtroom had already taken on the shabby, soulless look of the urban People's Courts. The single adornment was a crimson banner lettered in white hanging unevenly over the dais: THE COURT IS INDEPENDENT AND SUBORDINATE ONLY TO THE LAW. (Those are the words of Article 112 of the Federal Constitution.) The lay assessors sat on kitchen chairs, the judge on a high-backed chair marked

"R.S.F. . . ."; the "S.R." had rubbed away.

It is difficult to describe the flavor of that court session, for I have already talked of Moscow trials in terms of informality, and I know no appropriate comparative or superlative words to suggest superinformality. I can only mention that the supercasual public, many in barnyard clothes, wandered aimlessly in and out through the open door or (except for one strikingly beautiful young peasant girl who sat demurely throughout) sprawled on the benches gossiping loudly and spitting sunflower seeds onto the floor; that two drunks were made to leave; that all of us, including the assessors, kept on our overcoats in the damp cold; that everyone seemed to know everyone else and the fact that they happened to be in a courtroom made no difference in the way they addressed one another ("Hey you, Kolya, how's your cow?"); that the rules of procedure were relaxed beyond their ordinarily flexible limits so that the person talking at a given moment seemed simply the one most eager to say something; that the whole scene suggested less a criminal trial than a sergeant's dressing-down of a couple of errant recruits in a sloppy barracks.

The objects of rebuke, the ex-manager and the ex-saleswoman (both had been fired from the store when charges were pressed) looked almost alike except for details of nose and forehead. Both were about forty, short, stout, kerchiefed Russian peasants, strong in face and body, massive and solid, smelling of earth. They seemed the strength and sinews of Russia. (I shall never forget a taxi driver who looked much like both of them telling me how, after her four brothers were all killed by the Wehrmacht at Stalingrad, she picked up a rifle and crawled to the front.) With bulging breasts and stomachs, both stood up proudly before the court, imperturbably admitted their guilt, and said that they did not understand the great fuss over *meloch* ("trivia," or "details"). They could have been a reminder to jurists that the law is sometimes a great waste of time for people involved in more essential and understandable things.

The judge was a woman too, fat and florid, in a man-tailored suit (her husband's?) with bulging shoulders. She was new to the case; the judge who had presided at the earlier trial was now on a three-month maternity leave. Her questions were angry; but it was one of the assessors, an irascible, parched old man with, apparently, a personal axe to grind, who led the attack on the defendants. I had noticed before that in the rare instances when assessors participated actively in the questioning, they were almost always harsher than the judges. They seemed to have no feeling for procedure or restraint, or for their role as impartial arbiters; perhaps they thought of themselves as prosecutors charged with exposing the defendant, or perhaps they felt compelled to show themselves tough by being more "just" than the judge. Whatever the reason, defendants suffered at their hands.

This dried and brittle little assessor was of that breed. He fairly shook with rage as he interrogated the manager.

"You don't understand the fuss, you say? Excellent! Maybe I'll *make* you understand once and for all, cheater. Whose money was it, yours or the state's?"

"The state's, of course."

"Then why did you squander the state's property? Don't you know that is the same thing as stealing?"

"It's not the same thing. I lent it to her because I knew she would return it in an hour as she promised. I knew she wouldn't steal. And she didn't. Why, she's trusted with more than two hundred rubles every day in the store. She could have simply taken it herself without asking me."

"Incredible! You still refuse to see what is involved here—that you deliberately violated a criminal law. Well, we are going to have to teach you that some way."

"Whatever you say."

"All right, don't be so smart; we know what you were up to in that store. Too bad we finally caught you. Now let's check on another thing: you claim that you were never convicted before?"

"Never."

"But you were sure enough previously *tried*."

"I was acquitted."

"But you *were* tried on a criminal charge, right?"

"Yes, I was tried—but found entirely innocent; they admitted that it was a mistake."

"What were you tried for?"

"I told you, I was acquitted."

"I'm asking you what the charge was. Stop stalling. The charge and the year."

"All right, have it your way. It was 1954. It had to do with some irregularities in a buffet in which I was working. But I was freed completely—they even paid me for my days in court."

"What precisely were you accused of?"

"It had nothing to do with me, I tell you."

"Answer the question. You are only going to make things harder for yourself here."

Resignedly: "Of watering vodka and resealing the bottles. But I was innocent."

"And were you not also warned for short-weighting in that buffet? Stop playing innocent; we know your game."

"I did get a warning, that's true. But it was unfair, it was all connected with the vodka business. Most of the girls were found guilty, so they gave me a warning too—*na vsyakii sluchai* [just to be on the safe side]. But there was nothing against me at all; I was innocent, even if *you* won't believe it."

"If you were innocent, I assume you protested the warning. Did you?"

"I didn't want to get involved more deeply. I let it go."

"Too bad for you. Next time maybe you'll take it seriously. You don't get warnings for nothing. . . ."

"Did you know that she [the saleswoman] was in the habit of short-weighting vegetables?"

"No."

"You should have known; that was your responsibility. We pay you managers to find out when their employees are cheating, not to help them out."

"She wasn't in the habit of *anything*, and she wasn't cheating. She might not have weighed everything to the gram during rush hours. All right, that's her mistake, it's my fault too, but she's not a cheater."

"She systematically cheated innocent customers. She had a criminal system worked out—you heard the indictment. And it was your job to stop it, to stop that disgusting racket. How irresponsibly you acted! Do you agree, defendant?"

"If you like, I agree."

"Oh yes, irresponsible—and for that you will be sitting in jail."

"As you choose." She suddenly grows angry. "Do whatever you want with me, I don't care. Just stop attacking me like that, stop making things up. I told you what I did wrong. I made some mistakes, maybe I even broke some law, but I'm no criminal. My conscience is clear."

"Of course it was irresponsible. And 'irresponsible' means 'criminal,' just like your handing away the state's money to unauthorized outsiders. Whose money was that, I ask you? Whom were you swindling? You were swindling us, the ordinary workers. The people of the working class, just like yourself."

"Maybe worse than me."

"Why did you do it, I want to know. What was your reason for cheating the working class? What made you work out a system for thieving the bread of the toilers?"

"There was *no system*."

"Answer the question!"

"I can't answer that question."

Finally the judge restrained her incensed colleague.

The evidence was heard in normal fashion—the affair of the coat retold about a dozen times by everyone involved, and the short-weighting and overcharging discussed by a parade of expert witnesses as well as by the control purchasers. But the major part of the trial was given over to a general critique, by judge and assessors, of the daily operation of the food store. The women were grilled about a dozen faults: Why were the keys entrusted to workers not "materially responsible" by contract? Why was the floor dirty in the evenings? Why was the cleaning woman allowed to sell vegetables during the rush hours? Why were the tops of cans rusty? Why was spoilage determined without the approval of a vegetable expert? Why were prices reduced on substandard goods without authorization? Where were the invoices with the official prices? *What?*—prices were sometimes fixed by the look of the vegetables instead of by the invoices?"

The excoriation went on for an hour, and things looked very bad for the women. Now and then they protested, halfheartedly, against the "unfair attack" by the court, the manager explaining that she relinquished the keys to trusted workers only on mornings when she had to go to the warehouse, that spoilage was a tricky business, and that official prices were sometimes unreasonable, inferior pickles being priced higher than better ones; and the saleswoman saying that any mistakes she made in weighing were the result of overwork, and that the cleaning woman sometimes pitched in at the counter for the same reason. But for most of the hour they sat silently without defending themselves. Their lawyers appealed for moderation, and they introduced certificates of socialist merit which the women had won in the store. (The women themselves had forgotten about these awards, and they asked to be shown them after the court had examined them.) But the court seemed impervious to their explanations, dismissing them with waves of the hand. The old assessor kept on cutting in with "We know their cheating little game."

The lawyers fought valiantly, even though they knew that it was an almost hopeless cause. Aleksandr Solomonovich made one of his impressive speeches, urging that the manager be exonerated completely because the elements of a crime were lacking in her lending of the two hundred rubles. He read aloud the relevant article: "Misuse of . . . an official position is *intentional* utilization by a responsible person of his official position contrary to the interests of his office *if it is committed for mercenary or other motives of personal interest* and causes *significant harm* to state or community interests . . ." The text of the statute, he said, made it absolutely clear that the manager did not violate the law—perhaps the regulations of work discipline, but not the criminal law. "But I will say more," he went on ardently. "Sometimes you have to put your hand on your heart and speak frankly. Would this case have come to court had there not been that unfortunate oversight about the rotten pickles? I think not. *Surely* not. That charge was a mistake and happily it has been corrected, but there lingers on a certain suspicion, an undocumented, unfair suspicion, that there were evil doings in the store. Comrade Judges, you know that these are not grounds for a criminal conviction in a socialist court. You must consider here only whether the actions of my client are described by the words of the article with which she is charged. It is plain to see that they are not. She must be acquitted. We are all fighting to strengthen socialist legality, but that doesn't mean sentencing innocent people. That doesn't mean building up the statistics by adding one more 'criminal' to them."

But it looked very bad, and while the court was deliberating, Aleksandr Solomonovich paced about nervously among the villagers in the muddy vestibule, second-guessing. It was not so much the specified acts that bothered the court, he reflected, as the general condition of the store; the court seemed bent on righting wrongs—personal wrongs suffered by them as customers of the store. The critical references to the general operation of the store obviously violated a cardinal rule of procedure,* but he thought it prudent not to antagonize the court further by protesting on these grounds. "You see, my tactics were to emphasize, by my own silence, the insignificance of my client's involvement. I wanted to play it down so it took on perspective. That's the way it goes. . . . And besides, I've rarely seen such an accusatorial tendency in a court. I didn't want to feed the fire. It's going to be bad enough."

One more circumstance worried him: the general attitude toward salespeople. Soviet people are inherently suspicious of taxi drivers, waiters, repairmen, theater managers, tailors, ticket vendors, and anyone who deals with consumer goods or petty services and handles petty cash—especially saleswomen. The trades are a hotbed of petty cheating. It is *expected* that people who work in them are reaping private profits on the side and kicking back to their superiors. Like queues, petty cheating and petty bribery are part of the retail landscape. (In fairness to the two defendants in this case, however, it should be reported that when the investigator searched their rooms for evidence of profits, he found only a bed, a bureau, a table, and chairs, in each dwelling.)

To what extent this is a consequence not of socialism or of

* Article 254: "Examination of the case in court takes place only . . . on the basis of the indictment under which the accused has been brought to court trial."

the Russian character but simply of shortage, it is hard to say. "Under the table" transactions, after all, were commonplace in American free enterprise during the shortages of World War II. In any case, Soviet salespeople are mistrusted. I often heard it said that people behind counters double their (paltry) monthly incomes by selling scarce articles at a premium to contacts instead of to the first customer or by juggling grams and kopeks on the items in reasonable supply. A few grams less of bologna or of wine adds up to a tidy profit for the countergirl at the end of the day, and—to be fair to the village court—I saw a number of cases in which the seemingly innocent mistakes in weighing were in fact part of a quiet, systematic racket. Aside from the crimes of violence familiar everywhere, these kopek-crimes of exchange seemed to be the most common in Soviet courts. And there were cases in which more than kopeks were involved; I know, for example, of one in which a man paid 275 rubles under the table for an expensive Hungarian buffet.

Once an earnest witness in a higher court summed up the Soviet attitude nicely: "Everyone knows salespeople are all thieves anyway." And the lawyer, who was defending a salesman, countered: "That's simply solved: build a giant concentration camp in Siberia, shove all salespeople into it, and Soviet crime will be eliminated." The judge let the remark pass.

This is what depressed Aleksandr Solomonovich. "They always like the chance to get back at a salesgirl," he muttered between puffs on his Bulgarian cigarette. He was chain-smoking and uncharacteristically subdued, and surprisingly nervous, I thought, for a man of his experience.

But surprise! The verdict jolted him back to his normal good humor. Both women were found guilty, but sentenced to only a year's corrective labor at new jobs, as unskilled laborers, with 15 per cent of their wages deducted as fine.

As we squeezed into the little red Moskvich for the ride

home, the husky manager ran up to us. "Aleksandr Solomonovich, let me shake your hand again. Where would I have been
without you? Only *there*." She winked. "You're a good man."
And she pumped away hard at his arm, grinning.

Aleksandr Solomonovich grinned too. He was convinced,
he repeated as we sloshed off through the mud, that she was
in fact legally innocent, that no *crime* had been committed. A
mistake is not a crime. "But that old geezer of an assessor
worried me and I've got to admit I'm glad she got off as
lightly as she did."

He drove back in good spirits, and we stopped for vodka
and a late lunch in a café, where he joked with the waitresses,
whom he called by their first names.

XII

Speaking for the Defense

Here and there still persists that strange sort of attitude toward lawyers as people who interfere with, rather than contribute to, the exercise of justice . . . and some lawyers, fearing to enter into a genuine debate of principles with the representatives of the prosecution, encourage such an attitude toward themselves. We must put an end to this situation and regard advocates as real, persistent and courageous defenders of truth and justice.

—From a deputy's address to the Supreme Soviet, 1957

How DID Aleksandr Solomonovich own a car? Some lawyers do, for the successful ones live luxuriously by Soviet standards. Although the profession is almost never a point of departure for bigger things—it offers neither status nor a path to importance in Party, government or "business"—it can provide comfort. A young lawyer ends an old lawyer, but along the way he may become relatively affluent with rubles and hours to spare. I say "relatively" because the thought of a prosperous lawyer of the six-figure, Wall Street type is almost as absurd in the Soviet environment as the thought of a Wall Street broker.

One meets, therefore, men and women (sometimes couples) who have left other occupations in the legal world to practice trial law: former procurators, judges and legal consultants. One of the best-known Moscow criminal lawyers—although his fame is a fraction of what it would have been, *mutatis mutandis*, in New York or London—worked for many years in higher strata of the city procuracy. His new job gave him less prestige, but something like thrice the income. There is even a tendency, curious for Americans and Englishmen since it reverses their natural order of things, for judges, retiring or practicing, to become trial lawyers. The reverse very rarely happens.

Officially, an average Moscow lawyer earns only about as much as an average judge or procurator—between 110 and 125 rubles a month (working, however, many fewer hours than a judge or procurator). This is somewhat more than the wages of an average skilled factory worker. But lawyers can turn a penny *pomimo kassi* ("on the side") much more easily than the latter. This is simply done and so widespread that no one tried for long to conceal it from me.

All lawyers are organized into Collegia, "voluntary" collectives under the supervision of the Ministry of Justice. A lawyer must belong to one in order to practice. In Moscow, there are two such organizations: the Moscow City Collegium of Advocates and the Moscow Oblastnoi (Regional) Collegium of Advocates. Lawyers work in one or another of the Juridical Consultation offices, which are spread out over the city by districts and are subordinate to the Collegium. Here lawyers either are assigned to cases by the Consultation office's administration or take them on from contacts of their own. (Almost always, it is the relatives of an accused in jail who engage a defense lawyer, and this is usually done on the basis of previous acquaintance or recommendation by friends.) But in either instance the fee must be approved by and is paid through the Collegium and there are, as one might imagine, more or less standard honoraria for every kind of case, based upon complexity and length of service. On paper, then, engaging and paying a lawyer is a private affair within narrow public limits.

Often in practice, however, lawyer and client arrange for an additional fee, which is not reported to the Collegium; it amounts to about as much, by a rule of thumb, as the legitimate fee. This happens most often in serious criminal cases, and the *raison d'être* for this curious arrangement is always the same: the client feels more confident—and the lawyer does all he can to encourage this feeling—that he will be better defended if he awards a "bonus." And so a lawyer with some reputation can earn 250 to 350 rubles a month instead of 125.

Everyone knows about this bonus custom ("That's why the judges and procurators are always so angry-looking," an artless young lawyer suggested), but it has gone on for decades. Why? I asked. Because obtaining evidence about it—getting a defendant, involved himself, to testify—is difficult. "And because, if they cracked down, no one would work as a trial lawyer any longer." Nevertheless, while I was in Moscow, a case was brought against a well-known lawyer who had worked the system. He was charged with misuse of an official position; for the first time, a lawyer was designated an "official," and criminal sanctions were applied. The charges were dropped, however, before the case came to trial, and now, again, the most serious punishment a lawyer can expect for payment *pomimo kassi* is administrative: permanent exclusion from the Collegium, meaning, of course, loss of the right to practice law. Since this remains the extent of the deterrent, successful lawyers continue to live well.

I would like to say more about the lawyers. Taken together —there are only about a thousand in Moscow, and after a few weeks one keeps seeing the same more-or-less well-bred faces —they were the most attractive of all the people connected occupationally with the court. There was a keener look in their eyes, a quicker smile on their lips, an easier gait in their movements, than among the judges and procurators. They were also better dressed, their clothing neater, more fashionable, more tasteful. The difference among women was most vivid. Female judges and procurators invariably cultivated a severe, un-made-up, contemptuous-of-appearance look, while lawyers worked at getting themselves up. Some succeeded well enough to have looked in place on a West European boulevard.

And lawyers were more friendly to strangers than the others. It was almost always they who, seeing me scribbling my notes, asked who I was and whether they could help me. And, learning who I was, they were the most curious about the world abroad. What about American procedure? How would the last case have been handled there? What are the West's methods of legal education? How are lawyers regarded in Western society? How do lawyers make out there, and what is life *really* like for the likes of us? Judges and procurators asked these questions with little enthusiasm, if at all. And they almost never asked me to join them at lunch.

I do not want to make too much of the difference between lawyers as one group and procurators and judges as another. They often ate together and chatted cordially between cases. They belong to the same stock, the same culture and class. Yet, the separateness of the two groups is inescapable. In the textbooks, for instance, judges and procurators are always mentioned in one breath as allied official agents charged with almost identical functions—administration of justice, elimination of crime, protection of socialist legality—and the lawyers are treated in a passing half chapter. At work, the textbook situation prevailed: procurators and judges were hand in glove on every level. The procurator prosecuting a case frequently entered the courtroom from the judge's chambers, and I often saw his superior, the District Procurator, working with the judge's superior, the chairman of the People's Court, in the latter's office. (Sometimes they were on *ti* ("thou") terms with each other.) This was natural to them; they were members of the same team.

But the lawyers didn't make the team. They were, so to speak, in a separate league, a minor one. Again, the textbook difference manifested itself in perceptible ways. Lawyers were apt to be less "Soviet," not only in the cut of their clothes, but also in their speech, manners and sense of humor—less Victorian, less provincial, less apt to speak in newspaper clichés. However one measures the distance that separates people of different cultures, it was shorter between myself and the lawyers than between myself and the others. What we had in common was, somehow, more. One world?

Many of the lawyers are maimed—an arm missing, a leg, an eye. The numbers of crutches, black gloves, flapping sleeves and twisting scars at courtroom tables stand out even in Moscow, where one grows accustomed to seeing middle-aged men with missing parts. I have tried to imagine what the war meant to these people—they went to it as boys, and afterward, as cripples fit only for paper work, they entered the law—but I suppose I can have no real understanding. No American can understand what Russians experienced during the war. Soviet patriotic propaganda gives only the surface details of the story.

I met one quiet lawyer who specializes in labor cases (he had just won a difficult case for his female-mason client against a construction firm). A grotesque scar ran from his ear to his lip; he had been wounded by a grenade on the Austrian front, and while he lay unconscious in a field hospital he was wounded again, this time flush on the face. His nose was partly gone. "I should have died in 1945," he said. "But now I'm happy, especially in the morning when I wake up, because I look on each new day as a 'find.' " When these Russians talked about disarmament, there was a ring of honesty to their appeals.

Many of the lawyers are Communists too. I have forgotten what impression I had of a "Communist" before I lived in Moscow. Probably I pictured a steely, snarling, remote-controlled authoritarian. Since then I have learned that to appraise a man solely on the basis of whether he is or is not a member of the Party is stupid. A violinist I knew in Tbilisi joined the Party to get more concerts, and an engineer-Communist I knew in Moscow said more sensible things about the cold war than any other Russian I met. One of my roommates was a Party member, and this seemed only to make him especially concerned about my attitude toward his sneaking girls into the dormitory overnight. The Communist "boss" of dormitory section "G" was relaxed and open-minded (while the "boss" of neighboring section "ZH" was a vicious careerist). Communists sometimes invited me to dinner and sometimes were the most gracious and human friends. There are some ten million people in the Party, and they include the best and the worst types. I met only a few stereotyped, acid *apparatchiks*.

The best and worst types are in the legal profession too. Maybe it was natural that a stranger like me would meet more of the best. The lawyer-Communists I knew all believed that a guilty man should be punished, but fairly—for what he did, and not for what the procurator (almost always a Party member too) said he did. As often as not, the best defenses were made by Communists. They were consistently the courtroom's top performers, better prepared and far more eloquent than the procurators, and more intelligent than the judges. They put the case for the accused as well as it could be put. "It is true that this kind of crime is deeply foreign to Soviet society and must not be tolerated," they would begin, "but when we look at the facts in *this* case, we find that the

238

accused was a victim of circumstances beyond his control."

A Soviet trial is so conducted that the lawyer's concluding statement is more often a collection of mitigating circumstances than a denial of guilt or a presentation of purely legal arguments. But sometimes one does hear legal arguments as well (though never that a law is unconstitutional, that the government has exceeded its powers, or that a citizen has inalienable rights not to be infringed upon by the state). I remember a particular bribery case; like most, it involved many defendants. One of the lawyers, a Communist, talked brilliantly for an hour, demonstrating the lack of concrete proof for each of the charges against his client and insisting that it was intolerable to shift the burden of proof upon him. He said that to convict the accused on the basis of a witness' boast that he had given him a bribe would be dangerous because it would stretch the meaning of bribery beyond the legislative intent, and that was deeply alien to socialist legality. His defense would have done an American Civil Liberties Union lawyer proud.

In a word, Communist lawyers, as much as other lawyers, want a fair trial—that is what Communism means to them.

I have been trying in this report to give the flavor of the typical and to leave out most of the rest. Sometimes, writing as fast as I could, I took down the summation of defense counsels word for word. Here is the most typical of these from a case in Leninskii District. Two youngish women, disheveled and homely, were the accused; each had once before spent time in a labor colony for an offense similar to the one that was now being dealt with. The lawyer who spoke first was a round-featured, round-figured young woman who, it seemed sure, would be making a massive dinner for her family later in the afternoon. She spoke without notes, starting in a spiritless voice which gradually gathered body and emotion.

"Comrade Judges! . . . The case we have heard today is a

special one because in the dock sit two young women, two mothers, whose children depend upon them for guidance, support and upbringing. This crucial circumstance must make us proceed here with particular care. Whenever children are involved—the new Soviet generation—we all await the sentence with special emotion. I ask you, therefore, to take this into account.

"Zharikova, my client, is accused of actions qualified under Article 144, Paragraph 2, of the Criminal Code. The facts are not complicated, and were carefully and conscientiously examined here in court. On the fifth of August of this year, at the outdoor market at Luzhniki, near Lenin Stadium, Zharikova removed a purse, a mirror and some cosmetics from the handbag of a stranger, Citizeness Lebedeva, and passed them to Kushelova [the other defendant]. The act was seen by several passers-by, and the stolen articles were discovered on their persons. There can be no question about the facts.

"Comrade Judges! The story which we have heard today is deeply repugnant to our morals and to our Soviet concept of living. It is particularly objectionable and intolerable now, when we have reached the stage where friendship, brotherly co-operation and honesty are the principles underlying our society. Zharikova took a purse which belonged to someone else. The fact that it contained only six rubles and ninety-six kopeks has no bearing on the case. She stole someone else's belongings; she tried to live at someone else's expense; she violated Soviet norms and feelings. And this is repugnant.

"Of course I will not ask you to forgive this action. Zharikova stole; she committed a crime. But it is my duty to defend a living person, not an act, and I ask you, therefore, to consider the following circumstances. You must weigh not only the crime, but also its causes and the person and, most important, what must be done now in the way of reforming her.

Speaking for the Defense

"How did it happen that in a socialist society such a crime was committed by so young a woman? How can it be prevented in the future? Comrade Judges, I suggest that the war was the real cause of Zharikova's misfortune. The war. When she was still a young girl hardly separated from her mother's breast, her father died on the front, defending the Fatherland. That was in 1939. Her mother was wounded too, later during the war, and remains an invalid to this day. You heard her mother and sister testify today. You know what the war meant to the infant Zharikova. It deprived her of a normal upbringing in a normal family. The strength and support of a father was lacking, and her mother, sick and alone, was terribly hard up during those years. All of this misfortune meant that Zharikova never had the kind of spiritual and material support that every person needs to develop normally. Her mother simply could not cope with all the work of raising a family and earning a living. Zharikova was left alone most of the time and, because of this, sat for the first time in the dock of a criminal court at a very young age. A terrible misfortune. Almost certainly her life's path would have been very different were it not for the war.

"Later, Zharikova fell in love with a certain man. A son was born. But the marriage was never registered, and the man turned out to be a good-for-nothing. Another misfortune. After the child's birth, he abandoned her. The son never knew his father. Now this little boy is nine years old, and he loves and needs his mother. The boy asks, "Where is mama?" and no one wants to tell him that she is in jail. All sorts of excuses are resorted to.

"Before this unfortunate incident, Zharikova was earning forty-two rubles [a month] and raising her dear son on this. You yourselves, Comrade Judges, realize that this is very little, that her material situation was not easy. Zharikova has hinted that she was motivated to commit this crime by material need.

This is wrong. Her plight cannot be considered justification for her action. She had enough to eat. She was neither cold nor hungry. But it *is* a consideration nevertheless, and I hope that you will remember it. She had to struggle.

"From the testimony of the neighbors today, it is clear that the young son is a good, a happy boy, who adores and trusts his mother. I ask you to remember this too when you decide Zharikova's fate. Singlehanded, she is raising a fine Soviet lad.

"Zharikova has admitted everything openly and frankly today. She has not attempted to hide her guilt, because she knows that she must redeem it. And she has already started on the right path. I *know* that she is in court for the last time. She realizes that her pattern of illegal behavior cannot continue, that society will not permit it, that it is ruinous for herself and especially for her beloved son. I know that she has already suffered very deeply as a result of her errors. She eats very poorly; she hardly sleeps. I saw this myself when I visited her in jail.

"She told me there, in jail, that her one desire is to reform, to return, an honest woman, to her son, whom she adores, and to Soviet society. She told me that she understands that she committed a serious crime and that this is wrong. She regrets it deeply. I believe her. I hope that you will. I think that she can be worthy of the great title of Soviet Citizen. Sooner or later, she will be a free person again, and our major concern today is, How will she conduct herself then? I think there is no question about this; Zharikova has *already* experienced what punishment in our Soviet system is designed to accomplish. She has seen the error of her ways and is eager to reform.

"Yes, Zharikova is guilty—truly guilty. She must be punished. She committed a crime and in our society no crime can go unpunished. She must pay for her mistakes. But the punishment must be fair and sensible. This is what you must decide, Comrade Judges—you must decide her fate. To me, it seems perfectly plain that there is no need to punish her harshly. Our interest is that Zharikova return to society a useful member and this, I think, is already assured.

"I must now touch briefly upon another aspect of this case—the juridical aspect. My client has denied that she and Kushelova made a preliminary agreement among themselves to commit their crime. I must tell you frankly that I myself do not believe this. You have seen how mistrustful I was when I questioned her about her intentions. I simply cannot believe that she went to the Luzhniki market with Kushelova without having reached an understanding beforehand to take an illegal action. You, of course, will evaluate her testimony and that of the witnesses about this. But in any case, it is a matter of secondary importance. For Zharikova has been convicted before of theft, and the fact that this is a second offense places her present action under Paragraph 2 of Article 144, whether or not preliminary agreement was involved. There can be no argument, then, about the classification.

"Comrade Judges! But there are other factors involved in the story we heard today besides judicial ones. Unfortunately, I have not been able to obtain exact information about the illness of Zharikova's mother, but you have seen her today and heard the testimony of members of the family. She has long been an invalid and is now a very, very sick woman. She too needs Zharikova, and this is another of fate's burdens on my client which I ask you to take into consideration.

"One final point. In addition to everything else, the indictment characterized Zharikova in a negative way, claiming that her behavior in her apartment has been improper, that she drinks, causes unpleasant incidents and scandals and, in general, conducts herself in an unworthy manner. I do not know what sources the investigator had at his disposal, but I checked with her neighbors, and all of them had only good things to say about her: that she is a quiet, co-operative, friendly citizeness who maintains an orderly home and makes every effort to raise her son properly. There was not a single complaint about her behavior. Let us, then, put her crime in its proper perspective. Let us be fair.

"To me, Zharikova's role as mother and homemaker shows that she has the makings of a worthy citizen, that she will be able to reform and live in the future as a worthy member of Soviet society.

"I ask you, Comrade Judges, to take these circumstances into account when you determine the measure of punishment which Zharikova must be awarded. There is no need for severity here. Zharikova has had an unfortunate life; she needs help and encouragement now—encouragement from you, not harshness. I ask that you examine all these circumstances carefully and give her the minimum possible sentence under Article 144, Paragraph 2."

Some time in the middle of this talk, Zharikova's mother and sister broke into tears and by the end were sobbing steadily, though quietly. Zharikova herself covered her face to hide her tears.

Article 144, Paragraph 2, provides for "deprivation of freedom for a period up to five years." Zharikova got four.

I often walked out with the lawyer after his talk and tried to sound him out on the case just tried. If he was free, he would usually take time to answer my questions. Most often, what he said in private was nearly the same as his closing speech. Rarely were there hidden aspects to the case and rarely had the lawyer been mouthing a "sad story" which he did not believe.

When I controlled my curiosity and played innocent, a few lawyers went on from their discussion of that one case to treat me to monologues about the character of Soviet law in general and their place in it. I don't know why they were so open; some Russians are fond of baring their souls to strangers.

The best of the lawyers are cynical. (In what country are they not?) They have seen too much sloppiness and injustice, and they do not think it all accidental. Some have given up reading legal literature, because they feel that theory and scholarly analysis are irrelevant to their practical work so long as the actual, unwritten *règles* of the courts remain governed by other considerations.

The knowledge that they play second fiddle in the courtroom bothers these men in their serious moments. Unlike procurators or judges, lawyers are quasi-private agents with no official status, no official power or prestige. They are still regarded with suspicion because of their "bourgeois" occupation. And while bourgeois individualism suits them in their private, material lives (they are not self-sacrificing men who are eager to give up comforts for a cause), it depresses them as jurists. There is still the feeling that a lawyer is bought for a price and is not, therefore, to be respected. They complain that the court does not listen to their points of law, not even to their closing speeches; that the judge, who is usually less literate than they, assumes a disdainful expression while they speak and sometimes even laughs. This attitude is reinforced by the popular Soviet attitude toward the accused and the trial which undermines the lawyer's effectiveness. Even the law students on my floor in the dormitory thought of the trial as something of a formality and, consequently, of the lawyer's role as superfluous. "In *this* case, he is clearly guilty," I used to hear from students when we went together to court. "Why must the lawyer confuse the issue and waste our time?" The idea that guilt is determined only by the court, only after all the arguments are heard, is not firmly entrenched.

And so the feeling lingers on that the accused is guilty and represents a bother, if not a danger, to the state and that to defend him is somehow disreputable, obstructionist, opportunistic and a waste of time. Certainly lawyers are much happier than they were under Stalin, but since about 1960 they have come to feel that their greatest hopes for complete de-Stalinization will not soon be realized.

Most of the lawyers with whom I talked confidentially muttered that their own influence and sphere of activity is too limited, too restricted in some intangible way; that however strenuous their efforts in a given case, the sentence remains pretty much what it would have been without them; that other, bigger forces are at work, so that the decision depends less upon how they are able to work with the facts than upon these bigger, political forces.

I must qualify this notion. I saw many cases in which a revelation by a lawyer ("Look here, you forgot to consider the water content of the cucumbers; experts tell me that as much as ten per cent in weight can be lost in evaporation." Or, "I have documents to show that my client was on vacation for three weeks in July and could not possibly have worked eighteen shifts, as the indictment claims.") had an immediate effect on a given case. Their clients benefited. When they complained of impotence, the lawyers had in mind a more general phenomenon; they were thinking of the limits of defense as a whole in the Soviet courtroom, and the limits of the law in Soviet society. And the relationship of law to the campaigns. Let me try to explain.

Official life in the Soviet Union is a series of campaigns, with the press, radio, publishing houses, museums, universities, newsreels, television, schools, post office, and so on, joining efforts to hammer home their importance. There is a campaign to spread the planting of corn on collective farms, a campaign to greet spring with a burst of production, a campaign to celebrate Lenin's birth and death, May Day, Constitution Day, Election Day, Woman's Day, a campaign to commemorate the 125th anniversary of Pushkin's death and the 150th anniversary of Borodino, a campaign to free Antoine

Gizenga, to honor Soviet composers, to develop socialist basketball. . . . There is even an overpoweringly intense election campaign, although different from those we know, since there is only a single slate of candidates.

In normal life, one cannot avoid the campaigns.

The law too is subject to the campaign. I was in Moscow in the midst of an energetic, intense, sometimes violent campaign against certain kinds of crime, principally economic. During ten months in 1961–62, five decrees were passed extending the death penalty to formerly noncapital crimes, mostly economic. Currency speculation was one of these. (Although lawyers are skeptical of the long-term results likely to be achieved by the campaigns, this one directed against currency speculation seemed to have had the desired results. When I was in Moscow in 1959, hardly a day passed when I was not approached by someone trying to buy dollars. In 1962, after some publicized shootings of speculators, this was very rare. I was told that the old operators were well frightened and that dollars had become very difficult to trade.) Systematic bribery and graft and organized theft of state or communal property, when they involved large amounts, were other such crimes.

The current campaign led to the execution, in Leningrad in 1961, of the members of a gang of currency speculators convicted of running a highly profitable operation. The 1926 code, which was still in force when they were arrested, fixed a penalty of three to eight years' confinement for their crime. In spite of Article 6 of the Federal Bases of Criminal Law—"A law establishing culpability for an act or increasing punishment therefor has no retroactive force"—the maximum punishment provided by the new code, fifteen years, was applied to them retroactively. Then, again ex post facto, the Praesidium of the Supreme Soviet, on the recommendation of the Procurator General of the Soviet Union, passed a special decree permitting the death penalty for these men; and they were shot. Similar procedure was used to execute several gangs which had earlier been sentenced to lighter punishment for systematic plunder of state property.* The lawyers were dismayed by this action; they spoke as if they themselves had been wounded by the shootings. Many talked to me again and again about it. Some were ashamed. An elderly woman attorney, shaking her head sadly, complained: "They took their risks speculating, thinking they could get eight years. And they were shot. *Bozhe moi*—My God—what happened to socialist legality here?"

A lawyer I met in the corridor of City Court (I have him in my notes as Comrade P.) told me that "nothing, no procedural or substantive law, stands in the way of a serious campaign." He cited his most recent case: two workers testified that a third told them that he had bribed his employer. The accused denied having said it, and denied offering a bribe; the employer denied taking it. But the man was convicted on the basis of this evidence alone. "If you have a bribery case these days, you might as well give up," said Comrade P. dejectedly.

"The judges get the word," grimaced Comrade Zh. From whom? How? I asked. "Don't be so naïve. *S verkhu*—from upstairs. From the smell of things, from the way the wind is blowing." Are there specific instructions to judges in individual cases? The lawyers doubted this; certainly if direct interference happens, it happens rarely. "Why do you try to be so analytical about this?" asked G. "The *rukovodstvo* [leadership, or brass] makes known what it wants in a

---

* I heard the post-factum procedure described—with a sense of righteousness and determination—in a lecture by the Minister of Justice of the R.S.F.S.R. His intention was to enlighten the audience about the methods available to socialist legality for fighting economic crimes.

It can be argued that there was nothing *unconstitutional* about these retroactive shootings because the constitution itself says nothing about post-factum laws and the Federal Bases and Criminal Codes which prohibit them are, juridically, merely laws, subject to suspension by decrees which have the force of law. Nevertheless, the lawyers felt that the executions violated one of the most fundamental elementary principles of legality.

thousand open ways, and the courts make decisions accordingly. Every judge is reminded every day that there is a campaign against bribery. And no one tries to fight it, believe me."

I was indeed naïve; there is nothing secret about a campaign. Every recent issue of the law journals emphatically endorsed the new death-penalty decrees and preached the need to eliminate bribery, speculation and plundering by increasing penalties in sentences. Here is an example from the pen of the Chairman of the Supreme Court of the U.S.S.R.:

Unfortunately, not all court officials have yet realized that a severe battle must be waged against dangerous criminals who resist correction and re-education. Some judges and even procurators still underestimate the social danger of evils like bribery; they do not react against crimes of profit with the necessary sharpness; they do not come to the necessary political and practical conclusions. . . . Mercy toward bribers cannot be tolerated . . . the fight against bribery and theft of the people's welfare is not a short-lived campaign; it must be carried out permanently. . . .

In case judges missed hundreds of hints like these, printed in circulars, newspapers and magazines, they were repeated as directives in frequent obligatory meetings. I managed to attend two, and their theme was always the same: be tough on economic criminals. There were direct instructions from higher bodies too. The Plenum of the Supreme Court explained to judges that "they must take into consideration the dangerous character of the actions not only of those who take bribes, but of those who give them, and of middlemen." The Plenum noticed that "some judges are still too slow to overcome their underevaluation of the enormous social danger of these crimes," and urged that "stricter measures of punishment be applied." There were also daily reports in *Sovietskaya Rossiya* and *Moskovskaya Pravda*, less frequently in *Pravda* and *Izvestiya*, praising judges who gave the death penalty and long terms of confinement and criticizing those who were "indulgent." Editorials, feature stories and authoritative articles by leading officials were in every paper, dwelling on that one lesson.

So pointed and so overwhelming was the legal campaign that the women who cleaned streets near the university were aware of its direction. Surely no judge could fail to understand —no imagination was required of him.

Campaigns in the legal world are not always punitive. In 1958 and 1959 there was a short-lived, urgent campaign to be lenient with criminals—to trust them, give them the benefit of the doubt and another chance. Decrees were issued, plenums convened, and the legal and general press were set in motion to encourage probation, suspended sentences and early releases. Judges were warned of the danger of harsh punishments in standard cases. Conditional and suspended sentences and probations in the care of the collective jumped from 7.6 per cent in the first quarter of 1959 to 22.5 per cent in the last quarter under the "go-easy" campaign. "Hardly anyone was sentenced," said Zh. "There was talk of tearing down the jails. And the result was felt very quickly. Oh, very quickly. Crime rates soared. Every kind: murder, robbery, rape, muggings. People were afraid to walk the streets after dark. Everyone knew that *that* campaign had to be dropped." It was. In 1961 conditional sentences were back to 9 per cent and soon afterward the present "hard" campaign was inaugurated. In criminal law as in many other official aspects of Soviet life, sharp zigzag is the pattern.

Here is an indication of the nature of legal campaigns from the horse's mouth—one of the books assigned me by the dean:*

* *Juristic Guarantees of Legality in the U.S.S.R.* (Moscow: Academy of Sciences of the U.S.S.R., 1962), pp. 172–174.

The principle of the independence and subordination to the law of the Soviet court is one of the most essential of the guarantees which ensure legality in the activity of the judiciary. . . .

Organizational independence of judges means that they are situated in conditions under which not a single higher organ (judicial or otherwise) is empowered as a matter of subordination to influence the substance of trial decisions handed down by a court in a concrete case. The court is bound only by the law in its decisions. . . .

In reaching decisions, the court is not tied to any considerations whatsoever which are extraneous to justice, and is obligated to guide itself in its judicial activity only by the requirements of the law—this is established in Article 112 of the Constitution of the U.S.S.R. This article formulates a clear-cut demand: the court is obliged to function in its activity exclusively as an organ guaranteeing the strictest observance of the laws, itself acting, along with this, within the strictest limits of the law. In the determination of a case, the court is bound only by the law and its own convictions, based upon the circumstances revealed in the process of the trial and the facts established by these circumstances.

However, the principle of the independence of the court and its subordination only to the law cannot be interpreted in the sense that the court, in its activity, stands beyond politics, that in guiding itself in its decisions only by the law, the court somehow excludes itself from participation in resolving those immediate political tasks which the Party and the government place before the state and all of Soviet society in each concrete historical moment. . . .

The court does not stand and cannot stand beyond politics, beyond the solution of the tasks which face the state, beyond the direction of the Party. The court is an active, effective conductor of the policies of the state, a participant in the construction of Communism. . . .

Thus, in connection with the decision of the January Plenum of the Central Committee of the C.P.S.U. of 1961, the most serious task of combating various forms of antistate activity of officials in the area of the Soviet economy was placed upon the court. . . .

It is the whole concept of campaigns, rather than the contents of any one campaign, that made the lawyers unhappy. They felt that the law and the courts ought to be more insulated from the hots and colds of monthly political policy. I never heard lawyers talking about the need to give law a creative role in society, or the kind of independence which generally implies a system of precedents or a metaphysical attachment to "higher" justice. What the lawyers wanted was less: simply that the courts breathe more freely and serve less directly as an instrument of the campaigns, of Party policy, of the whims of nonlawyers who participate in their cases "from upstairs." They wanted their arguments listened to, even in trials that were related to the campaign.

The lawyers were not talking about terror. (The book from which I quoted is largely an analysis of the illegalities under Stalin and an attempt to prevent their return.) They were talking about pressure. About the weakness, the dependence, the "second-placeness" of the Soviet court and of their own voice within the court. About its ultimate subordination, not to the law, but to "them." About the easy malleability of the law itself in "their" hands. Not all of them would talk about this, and those who did were often not explicit, but I think that after a while I understood what they meant. I always heard phrases from the latest editorials repeated from the bench, and the trials always seemed slightly less than real for it. The third ear of Moscow judges seemed to be tuned not to the inner meaning of the case, but to those strong signals *s verkhu.*

In this framework, leave is given to speak for the defense. Out pours an emotional defense, often a solid, strong defense. But by the nature of things, it is a limited defense. The lawyers have mastered the art of sensing the limits.

Part Two

MOSCOW CITY COURT

XIII

Murder: Chernov

Imagine that you are creating a fabric of human destiny with the object of making man happy in the end, giving him peace and rest at last, but that it is essential to torture to death only one tiny creature, and to found that edifice on its unavenged tears—would you consent to be the architect under those conditions?

IVAN KARAMAZOV to his brother Alyosha.

Socialism, fully and finally established in our country, introduced fundamental changes in the consciousness and habits of the Soviet people, in the entire social body. Every Soviet person without exception now has a full opportunity to work successfully, rest normally, receive the necessary education, improve his professional skills and develop his talents. And if in spite of this we still find people in the healthy Soviet family who do not want to accustom themselves to a working life and make use of all the conditions offered them by the socialist system, if some people do not heed the voice of persuasion and reason, preferring to live dishonestly, committing dangerous crimes, then the state can and must apply the most strict and decisive measures to such people. . . .

—CENTRAL COMMITTEE of the Communist Party, 1962.

THE REGULAR Soviet judicial system, excluding administrative and quasi-judicial tribunals, is built on four levels, and courts of all four are located in Moscow. At the apex of the hierarchy is the Supreme Court of the Soviet Union, the ultimate source of interpretation, direction and appeal, roughly comparable to the United States Supreme Court, without judicial review. I was not permitted to watch it at work. One level below that, and about a half mile away near the Kremlin wall, is the Supreme Court of the Russian Republic, the highest court to which the residents of Soviet Russia (that is, the R.S.F.S.R.) may take their cases, except when national interests are involved and the Supreme Court of the Soviet Union enters. A few unusually important crimes are tried in the first instance by the Supreme Court of the Russian Republic, but it is usually a place for appeals. Of these, I watched several brought up from cases I heard in lower courts; but I shall not describe them here, because they lie beyond the realm of daily justice.

The third level interested me more. It consists of *oblastnoi* ("regional," or "provincial"; comparable to "county" in the United States) courts, but Moscow has one of its own, because, logically enough, the city is drawn on the governmental organization chart as an *oblast*. In Moscow it is called "City Court." Its judges are selected by the Moscow City Soviet—not elected directly by the people—to five-year terms.

The *oblastnoi* courts too deal primarily with appeals—from the People's Courts below. But it is also the court of first instance for such grave crimes as counterfeiting, desertion, crimes against justice, murder with aggravating circumstances, mass disorders (pogroms); and also for state crimes, such as high treason, terrorism, diversion, espionage, wrecking, anti-Soviet propaganda and agitation, participation in an anti-Soviet organization. I never came across any of these state crimes or saw them listed or mentioned anywhere except in the code.

Why? One likes to think that it was because they belong to the past, that the days of terror are over. But perhaps, conversely, it was because the terror has done its job so well; or because these crimes are still dealt with by swift machinery outside the courts. These are some of the questions that a year in Moscow did not answer for me.

In any case, I set out to the third level on a dark January morning after an apprenticeship in the lower courts. I wanted to see how the serious crimes were handled. Moscow by then was deep in winter. Every day was gray, the sky a single low gray cloud that held the threat of snow. My directions led me across the somber town, past old women, bent and wrapped in heavy shawls—all of them look so wearyingly alike—chipping and shoveling ice. And also past splendid children skating on the ice, and so bundled up in furs that they could hardly waddle—they all look so much more than two generations removed from their grandmothers. In time I came to a building with the look of a well-used mill, on an ordinary plot along an ordinary street. A dozen figures huddled around in the cold; a steady stream of trucks roared by, hardly muffled by the snow. Here and there a brick had peeled from the façade. A plaque at the entrance read: MOSCOW CITY COURT.

Inside, the lights were on. In one of twenty rooms the public benches were jammed, and the steamy air smelled of sweat and old wool. No flags, no banners with slogans, no red anywhere; nothing to inspire awe or fear of the Law. Just plain blond furniture, shoddy and old-fashioned, clean walls— and Lenin, larger than life.

In the dock a thickset young man with a sickly white face slouched down and fingered his cap. He looked like an average unskilled worker, and only his intense, deep-set eyes relieved the total ordinariness of his appearance. Over the prisoner, in full green winter uniform with high boots and wool-lined cap, stood a soldier at parade rest; three other soldiers with rifles, bayonets fixed, at their sides and pistols in their belts, manned strategic posts throughout the room. In City Court the Army is responsible for the security of defendants, and the Army is very thorough in its work.

"Comrade Judges! A man's life is at stake; we must be very careful. We face only one real issue in this case: the mental condition of the accused; and we know that expert opinion is divided on it. Two psychiatrists, who examined him directly after the incident, have concluded that he was disturbed, and not responsible for his actions. The court has not called them. I urge it to do so now. Hearing this case without them would only violate the defendant's rights and prevent us from doing justice."

Speaking was a tall, gray-haired lady, making her plea in polished Russian from in front of the dock.

"Your opinion, Comrade Procurator?"

From the table opposite, another woman rose, younger and less fine. "I remind the court that the accused was carefully examined at the best criminal-psychiatric institute in Moscow. I see no reason to question the competence of those doctors. I request that the petition be denied."

There was a flurry of whispers on the dais. (In Soviet law, as in Continental law generally, it is the court, not prosecution and defense, which calls witnesses.) The court in this case was a schoolteacherish judge without a frill anywhere, and two younger women in skirts and sweaters—one very young, obese and uncomprehending.

"The court has decided to deny the petition. The record shows that the accused was observed for fifty days in the Serbskii Institute. Further psychiatric expertise would be superfluous. We will proceed to a reading of the indictment."

I had come upon the opening movements of a murder trial. The charge was intentional murder with aggravating circumstances, and the indictment, which the judge read next, told a dreadful story.

The sullen man in the dock who appeared so average in everything—in features, size, background (Russian, *bezpartiinii*, ten years of education), in the whitish fear on his face—had killed his wife. The two were alone when it happened; there could be no question about who had done it, and the defense raised none. He killed her on a Sunday evening in July, exactly six months before. Together they had entertained friends in their room, and minutes after the friends left he savagely beat her to death.

Why? The prosecution charged "hooliganistic" motives and cited a record of minor misbehavior over the years, of unpleasant incidents in the defendant's premarital family life, of excessive drinking, and of truancy, lack of interest and poor performance at work. The personality of the defendant, the indictment stated, showed that he had consciously and willfully refused to reform, and that the murder was a direct consequence of his hooliganistic tendencies and attitudes. These were the aggravating circumstances—"hooliganistic" motives and killing with special cruelty—which made it a capital crime.

"Chernov, stand. Is the charge clear to you?"

A worker's body in an ancient tweed jacket and a threadbare shirt lifted itself heavily from behind the railing. "Clear."

"Do you admit your guilt?"

"I— Yes . . . I admit . . . my guilt."

"Tell the court what happened, everything you know about it."

For long minutes Chernov looked at the wall and said nothing. (He need not have said anything at all, according to the law, and neither could he, as defendant, be prosecuted for perjury. The court, however, is not prohibited from drawing an inference from the accused's refusal to speak. At any rate, I had never seen someone in the dock refuse to testify.)

Finally he whispered, "Comrade Judges, I cannot look you in the face. I know that I deserve to be shot . . ."

"Chernov, you may say all of that at your last word. We are interested now only in what happened."

At length, Chernov began to mumble his sad tale. He met a woman, Klavda, last winter at work at Coal Depot Number 4. She worked in the office; he drove a truck. She had recently been divorced, he knew, and now was free. They began keeping company; he courted her; they became close. He saw her every day at work and every day after work, and they pleased each other. Movies, walks, parties, just sitting—it was quiet and good. "In March, I don't remember exactly, she moved in with me—I had my own room, you understand. We got along together easily, the way it should be. We were married in April—"

"Chernov, you are twenty-nine; she was forty. Why did you choose a woman so much older? Neither of you saw an obstacle in that?"

"No. Age wasn't important; we didn't notice it. I liked her very much. I think she liked me. We were the same age, really, in spirit."

"Go on. You must face the court and talk louder."

They were married in April and lived tranquilly. Her children moved in with them. Together they built a home. It was a normal domestic life, except that they were together more than most couples; they traveled to and from work together and often saw each other during the day. There were arguments, of course, but trifling ones. Basically, they were good to one another; they liked each other. Klavda bloomed, grew fat, and told him that she had never been so happy. They were buddies and shared everything—she was his only *droog* ("intimate friend"). So it was, until that day.

That day, that horrible Sunday, began normally. Things at home were fine. They drank together, as they frequently did on days off, and later invited some friends. How often did they drink? Twice or three times a week. How much did he usually drink? Half a liter, sometimes more. Always with Klavda? Almost always; they like to drink at home, together. "Then— I don't remember what happened. What I . . . did, I can't remember. I can't remember how it happened. Nothing remains in my memory about Klavda that night. Everything somehow went blank, like I was in another world. Something took hold of me; it made me frightened. Oh, I know now what I did to her, but when the police came, I couldn't tell them—I didn't know myself. I didn't know anything, I— It was as if there was a heavy veil over my eyes and mind."

"Is that all? Have you finished?"

"Yes."

"What do you mean, you cannot remember? Tell us exactly what you *do* remember. Do you remember drinking vodka?"

"Of course I remember that."

"How much?"

"I don't remember exactly. Perhaps a bottle, I didn't keep count."

"You don't remember. But it was too much vodka in any case, wasn't it? There were four empty bottles on the table. You were drunk, weren't you?"

"I suppose I was high. We started in the afternoon—"

"In spite of the warnings? You have a record of too much drinking, isn't that right? Vodka has gotten you into trouble before. You were warned not to drink. But you paid no attention to that? You kept drinking?" The judge's voice was crisp, but not raised, a professional voice free of indignation and of sympathy.

"I didn't mean to get drunk. It was just a little gathering. We were eating too, not just drinking. It was *Sunday*."

"A man with your record who doesn't mean to get drunk

doesn't buy four bottles of vodka. Now, you say you can't remember what happened. Isn't that simply because you had too much vodka in you?"

"No, this was something else. Something strange—a veil, an empty blackness. I can't describe it, Comrade Judges."

"Do you remember the guests leaving?"

"Yes. It started after that. They went out, and Klavda was smiling at me, and . . . something came over me."

"Chernov, it would be better for you to tell the court everything you can. What really happened when you were alone with your wife? Did you quarrel?"

"I can't say. Honest."

"Do you remember hitting her?"

"I can't remember."

"You can't remember. You choose a convenient moment to forget, don't you? Can you remember anything at all about what passed between you?"

"No. Yes. I think I hit her. I think I remember fragments. It's all vague, like in a haze, like it was someone else, and I was watching. I think I slapped her three times. Like a silent movie —I didn't feel anything when my hand hit her."

Sharply: "What did you hit her with? Your hands? An instrument? Were you afraid that she was going to hurt you? What made you hit a defenseless woman?"

"I don't know, I don't know how I could have done it. She was my only *droog*. I loved her. Why did I do that to her?"

"That's what we're asking you. What prompted you to attack her? You had no argument with her? Did something come up when you were alone?"

"Nothing that I remember. I don't know what to say. Klavda and I had a perfect Sunday. Nothing was wrong."

"What *could* have made you do it? Take a guess."

"I wish I could explain."

"Did you beat her before?"

"No."

"Never?"

"I might have slapped her once or twice. She used to hit me too. It was nothing serious, just a flash of temper sometimes. We'd have a drink afterwards."

"There is evidence that you systematically beat her."

"No, that's not true."

"Well, we will hear the evidence. Why did she appear frequently at the depot with signs of beatings?"

"That's just not true. Maybe I slapped her once or twice. We got along well. Ask anyone at the depot. If we argued, it was nothing serious."

"To hit a woman is nothing serious? Don't you see where it led you? Don't you know that that was not the way to behave?"

"I loved her. I was good to her—until that day. You can ask anyone. I wish you could ask her."

"We will hear witnesses. Your story doesn't hold together. If you loved her, why did you drink and beat her?"

No answer.

"Let's get back to what you remember. Do you remember filling a pail with water and mopping the floor?"

"No, I don't remember that."

"When the door to your room was opened, the floor was sopping wet. You were scrubbing the blood from the floor. Now, does a man in a haze carry out such logical actions, or did you really know quite well what you had done?"

"I can't say. I didn't think Klavda was dead. I thought she was sleeping."

"Sleeping? With her blood spattered on the bed and floor? Do you expect us to believe that? Now Chernov, let us go to something else. The court would like you to describe your character. What kind of person are you?"

"Average, I guess. I'm usually rather calm."

"Do you think you are mentally ill?"

"No."

"Not mentally sick. Very good. Do you think you are a considerate and good-natured person?"

"Not much worse than others, I suppose—I *was*."

"Let's see about that. Your father left your apartment in 1959, is that correct?"

"Yes."

"For what reason?"

"I don't know. He thought it best. We hadn't been getting on particularly well since my mother died in 1957. He wanted to live alone."

"And what does *that* say for your character?"

"What do you mean?"

"Tell the court about the trouble you were always causing in your home. Isn't it true that the police had to intervene on several occasions when you behaved like a hooligan and caused disgraceful incidents with your family?"

"What can I say?"

"Did you try to mend your ways? Isn't it true that you systematically insulted your father—and your sister too—and that he left because of your malicious character? That your drinking made life impossible for them?"

"We got along all right. Of course, there was some friction, but nothing so serious. Just a squabble or two. We didn't need the police to settle our family affairs."

"But what was your *purpose* in life? Isn't it true that you never gave anything serious attention except perhaps drink. You switched jobs, you switched interests, you *drifted*. Where were you headed? What were you doing to improve yourself and Soviet society?"

"What can I say?"

"You were not working when the crime was committed, correct?"

"Yes, I was not working."

"Is all this accidental, Chernov? On what basis did you leave your job at the depot?"

"It was my own decision. I quit."

"You were not fired?"

"No."

"Why did you quit?"

"I wanted to find something more suited to me. I couldn't get anywhere in that job."

"But you had been switching jobs frequently, had you not? Wasn't it time for you to find a steady job and earn your living by honest toil instead of drifting around, drinking and quitting? Isn't that a part of your character, too? How long had you worked at the depot?"

"About half a year."

"And not very satisfactorily, not very interestedly."

"That's not true. I had no fines or censures."

"But the administration characterized you as a poor worker —not for nothing, we must assume."

"I don't think that's fair. There was nothing wrong with the way I worked. I worked hard."

"Let's go into that. Were you late to work?"

"Sometimes."

"Were you spoken to about it?"

"Yes."

"And you continued to report late?"

"How can I answer that? Once in a while."

"Then how do you characterize *yourself* as a working man?"

"I still say average. Not worse; I did my share. I was a good worker."

"Have you been fired from jobs?"

"Yes."

"For what?"

"That was a long time ago."

"Why were you fired?"

"For violation of labor discipline."

"What, precisely?"

"Truancy."

"How many times?"

"Once."

"Once is enough. Have you had reprimands?"

"Yes."

"Also for truancy?"

"Yes."

"And for drinking at work?"

"Yes. Once. But on a holiday—Soviet Army Day."

"How many jobs have you had since you left the Army?"

"I don't remember."

"Five?"

"Perhaps. I think so."

"And still you call yourself a good worker? Is that the way a Soviet worker behaves? [Pause.] Now let us get back for a moment to July twenty-sixth. Think very carefully, Chernov. Why did you kill your wife? What were your reasons? *Why?* It is better for you to tell us everything you know."

"I can't remember. I honestly can't remember. Comrade Judges, you must believe me; I am speaking frankly. I know these are my last words. I just don't know what made me do it."

"Did you feel angry? Depressed? Frightened?"

"I felt strange. Like it wasn't me."

"Have you ever been treated for alcoholism?"

"No."

"Why did you drink so heavily? Was life so difficult for you? Did something in particular bother you? Was there something you lacked for a normal life without vodka?"

"No."

"Now, tell us, did you ever have these spells—the strange feelings and losses of memory—before?"

"Yes."

"When?"

"Sometimes after I drank."

"When you drank too much?"

"Not always. They were very rare, anyway."

"You saw a doctor about your condition?"

"No."

"Why not? Why didn't you see a doctor if you in fact had spells?"

"I didn't think it was serious. I thought it would pass."

"Have you had any medical history of previous psychiatric illness?"

"No."

"What about your military service? What was your job in the Army?"

"I worked with rockets."

"Answer within permissible limits: were you subjected to any special danger or harm while in the Army—or on any other job?"

"No."

"So you insist that you didn't mean to kill your wife? You had no reason? No immediate reason? No long-term one?"

"I had no reason."

"You just lost control of yourself?"

"I don't know what happened."

"What usually happens when you drink five hundred grams [about a pint] of vodka?"

"I go to sleep."

"You are not aggressive?"

"No. The opposite—I become soothed."

"But before you were married, did you ever hit women?"

"Yes, I have."

"When drunk?"

"Yes."

"Was such an incident reported to the police in 1957?"

"Yes."

"You beat a girl with whom you had been intimate, isn't that right? Why did you do it?"

"I don't know. I didn't mean to."

"Do you see any connection between your past behavior, between the shortcomings in your attitude toward your family and your work, and your tendency to 'lose control' of yourself?"

"I can't answer that truthfully."

"What do you feel now about what you have done?"

"I feel like an animal—no; even an animal doesn't kill its mate."

"She was not only your mate. She was an honest Soviet woman, a mother and a worker. Do you understand that?"

"She was my *droog*—"

"And that such things are intolerable in Soviet society?"

Chernov seemed too exhausted to answer.

"And how do you feel now about your own performance as a Soviet citizen? Aside from this incident, did you fight to control your drinking? To become a first-class worker?"

When the judge had finished, there was little left for the "sides" to ask, and they asked little. The procurator probed more deeply into the flaws of Chernov's character, the domestic incidents in which he was involved, and the blemishes on his work record. "A man's intentions," she said, "show up most clearly at his job." The defense counsel emphasized his positive attributes: support of Klavda's children, successful service in the Army, endeavoring to show that Chernov's childhood had been severe, especially since his mother had died, and that shortly before the killing he had been tormented by loss of appetite, by nightmares, and by brief attacks of vertigo.

Murder: Chernov

"The defendant clearly has less than a normal emotional make-up."

In the afternoon nine witnesses were called. Their testimony was quiet and without incident, disturbed more by the shuffling of boots and the clicking of bayonets—the soldiers changed watch every hour and others not on duty came and went frequently from the room—than by a sensational revelation or a raised voice. A week after Chernov's trial I saw the film *Witness for the Prosecution* in a local theater, dubbed in Russian. Nothing could have been more unlike a murder trial in Moscow. Here there were no surprises, no battle of legal wits and professional reputations, no tricky questions or clever tactics, no intricacy, ceremony, "your Lordships," or "my distinguished friends." It was simply "Tell us what you know about this case," and self-possessed witnesses, starting almost at random and talking in vernacular until they ran out of things to say. The court did not frighten them; the judge was not "Your Honor"; there were no trained ears straining to pick at their every word for violations of the law of evidence. "I object" never interrupted the routine. Calmly, they told the Chernov story, without nervousness, pretension or confusion, but often with surprising articulateness.

The invited friends, the neighbors, the relatives, the policemen—those who had been with Chernov and Klavda (that was the way they spoke of the couple) that day, before or after the crime—all agreed about what had happened. Again and again the macabre story was repeated, each narrator, as in a Faulkner novel, adding slim new facts and new passions to a plot already well known.

It was Sunday in a sixth-floor apartment in northeast Moscow: three rooms shared by Chernov and Klavda, Chernov's sister, and another couple and their infant. Chernov's sister left early for a day at a friend's *dacha* in the country. Chernov and Klavda invited friends, another married couple who worked at the depot, to a Sunday "celebration." Late in the afternoon, before the guests arrived, Chernov set out for provisions. He was in so good a mood that he invited the neighbors to join them. The guests gathered after five, and there was gaiety from the start. There was vodka and wine, *zakuski* and cake, good feeling and singing. Chernov and Klavda were normally affectionate toward each other, and there was no hint whatsoever of what was to come. They spoke of their happy life together. Later both of them became rather drunk, and when they started to be openly amorous the guests thought the time had come to leave. When they parted, Chernov seemed happily and quietly drunk; they were sure that he and Klavda were about to make love. Minutes later, strange sounds were heard through the wall: frantic movement, Klavda's voice groaning sharply—not in pleasure—water sloshing on the floor. The neighbors were terrified. For terrible minutes they feared to go to the door. Finally someone was bold enough to knock. Chernov did not answer but shouted, "Klavda, get up and let them in." Then, after more fearful minutes, Chernov himself opened it upon a horrible scene: the room in shambles, blood spattered on his clothes, and a pail of soapy water which he had been slopping on the floor. Chernov had a strange look in his eyes; he seemed to be entirely distracted or in a trance, although he understood what was said and responded to conversation. They found Klavda's body on the bed behind a screen, half undressed and beaten to a pulp. At that moment when the discovery was being made, Chernov's sister, who had returned from the *dacha*, was trapped in the elevator, which had broken down between floors. The police were called frantically. When they arrived Chernov said, "What are you doing here? Go away. This is a family affair." He answered their questions strangely, seeming to have no clear idea of what had happened. "Chernov was not so much drunk as . . .

nenormalnii ['abnormal; not all there']. We took him to the station and there he admitted killing Klavda, but he would say nothing about how or why he did it."

"Did you determine immediately how much he had drunk?"

"There were four empty bottles in the room. Two of them were in pieces on the floor. We couldn't tell how much the accused himself had drunk."

"He answered your questions coherently?"

"Oh yes. He understood everything all right."

"Then in what did his 'strangeness' consist?"

"It's hard to say. He seemed far away. Possessed."

"Perhaps drunk?"

"Drunk too, but more than that."

"Have you any questions?" the judge asked the assessors. "No? Comrade Procurator? Comrade Defender?"

Here, as in the People's Courts, the judge did most of the questioning. Only after she heard the witnesses' stories complete to her own satisfaction were they passed on to prosecution and defense. And even then the clash of the "sides" was muted; they seemed less like adversaries than helpers of the court. Of course, both the procurator and the lawyer sought to elicit only the kind of information that would support their own arguments. But they put their questions almost neutrally. "What can you tell us about his school years?" "Why did he leave his job?" "Can you describe a bit more fully how he looked when he opened the door?"

But what stood out most about the testimony was that only a small part of it concerned those violent minutes in Chernov's room. The court seemed interested more in the man than in the murder, Chernov in his niche in Soviet society. The questions dealt with his childhood, personality, and production norms; the witnesses dealt in impressions and conclusions. The frictions of Chernov's past life—father rubbing against son, sister against brother, girl friends against lover—were aired and pondered. Who *is* this person who murdered his wife?

A neighbor: A month before the murder Chernov and Klavda were both drunk, and they beat each other. They were that way—hot and cold. Klavda never complained about this, nor about his behavior in general. She seemed pleased with Chernov. But something in the man frightened me. Frightened me, and aroused my sympathy. I could tell he was in some kind of emotional trouble.

When he finally opened the door that night it was awful. There was a terrifying look in his eyes. I asked for Klavda, but he didn't answer, he just kept staring . . . I had seen him in that mood before and it was weird: he would sit on a chair and stare at nothing, as though he comprehended nothing. Klavda would tell me to go away and leave him alone at those times. After the killing he was in that same mood again, looking at me as though for the first time.

Chernov's sister: My brother is really an unusual person, intelligent, knowledgeable and well-read, even though not formally educated. He knows and loves music and spends his time in all sorts of scientific and technical things. His range of interests is amazingly wide. Maybe that is his trouble; if only he had found something solid to which he could have applied his talents. I know he loved Klavda— What a ghastly thing, that he should kill her!

Procurator: And the difficulties with him in your apartment? Why did you quarrel?

"The quarrels ended about a year ago, when he met Klavda. He used to play music loudly, and late at night; it was hard to sleep. They started mostly with that. Then the usual things, bickering, nothing serious . . ."

Defense counsel: Did he suffer when your mother died?

"He wept; I think it hurt him deeply. He was a fine son to her, but less to Papa."

Defense counsel: And that is when the drinking began?
"Yes, in 1957 . . ."

Judge: You said at the preliminary investigation that he was sometimes malicious and hard to live with. What about his character?

"Only when he drank was he difficult. Vodka was his only real defect. He was more strange than malicious."

Chernov's father: I've tried to give you an accurate picture of my son. He has his faults—we had our difficulties—but he is essentially a good person. I don't know what went wrong here, how this could have happened; if you could have seen how good he sometimes was. Since 1941, when I left for the front, life has not been easy for him, for many reasons. His mother and I were sick. Something changed in him when she died in 1957. Sometimes, after that, he would get those little fits.

He is an unusually bright boy, energetic and versatile. Once he was going to play soccer full time. Then he got interested in opera and philosophy. Then science. But he never fulfilled his potential. I think his friends liked him. I don't know why he had to drink—that was his trouble, vodka.

After my wife died, my relations with him deteriorated. I moved to a separate place in 1959—I don't blame him for that —and I hadn't seen him for several months before the incident. I never met Klavda.

Procurator: What did you feel about his drinking and his shifting of jobs?

"I felt bad. I tried to talk with him about it, but he wouldn't listen to me."

Counsel: Can you tell us something about his service in the Soviet Army?

"I know he was decorated for good behavior and got a good-conduct award and a letter of commendation for his work."

Klavda's first husband: I never met Chernov, although he

was pointed out to me. He seemed O.K. Klavda continued to live with me after our divorce in 1960, but then began spending nights with Chernov. She left it to me to take care of the kids. I can't say she was very interested in bringing up the children. I can say nothing about the murder itself.

Judge (to Klavda's mother): Is that right—about the children?

"Oh, no, Comrade Judge, Klavda left them with me. I took care of them. He wasn't interested himself."

Klavda's first husband: That's not true. I'm sorry she's dead, but that's no reason to whitewash her.

Judge: Which one of you is telling the truth?

A fellow worker from the depot (called on the defense's request when the petition for the original psychiatrists was rejected): I know nothing about what happened on the twenty-sixth, but I have known Chernov for some time on our shift. He is an average worker, interested in his job. He seemed to act decently to Klavda. I saw her bruised once or twice, but she claimed that her *old* husband had hit her. They surely had a strong friendship.

Another fellow worker: Chernov was a good worker, although sometimes moody. There was always something strange about him. He seemed to take his job seriously. I visited his home twice, and domestic relations seemed to be normal—rather better than average.

Procurator: Did you know that he was reprimanded for tardiness?

"I did. That's nothing out of the ordinary."

Counsel: Would you say that Chernov did his job as well as the other drivers?

"Definitely yes."

Throughout the day, Chernov slouched motionless in his chair so that only the top of his shaved head showed above the railing of the dock. But late in the afternoon he inched up just high enough to peer over the edge of the rail, and signs of emotion began to appear on his coarse white face. His eyes watered when his father testified about his early childhood and when fellow workers called him a decent chap on the job. He began to take interest in his fate.

January 27, late morning. Until now several of the dramatis personae of the trial had been largely mute. One of them, a wrinkled, bent woman, a Russian *babushka*, sat in tears among the spectators; it was Klavda's mother. She was the "victim"— in Soviet law, one who has suffered morally, physically or materially from the crime—and as such was privileged to participate actively in the proceedings, questioning witnesses, making petitions and appeals, challenging the court, in addition to merely testifying. (She also could have been represented by a lawyer.) The theory is that justice must be done not only from the point of view of the defendant, but also from that of others directly affected by the crime. But in this case, as in most, the old woman was hard put to understand the meaning of the trial. She muttered about Klavda from her seat, and shook her head in bewilderment when, after each witness and every decision, the judge dutifully asked her whether she had questions or comments.

A second silent actor was the *obshchestvennii* accuser, a youngish worker from the depot. She too answered "No" whenever it was her turn to question, except when Chernov himself was standing. "If you were so interested in raising Klavda's children why did you report to work almost every day at ten instead of eight?"

Two more women had the rights of active participants: the expert witnesses, heavy ladies in sagging dresses, who sat at the procurator's table. But they too, watched silently until the second day, when they were called upon for their expertise.

The first expert delivered the medical conclusions, a long, detailed, painfully exact report on the cause of death, obligatory at all murder trials. Here nothing was left out, and although Klavda's body had already been described many times before, the medical examination, in its completeness and detachment, added a new dimension to the horror. Chernov must have been fearfully out of control: No part of the body above the waist, inside or out, escaped injury. There was evidence that sexual intercourse had been attempted, in spite of menstruation, but not achieved.

Next was the psychiatric report from a representative of the Serbskii Institute. His doctors found that Chernov suffered from symptoms of chronic alcoholism, that he was an inconstant and unstable personality for whom drink played an essential role, but that he was not mentally ill. No *nervous* disorders were uncovered. He must be considered to have been drunk on July 26, nothing more. When drunk he was usually good-natured, but he also had a history of another mood occasionally predominating. There was, for example, the incident in 1957 with the girl Galya . . . the instance reported by Chernov's foreman in 1960 . . . Most of the psychiatric information seemed to have been obtained from interviews with people acquainted with Chernov. With its absence of Freudian terms and even medical jargon the report sounded to Western ears more like the findings of social workers than psychiatrists.

Two questions were then put by the defense counsel—in writing, at the request of the expert—and they were answered after a short recess. (1) Was there anything unusual about the defendant's behavior when having intimate relations with women? There was a tendency to beat them, for no apparent reason. There had been a satisfactory sexual relationship with

Klavda; he sometimes beat her, but she did not protest. But these are not grounds, the expert emphasized, on which to call him mentally ill. (2) What was his exact mental condition at the moment of the crime? This was not possible to determine. He was drunk; his system had absorbed a considerable amount of alcohol, and his bodily functions were markedly affected. "Yet this was normal drunkenness, particularly for Chernov. There was nothing pathological, no derangement at the moment of the crime; he was mentally healthy in the legal sense. This was evidenced by his sense of reality and orientation immediately after the crime: he knew his neighbors and recognized the police."

"Comrade Judges!"—it was the defense counsel again, submitting a supplementary petition—"the procedural code permits the naming of additional expertise in cases where expert testimony has been insufficiently clear or comprehensive. This is surely such a case. What really happened at the moment of the crime? What moved Chernov to act as he did? His strange, fantastic behavior has not really been explained. Comrade Expert was contradictory: she said Chernov was inclined to beat women in sex, and yet to be mentally healthy. Furthermore, equally qualified doctors who examined him in July disagree about Chernov's mental condition at the moment of the crime. I urgently request, therefore, that these doctors be called, or that Chernov be examined again by new doctors to find out why he killed. Again, I want to emphasize that a life is at stake in this case. We can afford no doubts."

The court retired for fifteen minutes to deliberate the petition, and upon its return announced that the request had been declined.

"The trial examination has been completed. We will now hear the arguments of the sides . . ."

Throughout the trial something had been missing. Passion?

Legal oratory? Surprise? The prosecution's intentions? What had happened had long been clear to everyone; the real issue —what should be done—was approached only in the closing arguments.

"Comrade *obshchestvennii* accuser, your comments?"

A woman of about thirty, with the look of the English working class, rose from her place alongside the procurator to sum up first. She began by assuring the court that she bore no personal grudge against Chernov. She did not know him before he started work at the depot eight months before the murder. But since that time he showed himself to be a very poor worker, frequently late and totally uninterested in his duties. In April he was absent for ten days and fired, but when he returned, claiming that he had been sick, he was taken back as a loader. On July 1 he quit and never appeared there again. Is it purely accidental that he was not working when he committed the crime? The collective felt he consistently displayed "negative characteristics" at work. Chernov was a "rotten apple."

Besides, he was curt to Klavda. "Gimme money," he would snap at her; he wanted it for vodka. Sometimes she came to work with signs of beatings, and she would say, "He's a good sort, but bad when he drinks." The collective knew Klavda well (she worked there for ten years) and loved her as an excellent worker, a trusted comrade, and a good friend. She was plump and smiling and kind. Her death was a great loss.

"The collective held a general meeting on August 5, discussed Chernov's case thoroughly, and on the basis of these considerations instructed me to ask the court to apply to him the highest measure of punishment for his crime. Comrade Judges, we earnestly recommend that he be shot."*

Next, the procurator summed up, reminding, in the manner of a school principal, that "this kind of crime is a remnant of the

* See Appendix for a discussion of the death penalty.

past against which we must fight with all our resources. Murder is a very rare occurrence in our socialist land; the social and economic conditions which encourage it in capitalist society have long been eliminated here. Under socialism, Soviet man toils honestly, harvesting the fruit of the magnificent principles of the great October Revolution . . .

"Our law is the most humane in the world. But we must fight determinedly against murder. And, indeed, this too is humane: it means freeing our society of those who impede the building of a just society, the building of Communism. The Twenty-Second Party Congress and the historic Party Program have shown us the way to Communism, the best, the highest form of human society. Our law provides for the death penalty for those who hinder honest Soviet toilers, beloved toilers like Klavda, in their effort to reach this great goal. . . .

"The facts in this case are all too clear . . ." The story of July 26 again, a summary of the testimony, excerpts from the medical report—the procurator was building her case patiently, pointing always to the central fact: a woman was intentionally, brutally murdered. "I do not rest accidentally on this information about the eyes, the nose, the lips, the neck, the breasts, the ribs, the liver, the lungs; it shows the cruelty, the beastly method of killing, and that Chernov could not have been unaware that he was killing her. There is not the slightest doubt that he intended to kill her."

Finally the procurator sketched a detailed, if one-sided, portrait of the man Chernov. He was a hooligan type, manifesting these ugly tendencies consistently, even though his relations with Klavda were in some ways satisfactory. He beat her when he was drunk; he refused to stop drinking. His attitude toward work was negative. He had been counseled by the director of the depot and the secretary of its Party organization, but rejected all advice to change his ways. His record reeks of hooliganism and individualism, repugnant to the Soviet ideal. Compare him with Klavda, the woman he killed, whose children he deprived of a mother—a simple, good Soviet woman, respected by all, highly valued at work, a real member of the socialist community.

"Comrade Judges! The trial has shown beyond doubt that Chernov killed intentionally, with hooliganistic motives and special cruelty. There are no mitigating circumstances; there is no reason to question the psychiatric expertise, there is nothing to explain Chernov's consistent violation of the rules of socialist life except his own intention. I agree, therefore, with the *obshchestvennii* accuser and ask the court to prescribe the highest measure of punishment, shooting. We have no room for such people in Soviet society."

By the time the thin, gray-haired lady rose to speak in defense, the courtroom was hushed and tense, the way a Soviet courtroom seldom is.

"Comrade Judges! I speak in great agitation. We know that the defendant's actions have caused nothing but agony. He killed a good and gentle woman, leaving two young children without a mother and an old woman without a daughter. And for no reason whatsoever. I cannot attempt to justify this or seek the defendant's acquittal, but I feel it my duty to offer some few thoughts . . ."

It was a half-hour talk, an impressive, clearly reasoned defense, by far the most skillful performance of the trial. Its intent was to challenge the procurator's interpretation of the motive and method of killing, reducing it from capital murder to something less. "Chernov and Klavda lived happily together —every witness said that Klavda was happy, that they were *druzya* [close friends]. Yet he killed her, just a few minutes after kissing her. Why? The prosecution never explained why. All its talk of 'hooliganistic' motives explains nothing. We still do not know *why*, and that is why the defense feels that further psychiatric examination is essential. The medical report

280

indicated that sex had been attempted, and there is reason to believe that, Klavda being unwell and he drunk, Chernov was not able to resolve his drive in sexual intercourse and sought satisfaction in beating her. What has this to do with hooliganism? Hooliganism, as you know, refers to actions directed against or disturbing public order. [Here she read from the code.] This was an utterly private affair. Nor does the condition of the body have anything to do with hooliganism; this concerns the *method* of killing, not the motive.

"The Serbskii Institute has said that Chernov was sane on July twenty-sixth. Other doctors disagreed, but they, unfortunately, were not permitted to testify. In either case, is it not clear that Chernov acted *strangely?* Is it not *strange* to arrange a party when planning a murder? Not strange to yell to a person to open the door after killing her, to tell the police that it is a family affair, to act as though in a trance? Whether 'responsible' or not in those moments, Chernov was not 'normal.' Nor merely normally drunk, for Chernov has a history of these moods. The experts themselves admit that this is a complicated case. Too much has been left to doubt.

"As for killing with particular cruelty, this is undisputable. But it too was the product of his sickness—his frenzy, his loss of touch with reality. It has nothing to do with motive.

"You have heard the witnesses describe Chernov. He was never an ideal citizen. But he does have many fine qualities, and fine potentialities. The *obshchestvennii* accuser has said that he was a poor worker. That, of course, is her right. But other witnesses who knew him intimately on the job have praised his attitude and performance. It grieves me that the procurator chose to accept the *obshchestvennii* accuser's opinion as fact.

"Comrade Judges! The procurator's request for the highest measure of punishment is too cruel. In our law the death sentence is an 'exceptional measure of punishment' justified only in exceptional cases. Too cruel, and senseless. Chernov is a young man; he can be cured, re-educated, and returned to society as a useful member. This is the task that awaits us. I would like to believe that *this* is what socialist society means."

On its third day the trial was convened shortly after ten to hear Chernov's last word. Because the court must retire immediately after the last word, this short stage of the trial is often put off until the day following the summation.

Chernov swallowed, waited, and hung his head. The soldiers did not move. Few spectators could look at him.

"Comrade Judges, I am terribly, terribly sorry. I have done an awful thing. My life with Klavda was good. I miss her more than anyone. I don't know why I did it. I didn't mean to do it." Chernov choked. A long pause followed.

"Is that all?"

"I deserve to be shot. But I beg the court to spare my life. And nothing more."

This time everyone stood when the court retired.

I know no wait so utterly given to waiting as the wait before a decision. There was nothing to do in those courthouses to alleviate the fearful suspension of activity. Into the room, out again to the corridor, down to the toilet, outside and to the café in the basement for an irrelevant glass of tea, back again quickly to the room, as though that little bit of movement will change something. Russians are better at waiting in one place.

A group of workers from the depot, mostly youngish women who had been present from the beginning, gathered on the stairs. They were not of one mind about Chernov. "I can't agree with shooting him. What good will that do?" "But he killed her horribly. We have to eliminate that kind of thing." "Think of the kids—" "He didn't." "It will not be easy for them." "She was guilty too, to a certain extent." "Such a young man—he's *got* to live." "Young man or old— to do such a horrible thing!" The *obshchestvennii* accuser was with this group; she was a foreman at the depot, and chairman of the trade-union committee. "Don't think I always act as an accuser. Last week I *defended* a loader from our place, a good man who just got drunk and picked a pocket. I asked the court to go easy, and he got only a year instead of much more. Remember, this was a collective decision, not my own. If it were up to me personally, though, I'd still give Chernov what he gave Klavda."

A police lieutenant said, "They will shoot him. Not a trace of doubt. Good riddance." Klavda's first husband said he did not know what should be done. Chernov's father and sister sat on a bench in the corridor, arm in arm, silent, not to be questioned.

A gloomy older couple had been sitting next to me on the public benches—Klavda's sister and brother-in-law. "This is past the point for mercy. He killed her bestially—he took out her eyes." They had photographs: Klavda had looked about fifty-five, stout, with frizzy hair; far from pretty; tired. There was also one of the body in its casket: the face was beaten beyond recognition.

"I don't believe in killing another person, even through the courts," said an older schoolgirl in braids, a distant relative of Chernov.

"Never? Killing is never justified?"

"Only when it is necessary to prevent some larger evil. He needs help now, not shooting."

The lawyer smoked gloomily. She looked like a down-at-the-heels maiden aunt of aristocratic family. "I was counting very much on having those other doctors testify. I saw them just after I got the case; and they assured me that Chernov was sick and not in a responsible condition." She was graduated from Moscow State University in 1924 and had been practicing law since; she was for many years a consultant to the Ministry of Finance. (Her nephew had just returned from a year at the University of Pennsylvania in the student exchange program.) She was appointed to this case by the chairman of her division of the Collegium of Advocates, to whom Chernov's father had appealed for legal aid. Soviet lawyers cannot—except for reasons of health or conflict of work—refuse to take a criminal case assigned to them. "But I never would have refused this case anyway. I believe in it. He must be saved."

The procurator too sat alone. She had completed an evening juridical institute in Sverdlovsk and had been trying cases in City Court for four years. She did not want to talk about Chernov.

We waited for two hours. Some of the workers had brought lunch.

"In the name of the Russian Soviet Federated Socialist Republic . . ." Finally. The sentence was read in a different room, the accused standing, flanked by soldiers, not in the dock, but directly before the bench. It droned on for pages, but after the first minutes everyone seemed to know what it would bring, because it repeated the spirit of the indictment and the procurator's summation with little alteration. The court excluded "hooliganistic motives" as an aggravating circumstance (it classified the motive as "sexual-sadistic"), but since the killing was judged to have been committed with special cruelty, it remained a capital crime anyway.

No mitigating circumstances were allowed. Considering the plight of the children, the cruelty of the killing, and the weakness of Chernov's character, the court sentenced him to be shot. With this word, the stooped Chernov was immediately handcuffed, and he remained chained through the rest of the sentence.

When it was over, the court disappeared and the room

emptied quickly. The defense counsel remained, talking intently to Chernov. He turned away from her, facing the wall with the doomed look he had had at the trial's start.

"Will you appeal?" I asked.

Chernov did not look up. "Of course," said the lawyer.

As I left, the lieutenant in command of the soldiers—there were now five—was asking Chernov whether his handcuffs chafed.

I went upstairs to see the judge. She was surprised to see me —I had just walked in—but she was cordial. "You must not get the wrong impression. This was a terrible thing, very rare in Soviet society." She looked older now than I had thought, forty-odd, flat-faced, very neat and correct, cool and self-assured. She was serving her first term as a City Court judge, after having worked some few years as a People's Court judge, an office that she entered immediately upon completing her legal education.

She was, it turned out, Ukrainian-born; that was what gave her Russian a suggestion of accent. Like most of the legal profession she belonged to the Soviet intelligentsia, which means that her parents were poor peasants and she, with a higher education (at an evening juridical institute in Moscow), had risen from peasant to professional woman on her own, with almost nothing passed on from earlier generations. Women like her serve in literally every profession in Moscow, and there was something about them, even when doing this kind of disagreeable work, that made me proud. Something self-made, strong, adult; a "whole" woman.

Wasn't this case largely decided before it was heard? I asked. After all, immediately upon entering it at the investigative stage the defense counsel had asked that the other doctors be questioned. The investigator refused, the procurator refused, then the court refused—after having read, of course, the Serbskii testimony. The trial added nothing substantively new. It all seemed pre-ordained.

"Of course we have opinions before the trial—judges are people too, you know. We read the record carefully, and inevitably ideas form in our minds. But don't be misled. It often happens that as a case develops in court the feel of things is different from what it seemed to be when reading the record. When this happens, we change our opinions. Of course we change them."

She said little about Chernov. Simply, "Soviet society cannot tolerate people who do horrible things like that. They must be weeded out."

There was something about her that made me proud, but something too that disturbed. Something was missing. It took some time to recognize what. It was introspection. Life and death, society and the individual, crime and punishment—she had them all neatly solved. "We have no room for men like him." She was so sure of herself.

On February 14, 1962 (St. Valentine's day goes unnoticed in Russia), Chernov's appeal was heard by the criminal college of the Supreme Court of the R.S.F.S.R. Both Chernov and his lawyer had appealed, Chernov in a letter asking simply that his life be spared, the lawyer more formally, arguing again in a brief that the refusal to hear the other psychiatrists violated Chernov's rights as a defendant, particularly since both the motive attributed to Chernov and the method of killing could be explained in terms of mental illness. The appeal was rejected and the sentence remained in force.

Chernov then appealed to the Praesidium of the Supreme Soviet of the R.S.F.S.R. for mercy. The Praesidium, as the executive body of the Republic, is empowered to grant pardons and to commute sentences. It rejected Chernov's plea on May 5, 1962, and the sentence was executed shortly thereafter.

XIV

Three Appeals

ONE CORNER of City Court is reserved for appeals—the lowest level of appeals, coming from decisions of the seventeen People's Courts. I camped in that section for about two weeks.

Courtrooms for appeals resemble, in miniature, those for first-instance trials, except that there are fewer spectators and no witnesses waiting about. But in composition of the court there is a major difference: no lay assessors are present. The three men or women in the high-backed chairs behind the desk are all professional judges. A judge may not hear an appeal alone; the principle of "collectiveness" operates at all levels.

The accused does not appear at appeals unless specially called by the court; I never saw one called. In most of the cases I watched, a lawyer presented the appeal on behalf of his client; in the others, it was introduced by the court itself on the basis of a letter from the convicted person. In neither case, the law says, may the appeal court limit itself to the arguments of the appellants; once an appeal has been made on any grounds, judgment must be passed on all aspects of the trial and sentence.

Hearings of appeals and protests (it is called "appeal" when initiated by the defense, and "protest" when by the procurator) take very little time: half to three quarters of an hour, including deliberation, is standard; the courts dealing with them have ten to fifteen on their daily calendar. Procedure is remarkably simple. The chairman—the judge sitting in the middle—opens the hearing and attends to the formal matters in a minute or two. Then one of the members who has been assigned beforehand as *rapporteur* delivers a brief oral report, very general and conversational, on the essence of the case and the reasons for appeal.

"On April 11 [it is now May 9] Vasiliev, Viktor Andrei-evich, twenty-eight, Russian, *bezpartiinii*, a driver with five years' education, married, with two children, formerly convicted for theft, living at 12 Metrobuilding Street, Apartment 14, was found guilty of actions qualified under Article 120 (Lewd actions involving minors)* and was sentenced to two years in a labor colony under strict regime. The court found these facts: that on the afternoon of March 21, Vasiliev, a driver for the Ministry of Health of the R.S.F.S.R., invited four young girls, aged ten to twelve, and two young boys for a ride in the automobile to which he was assigned, and engaged in perverted behavior with the two girls on the front seat. The court based its decision principally on the children's account of the ride. Vasiliev denied his guilt throughout the trial and Comrade Solokov, his defense counsel, has appealed the verdict for lack of proof."

"That is correct." The lawyer had taken over. He was a young-executive type in a white shirt and striped tie. "I ask that the verdict be reversed. But even if my client *were* guilty, he would not deserve such unreasonably severe punishment. After all, he was not taken under custody during the preliminary investigation. Why, then, was he sentenced to a colony under strict regime?"

Comrade Solokov then elaborated, but simply and briefly, on his grounds for appeal.

* This appeal was heard behind closed doors. The court permitted me to stay along with Vasiliev's wife.

"The crime charged here almost always concerns a specific group of people: old men unable to satisfy themselves normally or others bothered by sexual abnormality. But my client, as you know, is a perfectly healthy young man, married, and blessed with a normal sexual life. I must tell you that not only did he categorically deny any improper behavior whatsoever with the children, but also that he was so shocked by the conviction that he attempted suicide in jail.

"What are the facts? Let's start from the beginning. The indictment charged that Vasiliev coaxed the children into the car, whereas it came out at the trial that they climbed in during his absence."

"*Nu*, so what?" It was the judge-*rapporteur*, breaking in without looking up from the dossier. "That has no bearing on what he did with them later."

"But it symbolizes the inaccuracy of the whole indictment. Nothing in it was proved at all. On the contrary. You can't talk about proof in this case, because the trial refuted the charges more than anything else.

"The point is this: the entire trip lasted ten minutes, during all of which time Vasiliev was driving. He had no time and no opportunity to do what he was charged with, even had he wanted to—and there is not the slightest reason for suspecting that he did want to."

"Nonsense. Not according to the girls, he didn't want to. The girls made it quite clear. I'd call that rather good proof."

"I am coming to the girls. You know yourself, Valentine Sergeyevich [the reporting judge], that the testimony of young girls cannot always be relied upon. You remember what trouble this gave us in that case last year from Oktyabrskii district."

"Oh, that case was something else again."

"Of course. But you know from personal experience what can happen in cases like these when the girls are prompted."

"There is nothing so complicated here. It's all quite clear."

"Not at all. Comrade Judges, I must touch on another point; and this goes to the heart of the insufficiency of proof. There was, as you can see, a most serious violation of procedural law during the preliminary investigation: the children were questioned not in the presence of a pedagogue, as required by the code, but in the presence of their parents. This infraction directly affected the outcome of the case. The record shows that, when first questioned, only one girl—who had been severely scolded by her mother for climbing into the car—accused Vasiliev. The others joined her only later, changing their original testimony. Obviously this was a direct consequence of the absence of pedagogues and the influence of parents on their children's testimony.

"The fact is that Vasiliev's own version was never refuted at the trial, and this version alone both makes logical sense and explains the girls' allegations. Comrade Judges, I suggest it was all terribly simple: he returned to his car from a toilet with his pants unbuttoned by mistake. He noticed this while driving when he unbuttoned his coat for a cigarette and the girls shrieked. He quickly closed his coat and let the girls out. That was it—that was the extent of his misbehavior. That is the only version that rings true.

"Therefore, on the grounds of discrepancy of the verdict with the factual circumstances of the case, I ask that the decision be reversed."

It was then the procurator's turn. The procurator appears at an appeal (he must appear at every appeal) not as an accuser but in his other role, as supervisor of the legality and validity, the "groundedness," of the sentence. That day the procurator, a very plain, spinsterish lady with gold teeth, was in uniform. She stood and, in an after-dinner voice, said almost in one sentence that there could be no question about the facts, that the testimony of all the girls coincided exactly, that

Vasiliev had been proved guilty beyond any doubt, that his record showed he had criminal tendencies, that she considered the sentence of the trial court to be fair, legal and "grounded," and that it was her opinion that it ought to be left in force.

"Are there any other comments? Comrade procurator? Comrade lawyer?"

"I really don't understand how the procuracy can consider the facts proved beyond any doubt. There is very great doubt here. The evidence is extremely tenuous; a man ought not to be convicted for that."

"I don't think so at all; the evidence is conclusive. The record speaks for itself—the testimony of the only witnesses. If you like, I shall review the facts and the proof."

The exchange subsided and the court retired for deliberation.

Throughout these fifteen or twenty minutes there was no description of the incident in Vasiliev's car. One could assume that no description was needed because all three judges had acquainted themselves with the trial record as they were supposed to have done. But it seemed to me that this was not the reason. From the look of things—and the consensus of the lawyers—it appeared that only the *rapporteur* leafs through the dossier beforehand and that his opinion predominates among his colleagues somewhat the way the opinion of the judge predominates among the lay assessors at the trial. The others simply have not time for more than a cursory glance just before the case is called. And so they ask few questions, make few comments, and rely on the *rapporteur*; the hearings are run through quickly, without lengthy descriptions and detailed analyses. The briefs are rarely longer than a page.

I spoke with the lawyer while we were waiting. He said that Vasiliev was convicted of fondling the girls' thighs, exposing and stroking himself, and ejaculating into a handkerchief. "What horrible nonsense! It would have been impossible under those circumstances; he was driving the whole time. I know he's no angel—I defended him before for theft—but he's not capable of *that*. What for, with such a wife?" The wife, in her early twenties, was unusually slim and pretty. She sat without a word or movement during the hearing, the wait for the decision, and the sentence.

The court returned in ten minutes. It found the sentence grounded and ruled that it would remain in force; the appeal was "not to be satisfied." The trial court, it reasoned, had sufficiently examined all the facts and circumstances, and there was no doubt about Vasiliev's guilt. It was the chairman who read the decision, reviewing the girls' testimony at the trial and quoting some of their descriptions of the ride given at the preliminary investigation.

No mention was made of the alleged violation of procedure.

By the time I collected my notes and coat, the judge on the other side of the chairman was reporting on a new case.

Next door an overdressed woman lawyer presented the appeal. She represented a twenty-six-year-old butcher sentenced to three years for malicious hooliganism. It was an uncommon tale. In February he downed three ounces of vodka, approached a stranger on a street (who turned out to be a policeman in mufti), and said, "I'm drunk, I'm a hooligan; take me to the police, I must be put in jail." The policeman tried to ignore him, but the butcher persisted and at last he was taken away, cursing powerfully. During the trial, in Leninskii district, it was decided to request psychiatric examination; he was a big, strong Russian, and three ounces of vodka could scarcely have had any noticeable effect on him. And the court arranged an appointment at the Serbskii Institute—an appointment in two months' time, however, because the Institute was booked that far in advance.

Meantime, he was sent home, and he did it again. In April,

after less than two ounces, at a bus stop: "Lock me up, I'm a hooligan . . ." Swearing violently, he pressed himself on a young girl, who hit him in the face with her pocketbook. Foreigners happened to be present at the bus stop, and the procurator later made much of the butcher's having "shamed" Soviet society. When this second case came to court, in Oktyabrskii district, the lawyer, learning of the impending psychiatric tests, asked that this case be postponed until the results of the tests were known and that the two cases be joined. The second court agreed and sent the request to the first one—which refused. Thereupon the second court changed its mind about the postponement and, after a superficial psychiatric examination (a half-hour questioning by one doctor, in the prisoner's cell), tried the case and meted out a three-year sentence.

The lawyer protested that the second case should have been joined to the first, and postponed until after thorough psychiatric evaluation. The second court's sentence, she said, violated procedural law and was grossly unjust. "It is perfectly plain what would have been the proper action in this case, especially since the accused had a medical history." (In 1957, when he was serving with the Red Army, he suffered a trauma during maneuvers and spent seven months in a military hospital recovering from shock and damaged nerves. "Tests" was the word used by the lawyer, who hinted that they were atomic but insisted to me afterward that she did not know.)

The procurator agreed that it would have been neater to hear the cases together, but insisted that once heard, the second case was heard correctly. Besides, she said, counsel for the defense had produced no evidence whatsoever to prove that the in-jail examination was, as she claimed, a "farce and a fraud." In fact, there were no grounds for appeal: the trial court had examined all the facts and circumstances thoroughly and there was no doubt that the butcher had committed malicious hooliganism.

The court very quickly agreed with this argument and denied the appeal, leaving the sentence in force. At this time, incidentally, the butcher was still waiting for his examination at the Institute, after which he faced the second trial and possible lengthening of his punishment.

One after another paraded the appeals with machinelike precision: new names, places, dates, incidents, all processed in one quick, automatic operation. No one wastes words in those rooms, perhaps because everyone is legally trained and tired of it all. There is nothing to be gained by a nicely turned phrase. Even the lawyers just *talk*, and they are frequently, arbitrarily interrupted by the judge-*rapporteur*.

The last appeal I saw through to the end stemmed from a two-day trial held three weeks before. Three teen-age boys had been sentenced to four, two and two years for a series of petty robberies in public places: a hat, a watch, cash, a bottle . . . There had been seven boys, five of them postal clerks, in the gang; four boys had been disciplined by *obshchestven-nost* in the forms of Comradely Courts and supervision by the collective.

Two lawyers presented the appeals, one of them defending two boys. They asked for lighter sentences on these grounds: the boys were young; this was their first conviction; they had been under the influence of vodka; the educative and preventive programs at the collective were weak; they had had unblemished records; a long sentence is not the best means of rehabilitation for youth . . . But one of the boys, a sixteen-year-old, had denied guilt, and the lawyer's efforts for him were more substantial.

An *obshchestvennii* defender, the same one, apparently, who had spoken at his trial, spoke for this lad now.

"Did the collective meet after the sentence?" the judge asked.

It had.

"Did you report the sentence of the trial court?"

He had.

"Did you discuss the sentence?"

They had, and decided to support the appeal. The boy was an excellent worker, an outstanding member of a Brigade of Communist Labor. Brought up with no father, under difficult conditions at home, he still had turned out to be a credit to the shop. "He is still very young. The Collective would like to take this lad and make him a good citizen. He has promised to serve the Soviet people honestly." Four or five spectators wept audibly during this appeal.

"The essential thing about this case"—the lawyer was speaking again—"is that there was no direct evidence against the boy whatsoever. The victims could not identify him; and the testimony about him by the other boys changed frequently. One of the boys said, 'I said he did it with us at the preliminary investigation because I was afraid things would be worse with me if I didn't. Now [at the trial] I am no longer afraid and I'm telling the truth: I never saw him take anything.' Such a flimsy case against so young a boy deserves only dismissal," the lawyer pleaded.

The procurator thought otherwise. "A sixteen-year-old knows perfectly well what is permissible and what is criminal." He knew that that kind of robbery could be performed only by a group and in confusion, and therefore he helped start fights at theater exits and on the streets. If he took part in the scuffles he *must* have known about the robberies. And all this was done to steal and to drink; at sixteen he already had a taste for vodka. "You people all talk a lot now about re-education. But why didn't you start the education before, when you saw those children drinking? You paid them no attention then, and you got the logical result: crime."

The judges found no grounds for changing the sentences.

Perhaps I came upon an atypical sequence. Certainly I had *read* of cases reversed in appeal, sometimes several times on several levels. But in those compressed, perfunctory cassational hearings in City Court there seemed hardly time enough —if indeed there was the inclination—even to review the cases seriously.

XV

The Conspiracy of
Kusin and Others

FIVE MINUTES' walk from City Court along a sometimes dusty, sometimes muddy, sometimes icy road dense with construction trucks, sprawls one of Moscow's sweeping, steppelike squares, Komsomolskaya ("Young Communist"). There, three great railroad stations stand together, Leningradskii, Kazanskii and Yaroslavskii. From the last of these, trains go north through woods to the ancient Slavic city of Yaroslavl and beyond to Archangel, and northeast through taiga over the staggering, empty distances to Irkutsk, Vladivostok and Peking. Look over the long, red routes on the Yaroslavskii station call-board in that spacious square and you begin to understand the meaning of *prostor* ("space"), the vast expanse of Russia.

Board a train from Yaroslavskii station, even for an hour's ride and, no matter how much you have read about the backwardness of Russian rural life, you are astonished by the contrast between life in the capital and life in the countryside. Moscow is gray, dulled by drab garments and façades; the contrast with the downtowns of Western Europe is appalling. Still, there are pockets of modernity interspersed amid the heaviness, and there is a hope that its streets may someday be fashionable. Young *Moskvichi* read Polish fashion magazines and do interesting things with their hair; cafés are beginning to appear; Glenn Miller and Dave Brubeck blare from open windows on warm evenings; and it is no longer easy, at important first evenings at the Bolshoi, to pick out "Western" from "Soviet" in the lobby at a glance.

But rural Russia has none of this. Peasant life still imposes its traditional, natural drudgery, with almost no refinement. "When the autumn rains come," said a fellow student who came from a Ukrainian village, "you cannot really call it human life; it sinks to an animal level of existence."

You need not even go aboard one of the trains leaving Yaroslavskii station to sense the contrast between city and country in Russia. Spend just an hour among the ragged peasant families who wait, seemingly since yesterday, for their trains—among the work-worn, starch-and-vodka-fed faces, the barnyard clothes, the dirty tattered bundles, the near-illiterate conversations—and you get a good idea of the backwardness and poverty of their lives.

The contrast between new and old, city and country, dynamic technology and stagnant custom, between the staggering progress that has been made and the staggering backwardness that remains, is so great that I left feeling that any visitor who does not come away confused about the country has only confused himself.

Somehow these contrasts one sees everywhere in Russia were reflected more than anywhere else in the case that comes up next. It was a stupendous extravaganza: for six weeks, thirty-one defendants, represented by twenty-two lawyers, confessed in detail, denied everything, incriminated and contradicted one another, bemoaned their drunken husbands and difficult lots, blamed the higher-ups and "the system," promised to reform, giggled and wept, and somehow laid bare a ring of nicely organized, smooth-working socialist illegality. The complexity, intricacy and confusion of the proceedings beggar description and whatever I can salvage of them will necessarily lack logical, to say nothing of legal, sense.

Still, I should try to suggest at least the central subject of inquiry during those forty-odd frantic days, for it is typical of the systematic cheating that infects the Soviet economy and inspires those sporadic emergency attempts at inoculation and immunization by the Party and legal press—and, from time to time, by local law-enforcement agencies. But the virus is rampant. City Court's docket overflowed with cases like this one, if usually on a smaller scale. By my rough count, over half of the first-instance cases there dealt with group crimes. On the "defendant's bench" (that is what the dock is called) would sit five, or fifteen, or more, "swindlers of communal property" —employees, from director to cleaning women, of a single firm or two or more associated ones, who had improvised a not-very-original variation on the familiar themes of elaborate, methodical theft, bribery and deception which ran through this mammoth case.

It was what Russians call *krugovaya poruka*, a "family circle," or "left-handed production," or more commonly a *bardak*, which is currently slang for a "huge disorder," and other things less polite. A naval skipper might have talked about the "rat's nest," but only Russian jargon does the conspiracy justice, because it was a typically Russian affair. A typically communal effort reflecting (it is the old dichotomy again, even on this level) traditional Russian collectivism or the stresses of authoritarian socialism, take your pick. Whatever the reason, Muscovites setting out to get something for nothing are not happy going it alone.

The scene of the crime was the Yaroslavskii railroad station.

The scene of the trial was the third floor of City Court, the largest room, set apart and used (it was almost never empty) for the more multipartite group crimes. Its furniture was neo-

Victorian-ponderous, yet it seemed lost in the stark *prostor* of the hall. Benches for about two hundred spectators were available; but about that many relatives alone attended regularly, so that each day, sometime after 10 A.M. or noon when the army officer signaled for the door to be opened, there was, as there is whenever a door is opened in Russia for people who have been waiting, a quick surge, a push, a roar, a determination, sharpened by years of shortage, not to be left out or without, as the entire mass of overcoated spectators battled to squeeze through the narrow opening at once. Both sides of the door were never opened together; no one thought of forming a queue. Twice I had buttons ripped from my coat in the melee.

The judge was a mild-mannered graying man, with a soothing voice who wore the same blue shirt and brown tie, it seemed, for the entire six weeks. Highly competent and experienced, he had great reserves of patience and endurance —which, nevertheless, diminished day by day; by the fifth week his nerves were frazzled, and he was desperate to get to the end. Both assessors were factory workers (curious how the office-face of the judge differed from theirs). One of them struggled conscientiously to follow the deluge of testimony throughout. The other one gave up; he grinned stupidly at the defendants nearest him, whispered to the soldiers standing guard at his table, stared for hours out of the double window, and after lunch cradled his head in his hands and dozed. He never asked a question during the month and a half.

The lawyers were of various types, from the deans of their profession, elderly, gray-suited gentlemen who had built their reputations in thirty-five years at the bar (they represented the general staff of the conspiracy), to young girls in worn turtle-neck sweaters who had left the university only a year before—and on some evenings left the trial to go back there for student dances. Some lawyers played truant on days when they thought they would not be missed, and all, except those at the head of their table who could be seen from the dais, read *Pravda* and *Izvestiya* during the drier hours of testimony. When they all attended, the overflow from their table had to sit among the public, exchanging notes with the main body.

Facing the lawyers, an angry procurator worked alone, a youngish man, vaguely handsome, with a rasping voice and a craving for authority. He pounded his table, shouted for quiet in the hall, snarled at witnesses ("We know you are lying; you had better redeem yourself now."), lectured the lawyers ("I refuse to tolerate such behavior from Soviet lawyers in a Soviet court"), and in general conducted himself as if he were the presiding judge.* But he was alert and persevering, the most dynamic person in the hall, and he stood up well under his enormous burden. The conspiracy crumbled in his hands.

There was also an expert witness, a soft and seedy accountant who left the trial in the fourth week, after it was clear to everyone that he had reduced the necessary figures to an indecipherable garble. And an alternate assessor was present too so that the trial would not have to be started afresh if one of the two regular assessors should be incapacitated.

Finally, there were the thirty-one defendants. I cannot, of course, describe them individually. Twenty-five were women, mostly between thirty-five and fifty years old, mostly overweight, round-faced and kerchiefed, peasantlike, and passive—except when, by a logic comprehensible only to themselves, their personal sensibilities were offended by the accusers. During the first three days two of the women held infants on their laps between nursings, and the opening stages of the trial were

* Once he demanded that a woman spectator who had been swearing on the outer stairs be removed from the courtroom. The judge was about to agree, when the lawyers protested that it was not the procurator's affair. The issue was not decided, because the woman had disappeared of her own accord.

periodically disrupted by lusty squalling. Finally the judge sent these two home, ordering them to report, minus offspring, in ten days, when their testimony would be taken.

Eleven of the defendants sat in two rows just below the veneered desk of the court; they were in custody, guarded by from six to ten bayonet-carrying soldiers—sometimes there were a dozen well-armed troops in the room—and were not permitted to talk among themselves. Behind them, separated, sat the remaining twenty defendants in three rows; they were free, whether on bail or on their own recognizance, and came to each session under their own power. At least once a day the hall was treated to a moment of comedy when an unsuspecting spectator, finding an empty seat among this second set of defendants, would sit down there. Everyone roared, even on the next-to-last day.

I could not discover on what basis the defendants had been assigned to the respective groups; those who allegedly were the leading conspirators, all of whom denied their guilt, were up front under custody, but the rest were assigned without apparent reference to whether they denied their guilt or admitted it. Perhaps the only criterion was the investigator's appraisal of each accused, taking into consideration his personality, past convictions, age, health, family situation, and so on, in addition to the seriousness of the charge.

The first morning of the trial was spent "introducing" the defendants and by the time the judge had finished, no one could have remembered who was Russian, who Ukrainian, who was married and who divorced, whose husband or father had served with distinction in the Soviet Army or had lived through the Leningrad siege twenty years before (the lawyers tried very hard to bring this out), and how many times another's husband had been sentenced for hooliganism (the procurator wanted to know this). There were simply too many similar biographies.

The indictment is as difficult to describe as are the defendants. Racing through it like a tobacco auctioneer chanting his spiel, the judge took the better part of a day reading it through. In all, seventy-four separate charges were made. I shall try to give only the essential elements of the conspiracy.

All thirty-one defendants worked either in one of the four buffets (inelegant snack bars) which served the Yaroslavskii station or in the station restaurant to which the buffets were administratively subordinate. Coffee and cocoa were among the thin fare offered at these buffets, and the norms for their preparation had been fixed by the Moscow Restaurant Trust (with the approval of the Ministry of Food and Retail Trade, and so on up the line): 400 grams of coffee and 300 of cocoa per 50-glass urn. But for at least a year and a half—no one could say when it had started or whether it overlapped with the previous variation of swindling by watering the beer —the *bufetchiki* (employees of the buffet) and *bufetchitsi* (the same, female gender) were mixing in far less raw material and putting the "surplus" to private use. Sometimes two bags—200 grams—were used, sometimes 100 grams; *never* 400. The watered brews were sold at the counter at established prices, ten kopeks the glass for coffee, fifteen for cocoa and, with the ingredients "saved," extra urns of the same quality were mixed and extra glasses sold at the same prices. This income, less expenses for extra sugar milk and sometimes chicory —to give some color and aroma to the water—was pocketed, each shift dividing its extra receipts among themselves. It was private enterprise. It was profit.

How many glasses and how many kopeks were involved remained a mystery, for although the indictment charged each defendant with a precise sum of stolen money based on a precise number of shifts worked and a precise number of glasses sold, the prosecution figures were disputed even by the employees who admitted their guilt fully, and in cases where they were checked in detail at the trial proved absurdly inaccurate. Holidays, sicknesses and absences were omitted in the prosecution's calculations, multiplication was confused and, it seemed, figures were imagined when they could not be determined. The payroll and bookkeeping accounts of the restaurant were a shambles, and the investigation was not able to put them in order. Day-long discussions before the exasperated judge about grams of sugar, bags of coffee, sizes of glasses, chemical analyses of content produced nothing concrete. The procurator insisted that at least 17,800 rubles had been pocketed. Various lawyers argued that that was mathematically impossible. The actual figure was probably somewhere near 12,000 rubles, and that, finally, was the way the court seemed to look at it. From The Beginning, 1917, Soviet jurists have sought to make their laws and courts simple, and the judge carried on the tradition, even in this complicated case. An average shift (which worked twenty-four hours and rested forty-eight, as in much of the nonfactory work in Moscow) netted an average woman employee something under two rubles, over the entire period about two hundred.

Whatever the gross amount, however, it was not all clear profit, for overhead was high. The head *bufetchik* of each shift took the lion's share, because out of it he had to bribe the *bufetchik* in chief. And so it went, up the chain of command to Kusin, Director of the Restaurant, Communist, Member of the Union of Restaurants, winner of countless awards for "distinguished service" and "contributions to Soviet consumer trade," and delegate to his district Soviet. The indictment claimed that Kusin had accumulated 4,500 rubles in bribes, and although this, like all of the figures, was vigorously disputed by the defense, it was clear that the restaurant-buffets' administrators profited far more than the ordinary *bufetchiki*. The latter, in fact, worked the system for the former, who ran it as proprietors. There were hints too of absentee ownership. The procurator kept referring to "pay-offs" in the form of entertainments and gifts given by Kusin to officials of the Trust and the Ministry, but no action was taken against the latter.

The system worked exquisitely while it lasted. Not a single consumer complained about the coffee—although each buffet dutifully displayed the Complaint Book required of every Soviet organization which serves the public. Perhaps the customers were satisfied. In all but a few restaurants with new Italian machines, coffee is so tasteless anyway that expectations are conveniently low. The police, from headquarters in Yaroslavskii station, went about the business of hauling in drunks and speculators, and apparently never suspected the existence of a conspiracy right under their noses. There had been one complaint that the buffets were serving Kusin's cronies free, but an investigation conducted by the restaurant administration itself discovered no irregularities. The restaurant and buffets went on winning medals for meeting their plans, often for overfulfilling their norms. In short, it was a neat little racket—ultimately exposed only through sexual misconduct within the ring.

For although coffee, cocoa and bribery were the principal subjects of debate during the trial and most of the questions concerned how the *bufetchitsi* prepared and sold the beverages and the *uborchitsi* (cleaning women) bought sugar from retail stores, and how the bribes changed hands and the profits were divided, there were related doings which reflected the general tone of the establishment. The chief bookkeeper took his cut; no one knew exactly why, but no one wanted to walk the five flights to his office in case he got fussy with chits, arithmetic, and regulations. The inspector of cadres (a medieval Director of Personnel) liked to sleep with women who applied for jobs or for promotions from *uborchitsa* to *bufetchitsa*; and when, rarely, they refused or did not meet his liberal standards, he took two months' salary instead. The *bufetchik* in chief was fond of doing the same and cultivated the habit of borrowing a girl or two from work for an hour in the afternoons and even treating a favored few to short trysts in the country. The director who replaced Kusin—he was promoted to an executive position in the Restaurant Trust shortly before the case broke—became, ex-officio, leader of the system, and ordered profits increased. It was a happy family circle.

Crimes in Moscow may be divided into two categories. One covers violations of the law in all civilized countries: robbery, counterfeiting, perjury, espionage, bigamy, plagiarism, murder, poaching, et cetera. A second is peculiar to socialism. For one of the corollaries of a planned economy—I speak as someone convinced that some form of socialism is essential and inevitable in a twentieth-century industrialized society—is that a certain range of actions which had been private when the market was free must become public when the Plan takes over, and that the criminal code must expand to regulate those actions. Thus the Russian code: Article 153, Private Entrepreneurial Activity and Commercial Negotiations; Article 154, Speculation; Article 156, Deception of Customers; Article 157, Putting Inferior, Substandard or Incomplete Merchandise on Sale; Article 162, Engaging in Prohibited Enterprise; . . .

Drink a bitter cup of coffee in Chock Full o' Nuts or insipid tea in a Lyons Corner House and you "punish" the offenders by never coming back. (That, anyway, is market theory. Why we sometimes put up with offensive liquids is a question which economists and jurists need not answer.) Sell a sweater or a rug to a willing buyer in Toledo and you are doing the community a service, even if a handsome profit goes into your cashbox. Buy a peck of pickles in Leeds and you yourself are responsible, within very wide limits, for taking home juicy, tasty ones that are worth the price. These are essentially private transactions in which the state is scarcely interested.

But in a socialist economy, more precisely in an economy planned to the extent that the Soviet one is planned, coffee, tea, sweaters, rugs, pickles and everything else command national concern. They have all been calculated in the Plan. There is a norm, a quantity and a price for everything, for the concentration of coffee in the water and of dill in the cucumbers, for the mark-up on rugs, for the quantity of sweaters. And deviation from the norm means violation of the law.

On a larger scale the reason is obvious. Sell a carload of steel to a railroad trust instead of to a tractor factory or ship an order of substandard sparkplugs to the tractor plant in order to meet your monthly production quota, and you spoil everything, from the goals of the tractor industry down to the corn crop and back up, through meat production and labor supply, to all kinds of industries. In all economies everything is interdependent, but when all the variables are planned, one deviation here means thousands of them there. It is not *your* business but the community's.

The most lucid illustration I know of the difference between a planned economy and a market one was a case heard in late May in the city of Frunze. A Moscow lawyer preparing to travel there as defense attorney told me about it. His client was charged with buying up rugs from officials in Moscow stores and shipping them somehow to rug-starved Frunze, where they sold at roughly double the established price. Had this man done the same in America—rugs in New York, no rugs in Cleveland, ship them there, enterpriser!—he might have expected honor as well as riches—certainly not a stiff sentence as an entrepreneur for large-scale speculation, which the Moscow lawyer anticipated. His iniquity in Soviet circumstances lay not only in making a profit and carrying on in the old spirit of private enterprise, greed, exploitation and backwardness which the regime is sworn to eliminate. He was also wrecking the distribution schedule for rugs—damaging the Plan. This is why, I think, the sanctions against "public" wrongdoing are always more severe than against private. Theft of private property, for example, is punishable by up to ten years' confinement, but theft of state or communal property by up to fifteen years or death.

In a way, the Kusin case fell between these two categories. Hoarding coffee from stock, selling it and pocketing the proceeds would, of course, constitute conspiracy in Western law—but such a scheme would not likely be put into practice in capitalist railroad stations. Nor taken very seriously were it tried. But in Moscow it was as common as cabbage in winter. Every tenth enterprise seemed to have devised some simple system of shredding profits from its proper operation—the kinds of manipulation that would hardly occur even to the writers of Alec Guinness plots, but which germinate naturally and spontaneously in the minds of simple folk under the Plan. And Soviet procurators, of course (when they are not themselves involved), work furiously to plug the ruinous holes in the socialist economy that are made by beating the Plan.

Of course all this is old hat to Moscow lawyers, and none of those in the Kusin case thought the charges strange: deception of customers, abuse of official positions, bribery within an organization. One supplementary charge, however, which was directed against almost all of the defendants, caused a crescendo of protest by the lawyers and became the great legal issue of the case.

That charge was theft of state property. While the case was still under investigation the lawyers had petitioned to have this part of the accusation dropped, and they continued to petition throughout the trial. They argued that it was a feeble fiction; that the state had had nothing whatsoever stolen from it since the norms for buying of coffee and cocoa were met exactly, all moneys due the trust were paid regularly and the accounts with all other state enterprises were in perfect order. Only the public was cheated, the individuals who drank half-coffee. This, said the lawyers, was precisely and completely described by the article on deception of customers, and nothing more serious could logically be charged. The *state* was not defrauded of a kopek; not a kopek of state money was missing anywhere. Besides, a crime cannot be qualified twice; if this was deception of customers, how could it be theft of state property at the same time?

For two reasons, the procurator answered. Since the extra kopeks taken in daily were put in the regular (state) cashbox with regular income, they became automatically *state* kopeks, and the sharing of them at the end of the shift constituted theft of state property. (Had they separated the good money from the bad, according to this reasoning, putting the latter directly in their pockets, the state would not have been defrauded. The lawyers pleaded that this was ludicrously weak. It was at trials like this that I heard bitter complaints about the "campaign.") Later the procurator found another argument: the defendants had used the state's urns, water and the facilities of the buffets for their private purposes, again stealing state property.

The court sustained his reasoning. Theft of state property was upheld. The lawyers sensed that stiff sentences were forthcoming.

The defendants were heard in order of the co-operation they had given the investigator, beginning with those who admitted everything, described the system, traced the chain of command, listed figures and dates, and named names, so that by the time, four weeks later, the chief *bufetchik* (he had worked twenty-five years in Yaroslavskii station buffets and had been proclaimed an "Excellentnik" of Soviet Trade) and his superiors had their turns, a mass of evidence against them had been produced. They presented their defense—that any irregularities had taken place without their knowledge, that they had never taken a ruble in bribes, that they ought to be exonerated because all of the norms and obligations of the buffets had been met precisely—without much conviction.

Log by log, the procurator built his case. "How could your conscience allow you, a Soviet worker and a Soviet mother, to cheat Soviet workers and the Soviet state?" was his favorite question. He did not ask it rhetorically. Most of the women answered simply that that was the way things worked in the buffets, that the system of cheating was entrenched because "the bosses" enforced it. "Either you went along or you were on the streets." "I didn't dare refuse—I couldn't afford to be unemployed."* "We all simply *had* to do it to keep our jobs. The bosses were in command, and they commanded it."

But in the background was another reason, which the procurator seemed less anxious to hear. It was based on need: the *bufetchitsi* and *uborchitsi* were abysmally poor. According to Western standards, even according to the average standards of Moscow, they lived on the fringe of existence. Unskilled Soviet labor is wretchedly paid; the simple women in these buffets got almost nothing. Thirty-five rubles a month was their average wage, just over a ruble a day, twenty kopeks an hour. I suppose a Russian woman accustomed to cabbage and potatoes can feed herself on that. Rent and medical costs are negligible, transportation is very cheap, and clothing is ignored. But over half of these *babas* were divorced or separated from husbands and were trying to maintain homes, mostly with children. They all had pitiful stories (which the procurator cut short) about unpaid alimony, unforeseen expenses, shoe money gone to vodka, and sheer fatigue. From

* How to reconcile this with Russia's labor shortage and apparent absence of unemployment I do not know. Several women made such statements.

the look of them, their life must have been a grueling routine. The extra three or four rubles a week from the profits soon seemed to them an absolutely necessary supplement.

Not that they whined in court. On the contrary; even as defendants, their endurance, or resignation, kept them to understatement. Nor was there personal antipathy, resentment or indignation against "the bosses" as such, even though many felt misused by them. No "we" against "them," poor against rich, worker against Communist. The socialist camaraderie of one class or one stock prevailed even under this stress. When the procurator snidely asked a particularly bedraggled and mistreated *uborchitsa* how she felt when Kusin won awards for excellence during the height of the cheating, he was unpleasantly surprised. "I felt very proud. I think he deserved it." Was this socialism's work or, perhaps, an old Russian instinct to huddle together when faced by common disaster?

When the judge has finished with a defendant or witness the order of his further questioning in Soviet procedure is flexible. Usually the procurator starts and the lawyer follows, but questions then go back and forth from both sides, and earlier witnesses are often asked to comment on what the current one just said. In the Kusin case this meant that two or three defendants were sometimes standing simultaneously answering the judge, procurator, and one or more of the lawyers. With that procedure it took great effort to finish with each defendant, and there was an audible sigh of relief each time one sat down.

Here is how about five minutes of this sounded. *Bufetchitsa* Anashkina, a typically hulking woman of middle age, is standing in front of the first bench of the second group. In her year at Buffet No. 2 she consistently used two bags of coffee to the urn and she has admitted taking 170 rubles in profits. The judge has questioned her exhaustively about her duties and instructions and about the preparation of coffee and cocoa. She has said that she had never been told and never knew how much coffee was supposed to be used, but did assume that her activities were illegal. She has divulged, apparently, everything she knows about the arrangements on her shift, identifying the makers of coffee, the buyers of sugar and the takers of bribes. The procurator has had her recount it all a second and a third time, and then goes on:

"You are telling this court that the cheating bothered you. A likely story! Evidently it didn't bother you enough to do something to end that rotten business. If it bothered you you would have done something. You know your duty as a Soviet citizen. Why didn't you report to the police station, which was two steps from your buffet?"

No answer.

"Answer me! Why didn't you lift your finger to end it instead of turning up your palm for profits?"

"I just couldn't do anything else, it was beyond me. I couldn't fight the system alone. I did what I was told, that's all; I wanted to keep my job."

"Self-seeking to the end. All right, when did you finally confess?"

"When I was questioned by the investigator. I told him everything. I was glad that it was all over and I could face myself again."

"From the very first questions you stood on the right path?"

"I did. I told you, I'm not a cheat. I was glad it ended."

The procurator then reads irately from the preliminary investigation. The record shows that Anashkina at first denied everything and confessed only at a confrontation with a fellow *bufetchitsa*.

"Despicable! So you did not confess until you saw no other way out. And now you want us to believe that the system troubled your conscience. *Ech*, despicable! Why didn't you at least tell the truth when the police came to *you?*"

Anashkina does not answer.

"Did you tell the truth in the end at the preliminary investigation? Can we believe you now, at last?"

"Yes. Everything is true."

"Who else besides you prepared coffee on your shift?"

"I told you, all of us did."

"Varabieva and Bielokurova?"

"Yes."

"And Krutova?"

"I think so. I can't be sure. When we were rushed, anyone made coffee."

One of the lawyers: "Question to Bielokurova, please."

Judge: "You may." Bielokurova stands.

"Bielokurova, can you remember when Krutova made coffee and what ingredients she used?"

"I don't remember exactly. I know that we all made it, and nobody used more than two hundred grams. I don't know what she [Krutova] is trying to hide. She took her cut like the rest of us."

Procurator: "Question to Krutova, please."

"Must you? She has already testified for two hours." Krutova stands.

"Now how about it, Krutova? Here are two disinterested people on your shift who saw you making coffee and dividing profits. Are you going to stick to your fairy tales?"

"I told you, I hardly ever made coffee, and when I did it was exactly according to the norm. I had no part in anything wrong."

"Not likely! Why would Anashkina and Bielokurova and Varabieva try to implicate you for no reason? It doesn't ring true to the court. Tell us the truth!"

"I do. You have to ask *them* why they implicate me. Maybe they're trying to lighten their own responsibility by implying that it was impossible to be honest in the buffet. I only know that I was."

Krutova's lawyer: "Comrade Judge, one question to Krutova, please."

Judge: "*Nyet*, this is *enough!* We heard Krutova for an entire morning and we are not going to go through it all again, just repeating. We shall never get done. Comrade Lawyer, you will have the opportunity to add anything you want during the supplementary testimony." He turns to the procurator. "Now let us get back to the witness and get *on*." Bielokurova and Krutova sit.

Procurator: "Tell us, Anashkina, whose idea was it to cheat on the coffee?"

"I can't say whose idea it was. It was just the way it was done, nobody questioned it."

"Nobody? But who did you *assume* invented the scheme?"

"I assumed it was someone smarter than I."

"Very funny. Your lightheaded attitude toward your sins is not going to help you."

"There was talk that it was planned by Kusin and Maievskii [the chief *bufetchik*]."

Kusin's lawyer: "May I ask an important question? I don't think it is right to—"

Judge: "Comrade Rosenberg, will you please wait until the procurator has finished? You will have your chance."

Procurator: "Defendant Anashkina, I want you to describe in as much detail as possible the passing of your first bribe to Maievskii. Who suggested it, where and when did it take place, and under what conditions?"

"How can I remember all that? It was more than two years ago. I just gave him ten rubles, there were no particular circumstances."

"For what reason did you give him money?"

314

"What do you mean, for what reason? It was expected."

"Expected by whom?"

"By the administration, by everyone."

"By Maievskii himself?"

"Of course."

"Who was present when the money changed hands?"

"No one. No one was ever present. He saw to that."

"Did you tell anyone about it?"

"Probably Shchedrina. She was on my shift then."

"Question to Shchedrina, please."

"Granted." Shchedrina stands.

"Did Anashkina tell you sometime in February 1960 that she passed bribes to Maievskii?"

"I don't remember whether she told me. I knew she was doing it."

"You knew she was doing it. Very well, you may sit down." Then to Anashkina: "How did Maievskii let you know that bribes were expected?"

"He made it plain—oh, his hints were obvious enough. Before I got into the system he came around a few times in the middle of the night to inspect the buffet, saying he could make my life miserable."

"And the bribes followed from that? And the cheating on coffee?"

"Of course."

"Then what followed between you and Maievskii? What else did you give him of yourself?"

Maievskii's lawyer: "Comrade Judge, I think that such a question is unfair to my client. Anashkina has testified three times that Maievskii never suggested that she be his concubine."

Judge: "Yes, yes, that's true. Comrade Procurator, why ask that question again? It's really not needed now."

The procurator is furious. "She lied before. Outright lied. I want to get to the bottom of this rottenness." Then to Anashkina: "Defendant, how often after that first time did you pass your bribes to Maievskii?"

"About once a week. Once every two weeks."

"Regularly?"

"Fairly regular."

"When was it done?"

"When he came around and let me know that it was time."

"You yourself passed him the money?"

"It wasn't hard."

"I'm warning you, stop making a joke of this. How much did you pass?"

"Five rubles."

"Every time?"

"Almost every time. Sometimes it was ten."

"What did he say when you gave him the money?"

"He said, 'Thank you.' " Laughter.

"Silence! I demand silence in the hall. This is a Soviet court! Either the spectators will remember where they are or we will throw them out. I have no further questions of Anashkina."

"Comrade defender, do you have any questions?"

"If you please. You understand, Anashkina, that some people may think that you have admitted your guilt and told everything you know so openly only to soften the punishment you may expect. Tell us, then, why you have been so frank and co-operative. What were your real motives?"

"Only to tell the truth. I want to wipe my record clean at last even if it means sitting [in jail]. I'm through with lying."

"That's very admirable. I'm certain the court understands how you feel. Now, you've admitted taking a hundred and seventy rubles. How did you arrive at that figure?"

"I didn't arrive at it, the investigator did."

316

"Is it the correct figure?"

"I haven't the faintest idea."

"You must have *some* notion."

"It's probably too much. They have me down for a hundred and thirty-eight shifts; I never worked more than a hundred."

"Is it also true that you bought china for the buffet with some of the extra money?"

"It's true. Plates and glasses. We never had enough."

"Why didn't you tell that to the investigator?"

"I forgot. Am I supposed to remember everything?"

"Do you remember how much you were earning in the buffet?"

"Thirty-seven or thirty-eight rubles a month."

"Tell us about your family situation."

"Separated, that's all. My husband left me. Let him stick to his bottle—he treats it better than me."

"And what about your daughter?"

"She's still with me, thank God. My own blood."

"You support her?"

"That's what I'm living for. Her father is supposed to pay alimony but sometimes he doesn't send it for months. The court gets him to pay for a while, then he starts again on vodka . . ."

In any group trial where some of the defendants confess, they provide the most damaging evidence against those who do not. So too with Anashkina and the other *bufetchitsi*. Before she was through, therefore, she was grilled by six lawyers representing defendants whom she had implicated but who protested innocence. (Four of the questioners were the lawyers representing Kusin and the other administrators.) During the next hour they hammered at the weak points and uncertainties in her testimony and, seeking to prove the opposite of what the procurator sought, were only slightly quicker and kinder with her than he.

The case dragged on, a comic tragedy in which confusion multiplied like yeast. On some of those long stifling afternoons I had the feeling of *déjà vu*. Was it Gogol?

Later, I stopped going every day, and sometimes when I went the doors had been closed for consideration of the sexual aspects, or an adjournment had been called to permit the lawyers and judges to return to private life for an afternoon. I got the gist of what transpired in the sessions I missed from the relatives of the leading defendants, most of whom attended every day, waving to their loved ones as if to heroes on a soccer field, not sad failures on the defendant's bench. These relatives kept assuring me that their husbands and wives were innocent, but they said it unconvincingly. Their resentment, significantly, was directed mostly to peripheral matters like the arrogance of the procurator; the distortion of the article in the Sunday supplement of *Izvestiya* which omitted the word "alleged" and demanded the "strictest measures of punishment for the accused"; and the reasoning of the prosecution according to which a *dacha*, television set or sewing machine was *ipso facto* proof of illegal earnings. Nevertheless, family loyalty seemed extraordinarily strong and I do not know how to reconcile it with that other phenomenon I saw in the courts: the high incidence of broken homes and divorce.* Even the wife of the lascivious inspector of cadres, whose conquests were legion, blew him a soulful kiss whenever he turned around.

As weeks dragged by, it became more and more certain that

---

* Perhaps, however, the courts gave me an exaggerated impression of the frequency of divorce. Until recently, most Soviet social statistics were kept secret; now they are becoming more available. One official report, made after I left Moscow, put the Soviet divorce rate at 13 per 10,000 persons compared to 22 per 10,000 in the United States.

everyone was in fact involved in the conspiracy, and also that no one was going to find out to what extent. The lawyers and one defendant, the chief bookkeeper, continually attacked the prosecution's case for inaccuracy, scoring the procurator's explanation that his figures were "minimal," and therefore merciful. "That is unheard of. Our law knows no such thing. An investigation must establish exact figures, not guess at minimums or grant mercy." One after another the lawyers pleaded that the indictment was meaningless because it was based on meaningless information. This "deliberate stalling and confusing" turned the procurator purple. After two weeks the judge seemed utterly uninterested in the figures—what was five hundred glasses more or less? "That is enough, for God's sake! Maybe some of the information is not a hundred per cent accurate. So what? We are not going to listen to all twenty-two of you make the same point." He rejected out of hand the lawyers' petition for a new investigation to start from the beginning and "do it right."

Somehow all this emphasis by the defense on the inaccuracy in detail made it appear *more* certain, rather than less, that the defendants were guilty.

Thirty-nine witnesses were called: inspectors of all sorts, control-purchasers, bookkeepers, chemists, employees of the station, ice-cream vendors, policemen, deliverymen, customers. A circus parade. By this time the brewing of coffee and splitting of profits had been described so often that the witnesses stepped up and down from the stand quickly, and when some testified that they knew "nothing" about the case—an old grandmother said, "I remember nothing." "Not even whether you told the truth to the investigator?" "No, nothing."—neither judge nor procurator pressed them seriously to talk.

Slowly the epic approached its end, though no one believed it. In his closing speech the procurator quoted Lenin, Khru-

shchev, the Party Program and *Pravda*. It was a textbook presentation and made much of the arguments stressed in texts:
that since there are no "objective" social or economic reasons
for crime in Soviet society, people who committed them, who
lived by the old, bourgeois rules, are *personally* responsible
and deserve severe punishment; that people who steal from
the state are stealing from the toilers; that cheaters are doubly
dangerous because they also hinder the building of Communism; that strict penalties are needed not only to punish
the guilty but also to warn the public. He concentrated his
wrath on the administrators, emphasizing the fatal danger of
bribery, especially systematic, organized bribery, to the Soviet
state. Then he cited the two-month-old decree establishing
the death penalty for economic crimes as proof that the Soviet
people (*sic*) demanded an end to them. For Kusin and his
staff, he demanded from ten to fifteen years each.

Coming to the *bufetchitsi* and *uborchitsi*, he spoke of "understanding one's mistakes," of "socialist re-education," of
"the misfortune of being misled," and of "the humanity of the
Soviet court"; and he asked for terms of two to seven years.
Two women, he felt, deserved conditional sentences.

The lawyers' replies varied. Those whose clients had confessed expressed shock at the severity of the procurator's
recommendations after his "fine words" about humanity and
re-education. Those whose clients had denied guilt attempted,
sometimes brilliantly albeit futilely, to refute each episode
charged in each part of the indictment as lacking concrete
proof. But all of the lawyers protested again the accusation
of theft of state property; passionately and persistently they
pleaded that that qualification was superfluous, erroneous, and
detrimental to the integrity of the Soviet court, because, as
one of them put it, it was so obviously unfair that sustaining it
would weaken the people's confidence in the court.

By the time the sentence was read, the soldier-guards had

changed to summer cottons, but they sweated through them nevertheless. The hall was like a Moscow bus during rush hour: physical contact to the breaking point, then a dozen more people ram themselves inside.

A total of 127 years in labor colonies was dealt out among the defendants much the way the procurator had recommended, although in somewhat smaller amounts. (He had asked for 153 years.) Everyone was found guilty—and, predictably, of theft of state property where it was charged—although some of the less important women were acquitted of bribery for lack of evidence. The five restaurant officials were sentenced to ten years each in colonies with strict regimes, and their property was confiscated. Most of the women got from two to five years; two were given conditional sentences as the procurator had suggested, and the women with infants were directed to delay in reporting for their terms until weaning could be satisfactorily arranged. The others were marched off after a minute of mass goodbyes that was a living re-creation of the melodramatic parting-at-the-railroad scene in every recent Soviet film about the war.

When the trial ended I was at loose ends. Something inexplicably meaningful was over forever. Kusin, Maievskii, Anashkina and Bielokurova, the irritated procurator, Rosenberg and the other lawyers—involuntarily, the Yaroslavskii affair had become my personal epic, and I felt lonely at its end, as one feels at the close of a long novel.

I was sure that the weary judge would take a vacation when it was over, but I happened to notice him in the metro the following week, reading his morning *Pravda*. He was on the way to work, in his blue shirt and brown tie. I followed him. He had another group case, this time the meat-pie, hot-dog and payroll manipulations of a large café at Lenin stadium, and he conducted it in the same mild, soothing tone with which he began the case of Kusin and others. Later I saw him frequently: again "family circles" operating grandiose, ludicrous bookkeeping and payroll schemes, producing secretly and selling privately on the side, systematic short-changing, short-shipping, short-weighting. (Only the wholesale cases were heard in City Court.) Once it was a group of furriers using sixteen stretched pelts to the coat instead of twenty, and making coats out of the extra pelts for their own profitable trade. Another time, a group of speculators who would buy up an entire shipment of clothing and sell it piecemeal at triple prices. Several times it was factory personnel which produced fifteen units instead of ten, and sold five through private distributors for profit. What an amusing book that gentle judge could write!

XVI

Nikolai Nikolaievich

*Philosophers have only explained the world in various ways:
what really matters is to change it.*
    —KARL MARX (quoted on page one of the latest Soviet
                      philosophy textbook)

*The law embodies the story of a nation's development
through many centuries, and it cannot be dealt with as if it
contained only the axioms and corollaries of a book of
mathematics. In order to know what it is, we must know
what it has been, and what it intends to become.*
    —OLIVER WENDELL HOLMES, *The Common Law* (1880)

A STOUT lady with hat and handbag walked in, looking feature
for feature like a woman detective. (She was a social worker
in juvenile cases.)

"Nikolai Nikolaievich, hello, greetings. Sorry for rushing
so, but be so kind, please, and hear my grocery case today,
yes? I have a conference tomorrow and it ought to be cleared
up first."

"Wait, Anna Mikhailovna, can you wait just a *minutichka*,
please?"

He turned back to the gold-toothed official in blue serge
seated across from him—the district procurator.

"*Nu*, Viktor Romanovich, have we gone over almost everything? I'll see you at the meeting then, eight P.M. Don't forget the notes."

"And the other thing, Nikolai Nikolaievich? It's important."

"Don't worry about a thing. This week or next, it will be done. Only I think you ought to talk about it first with the others."

"Right."

"Right then. *Do svidanye*. See you soon."

"*Do svidanye*."

"Now, Anna Mikhailovna, come sit down. Where have you been keeping yourself? What can I do for you?"

"You remember, my petty-theft case—the two kids in the grocery?"

"Yes . . . oh yes, of course! Well, we'll try to get it heard. I'm overloaded today, as it happens: two judges sick. But I'll do my best."

He made several short interoffice calls, offering the case to his staff. "O.K. . . . All right . . . Well, if you can't, . . ." No luck.

"Come back in half an hour, will you, Anna Mikhailovna? Nothing doing so far, but we'll try to work something out for you."

A broad-shouldered Burt Lancaster had come in. (He was a young People's Judge.)

"Nikolai Nikolaievich, I'm stuck. I think I've got to send this darn case back for supplementary investigation."

"What's the problem?"

"The problem is that it's robbery, obvious robbery—not hooliganism. He stuck his hands right in her pocket. I had a funny feeling about this case from the start."

"How far have you got?"

"Questioned the witnesses. They all agree. And he was

freed only last August for exactly the same thing. It's his handwriting, all right. Robbery; perfectly plain."

Nikolai Nikolaievich glanced professionally at the dossier, flipping pages.

"Hmm . . . yes, hooliganism is wrong. But what about those hands—you sure it wasn't attempted rape?"

"Pretty sure. She's an old woman."

"All right then, robbery. Here's what you do: Article Two thirty-two, Paragraph three, of the procedural code—base your decision on that. You'll have to send it back for supplementary investigation even though it looks quite clear. That way there'll be no grounds for a protest."

"Right, Nikolai Nikolaievich, no reason for protest. Do I have to hear the lawyer first?"

"Makes no difference. You're going to send it back anyway. It's up to you."

"Right."

"Wait—how long will you take with that one? Can you hear something else for me this afternoon? A short one, kids stealing."

"Nikolai Nikolaievich, I'm swamped. I've got office hours and another case this afternoon."

"All right. O.K. Article Two thirty-two; go to it."

Next was the turn of another People's Judge. The defendant had denied his guilt but changed his mind midway through the trial. Need the case be returned to the investigator? Then a matronly woman came to whisper something into Nikolai Nikolaievich's ear.

Then Anna Mikhailovna returned. "Don't worry," he assured her, "I'll hear the case myself if I can't get anyone else."

A peasant type in dirty boots and an untrimmed mustache barged through the door shouting, "Comrade Chairman, I *must* see you for a minute, just one minute." Nikolai Nikolaievich muttered to himself, "I need a secretary. Someone to keep at least the strangers out of here."

He was Chairman of People's Court, X District. We were sitting in his sparsely furnished office. I had sat there many times during the year—he invited me in to chat whenever I knocked. Now I was waiting to see him alone, for it was time to take leave.

Nikolai Nikolaievich was thirty-eight, maturely handsome, happily energetic; a rough-cut, self-made man. He limped and had a shrapnel scar on his neck. In 1941 he finished middle school at seventeen, volunteered, and was wounded three times as an infantryman on three fronts. He finished the war a captain, in command at age twenty-two of six hundred men. (This was in 1947. Soviet troops in Europe did not cease fire on V.E. Day; there remained Polish and Ukrainian nationalists to suppress.) Demobilized, he drifted in Moscow for two years in vegetable warehouses, bottling factories and gravel trucks. In 1949 he entered a juridical institute and, after completing a two-year course, was elected a People's Judge in a town not far from Moscow. He was transferred to a Moscow district in 1955 and transferred again in 1959. In 1961 he was elected chairman of his present court, the administrative supervisor of twelve People's Judges.

Nikolai Nikolaievich seemed honest and straightforward. He never hid the unpleasant cases from me and never used the old clichés "imperialism" and "exploitation." (And when someone in his office did, he sent me a wink.) He liked best talking about his sons, about hunting and fishing, and about the joys of the Russian countryside in changing seasons.

"I can't tell you how I ache to spend more time in the woods. I'm just going to get another job one of these days, that's all. I'm tired of this. It's too hard on a man."

"Something in particular got you down, Nikolai Nikolaievich?"

"No, nothing in particular. My court is running smoothly, I think. It's just too demanding for me: administrative work, records, trying cases, Party duties, lectures and meetings, preventive work, *obshchestvennost* . . . Too much pressure for me; I need something slower."

"But is all that work getting anywhere? Is there progress? I mean, is the rate of crime actually decreasing?"

"Decreasing? Oh, yes—most definitely yes, positively decreasing."

"Definitely?"

"Absolutely. I've seen it myself going down from year to year. Well, not *every* year. Sometimes it goes up temporarily; especially, for example, after the amnesties of 1953 and 1957. The trouble is that all kinds of cutthroats were freed, not just political offenders. But the general trend is perfectly clear: steadily down. No doubt about it; steadily, surely down.

"And not only the *rate* of crime, you see; the character is changing too. I remember the postwar years—*uzhas!* [horrible!] Violent crimes every day. Murder. Holdup. Rape. And even in the early Fifties we were often getting armed robbery, banditry, professional strong-arm stuff of all kinds. But you know, I haven't seen a case of banditry now in two years. Look at it this way: forty-four per cent of our cases this year have been for hooliganism, and the majority of these were in the family; drunkenness, insults, beatings, swearing—you know, the kind of thing we didn't even bother with years ago because we had no time. Oh no, there's no question about the general trend. *Kulturnnost* is increasing, legality is increasing, and crime is falling, all right. Steadily falling."

"Then why are there no statistics? The government's not usually reluctant to publish statistics which do it proud. Why aren't your own lawyers permitted to see the criminal statistics?"

"I can't answer that. I think it's a mistake. It would be very much in our favor to publish them, because we are defeating crime while in the West it is defeating you. And not only for that reason; we need to start using statistics for our own good to help with tactics for wiping out crime. I don't know why they're reluctant to publish figures. Maybe because the *absolute* numbers are still too high; it's still too early to make them known. The wrong kind of people might use them for the wrong purposes.

"All I can tell you is that the figures in *this* court are pretty encouraging. Pretty good progress. See this chart? It's got every criminal statistic imaginable from my district during the last quarter. I send these charts to the Ministry of Justice, where the figures from all over the country are analyzed. I *know* my district is making progress. The point is not publishing statistics, but making progress. You Americans publish very careful statistics for all the world to see, and what good does it do you? Maybe it even does harm. Your statistics show a disastrous spread of violence and illegality. We could never permit that."

"What do you attribute your progress to?"

"Hard work, mostly. You see it yourself. The Party is going all-out to eliminate crime—to root it out completely. Lectures, meetings, propaganda, publications, agitation, rehabilitation— we don't stay in the courtroom sentencing people and waiting for them to come back. We go into the community. *Prevention* is the thing; not only eliminating crime, but eradicating the *causes*."

"Seriously, Nikolai Nikolaievich, just between us, can the causes of crime really be eliminated?"

"They can, of course they can. I think we've eliminated the main ones already. Everyone has enough to eat, everyone can get work and support himself honestly, and rest and be treated like a human being, and have a decent old age. We've wiped out hunger and exploitation, unemployment and class hatred. You see, socialism roots out the objective causes—except, unfortunately, that some of our people still live too poorly. Everyone's got to have a comfortable life before we can *fully* eliminate crime."

"Fully? Do you believe that? Crime will disappear?"

"Of course it will. Crime is a disease. We've cured tuberculosis; some day we'll conquer crime."

"Maybe that's why you want another job, then? To assure your future?"

"*Nyet, nyet,* this has nothing to do with my lifetime. Eliminating crime is going to take a long time, a very long time. The propagandists are kidding themselves if they think it'll be done in thirty years, Communism or no Communism. It may take a hundred years, maybe five hundred. It's a fantastic task and we've only just begun."

"But the court will eventually wither away?"

"Certainly it will wither away. It could be one of the earlier state institutions to go. Why do you think no new courthouses are being built in Moscow? It would have a retarding effect, psychologically."

"And all you need now is to raise the standard of living? But plenty of rich people in America commit crimes, you know."

"Aha, that's exactly the point. The social system is the key. Socialism eliminates the objective reasons for crime but capitalism encourages them. The fundamental principles are diametrically opposed. You know what I mean—don't take personal offense. I like Americans."

"Then what's needed is a high standard of living *and* socialism?"

"That's still too simple. We have socialism already, and

329

it's just a matter of another twenty or thirty years to build the material base for the highest standard of living in the world. So there you have it: a few decades and there will be absolutely no reason for crime. But that's not enough, that's only the beginning; the real work will still lie ahead. The main thing is to make everyone *realize* that there is no reason for crime. That's our real job. Every living person must be made to understand that society is *his*, that to rob his neighbor is to rob himself. We've got to undo the work of hundreds of generations which were taught the opposite; we've got to root out the evils that still infect Soviet man from the past, even though the actual causes of the disease have disappeared. But I am boring you, eh, Giorgii Giorgievich?"

"Please go on, Nikolai Nikolaievich."

"You think this is crazy utopianism. Well, maybe. But the point is that we are reconstructing men's consciousness already, and that is far more difficult than pouring metal and making tractors. Lenin knew this; he said that remaking men's minds was the most important job in building Communism, infinitely harder than making dams. Only when everyone is fully conscious of what it means to be a Soviet citizen will there be no crime."

"And everyone will become fully conscious through—"

"Through the work of the courts, for one thing. First of all, every single violation must be uncovered and punished. With no exceptions. Everyone must know for certain that it is futile to break the law—that he has *no* chance of getting away with it; and, if necessary, that he will be punished severely. That's why law enforcement must *expand* before it withers away.

"Secondly, there is education, or re-education. People have to be taught that they are living in an entirely new world— that they must think of society and their neighbors in an entirely different way than when everyone was trying to ex-

Nikolai Nikolaievich

ploit everyone else. But perhaps this is still too vast an idea
for you to grasp.

"Anyway, don't think we haven't started on this change
already. Soviet man has very different feelings about his society and responsibilities than he had forty years ago. In two
generations we've already undone a surprising amount of the
evil built up over thousands of years. In 1917 we were damned
close to anarchy: incredible backwardness and crudeness,
crime running wild—nobody *cared* about the community. But
slowly—faster in these last years—we are molding a conscious,
responsible citizen. The kind for whom crime is unthinkable,
and not only for himself; it is unthinkable that he would permit his neighbor to practice it."

"Some philosophers say that crime is part of human nature,
inherent in the human condition."

"Nonsense, I must say. There is no such thing as human
nature. Man is the product of his surroundings, of the social
and economic system which molds him. Change the mold and
you change the man. And that is what we are doing. You
know, the church used to talk loud and long about original
sin: it was a good way to keep the masses in their miserable
places. But we junked that idea long ago.

"We are doing something, we are doing a great deal, about
removing the artificial societal arrangements that foster crime
—and this is where I think socialism shows its greatest advantage over capitalism. Don't damn us because we haven't
yet succeeded. We know that. But you aren't even trying.
You laugh at our goals and let yourselves slide deeper into
crime in the name of a theory of man—and then call *us* dog-
matic.

"You ought to read Engels about human nature and crime:
he proves that the growth of greed grew out of the growth
of private property and profit. Of course, these attitudes have
been brewing a long time; of course, they won't be easy to

331

change. Of course there are even some Soviet citizens who don't believe in the change, and some—you've seen them here— who do their best to hang on to the old ways. But give us time. We'll prove that there's no 'law' that man must be a cheat."

"Are you saying that none of the causes of crime is rooted in the make-up of man himself? In the raw material?"

"Look, Giorgii Giorgievich, I've been a judge now for twelve years; I've seen the worst of men and the worst of deeds. But when someone tells me that crime must go on as long as there is human civilization, I feel sorry for him. He's in the dark ages. If the forces that shape society are under-stood and properly channeled—and this is what Marxism-Leninism does for us scientifically—all sorts of good things are possible. You see, man is essentially good; only private prop-erty and everything he learned from it corrupted him. We're restoring his goodness and at the same time making him in-finitely richer in every way. Don't you see the glory in that?"

"But even Nikita Sergeyevich has said that there may be some crime under Communism."

"Well, maybe some; we can't tell yet exactly. Accidents there will certainly be. And maybe some minor violations due to jealousy or loss of temper—weakness of character. But that'll be very different from what we have now; that'll be in-dividual slips, not organized crime or crime for crime's sake. Not crime as we know it now. Not hard-core crime. There may be some wrongdoing, but the kind of thing dealt with by *obshchestvennost* in some sort of general meeting, not by po-lice and a formal court system."

"Aren't you sorry that you won't be living in such a glori-ous society, Nikolai Nikolaievich?"

"Sorry? Well yes, of course I'm sorry; that will be a time to live! I hope my grandchildren will see something of it . . . ahh, yes. On the other hand, you know, I like it now, too. I like the satisfaction of helping to *build* this great thing. To tell the truth it may be more exciting now than when almost everything is already done and everyone is well-behaved."

With everyone I spoke it was the same—the same matter-of-fact conviction that crime, contracting now, will someday disappear. Not only propagandists said it, but also judges, procurators, criminologists, and even lawyers—people who have lived with illegality and know the worst of it. They would look me straight in the face (even after an unpleasant case) and explain: "We are curing the disease of crime. We are making a new man and a new society, cleansed of criminality. We are far away; the distance to go is colossal; but we are putting one foot after another and some day we shall arrive. This is no dream, but objective reality."

This "objective reality" ought to be reckoned with somehow, when adding the goods and bads of Soviet courts. *I* was trying to weigh severity and compassion, accuracy and arbitrariness, protection and highhandedness—on traditional scales. But according to Soviet reality I was weighing superficial things.

And it is true that court procedure is not the only measure of the law; in Soviet society it is perhaps not the best measure. For the real work of the Soviet court eludes the naked eye. Its product is mankind, not individual men. Not the case at hand, not the fate of Ivanovich or Petrov, not even Dispensing Justice is its duty, but waging the Great Ultimate Campaign for a new world, free of evil and unhappiness. "The most important function of the Soviet court is the fundamental remaking of the consciousness of the people," said the Chief Justice of the Soviet Union. This is the difference: Soviet courts try for far more than Western ones. The ambitions are more lofty, the goals more shining. The courts are doing away, once and for all, with the sad business of courts.

333

A far better world is being built. And suppose unpleasant methods must sometimes be used to finish the work? Communists have always accepted this; they are not utopians. Lenin's advice, the Bolshevik tradition, shouts from thousands of posters all over town: bear down when necessary, be hard, be merciless; the pain caused will be infinitesimal compared to the pain of the old order, trifling compared to the pleasures of the new; only bourgeois liberals shrink from using strong methods—and thereby compound the world's misery.

"Glory to Communism, establishing peace, work, freedom, equality, brotherhood and happiness for all peoples on earth!" This is the ultimate difference: Communists *know* the world. They have discovered the laws, they understand man, they are certain where they are headed. They have a cosmic goal. Man and society as they are do not please them; therefore they are remaking them with their scientific tools. Their reformation is unparalleled in history. In the "socialist spring of mankind," the "sun of Communism" is dawning, the "shining new era," the "brilliant tomorrow" when "splendid, noble new man" will be *"happy."* Happy at last in that land tyrannized for centuries by sadness and misfortune.

Can bourgeois liberals like myself—for whom man is still incognoscible, still doomed to unhappiness and to ignorance about the great questions—sensibly criticize the methods of the enlightened? Not knowing the road, can we question the guide's directions? On the basis of the old, bourgeois standards?

It would be easier to scoff if no progress had been made toward the new world. But in some areas Soviet achievement has been magnificent. The legal system has benefited less than other pursuits, because in that nation of priorities judicial excellence is not yet high on the list. First place, and second and third and fourth, go now to production, to building the material-technical base for Communism. But when the country

334

is immensely rich—and it is certain that it will be—who can say that great progress will not then be made in dealing with crime? Or that a precise court system, faithful to liberal-capitalist standards, is the best way of doing it? The pride in human accomplishment that tingles the spine while an English judge charges the jury ("The price of making sure that the innocent are not convicted must be that the guilty sometimes must go free") may be replaced by a greater glow fired by greater human accomplishments under socialism. Rigid rules of evidence and proof are hardly man's *summum bonum*.

Is it fair to taste the pudding while it is still cooking?

"*Do svidanye*, Giorgii. All the very best to you, good luck. I hope you can come to Moscow again soon. Don't forget old Nikolai Nikolaievich when you do. Give my warm greetings to your people at home—and don't forget to tell them the *truth* about us here."

Next door to his office I watched some late afternoon cases, just for a last look. The first was open-and-shut—a worker had walked out of his factory at lunch hour with a 3-horse-power electric motor—and more time was devoted to one witness, a tattered, bearded peasant grandfather, keeper of the factory gate, than to the accused.

On the basis of *what*, the judge asked him, did he permit valuable objects to leave the gate. On the basis of documents. What documents? He didn't know. Laughter. Who signs the transfer papers? He didn't remember. Why, then, is he stationed at the gate? To open and close it. Belly laughter. But mightn't he just as well leave it open altogether? No, for then he would be out of a job. Pandemonium. Then why *did* he sit there? That was his job. *What* was his job—what exactly was he supposed to do there? He wasn't sure. Didn't he know that he was supposed to prevent theft? Sure, but everyone at the factory steals anyway. A tittering.

The judge grew purple. "You are incredible, simply incredible—a figure out of Chekhov." He delivered a passionate lecture on the need for strict security and supervision to stop thievery. The lawyer also based her defense on this; the real villain, she said, was the intolerably lax security arrangements at the factory. Had the property been properly guarded, the defendant would not have been tempted to steal. She produced a paragraph from the factory rules which had been violated: not the tiniest scrap of anything was permitted to leave the gate without documents signed in quadruplicate.

This is the spirit of Moscow today: Lock it up! Put a guard over it! Sign for it! Security arrangements (on paper, at least) are grandiose: passes required everywhere, old women sitting on every floor and at every gate, contracts of personal responsibility demanded of everyone with access to money or material, checks and double checks, guards, elaborate preventive measures, the buddy system, weighing to the gram and measuring to the millimeter, locking windshield wipers inside cars to remove temptation. Nothing is left to chance—that is, to simple trust. And under Communism, will there be fewer guards or more, or simply better ones? Will the new Soviet man be scrupulously honest only because vigilance will have been perfected and temptation eliminated—because it will be *impossible* to be dishonest? "Not a single citizen must be allowed to imagine he can 'get away with it'; not a single infraction must go unpunished," admonish the texts. Is there a dialectic logic here which escapes me? If eliminating crime depends on security, what has Communism to do with it? If Communism will stop stealing, what need for Moscow's ubiquitous guards?

The next case was Intentional Heavy Bodily Injury: a drunk had pummeled an acquaintance in a dispute over a motor scooter. The defendant was a nervous man with a sad history. In 1941, at fourteen, he came alone to the capital from his small village where he had been spending his days gathering firewood and dreaming of food. His parents had been killed. ("Things were terribly difficult for me then," he said. "It was the war," snapped the judge; "things were difficult for everyone.") In 1943, a factory worker at sixteen, he was sentenced to five years for banditry—his gang of adolescents had been raiding potato dumps. In 1951 he got six years (but was released under the 1953 amnesty) for stealing a leather jacket. He protested the second conviction—"I swore that I was innocent then, and I swear it now. The investigator simply said I was rotten and didn't even listen to me."

After 1953 he settled down to work in a factory and worked hard, often overtime and Sundays, until he was made foreman. He earned sixteen prizes for introducing new techniques and a regular 30 per cent bonus for overfulfilling his norms. There were many mitigating circumstances in the pummeling incident: a nervous ailment that stemmed from his childhood and often took him to a doctor; the fact that the man he hit (who was drunk too) had taunted him and refused to return the key to the defendant's motor scooter; the defendant's immediate, and apparently genuine, remorse for his action.

The procurator mentioned none of this, but concentrated instead on his shortcomings: the old convictions, the few times absent from work, the neighbor who said he sometimes swore, a history of petty family quarrels. She said that the unhappy childhood and the nervous ailment were entirely irrelevant. ("It might have affected him in 1943, but by 1962 nothing stood in the way of his living a normal, well-behaved life. He had all the opportunities open to a Soviet citizen. There are no possible mitigating circumstances in this case.") But that was not all. She added a second charge, hooliganism, for a disturbance the defendant had caused in his home seventeen months before! His sister and father said that this earlier (unrelated) incident had been long forgotten and begged the court to ignore it, and the lawyer pointed out that it had already cost the defendant fifteen days' confinement by way of administrative discipline; but the procurator refused to drop this added charge. "The earlier episode shows his true character, shows that he is truly a hooligan, that his beating a friend was not at all accidental but one of a series of offenses, a natural product of his hooliganism. He is a socially dangerous person, who must be taught a lesson he will understand."

The court agreed and sentenced him to three years for the two charges.

This too is a spirit of Moscow I do not understand. Logically, it may be argued that the causes of crime are purely environmental; that such concepts as original sin and inherent evil, the ego, flaws in the soul, the devil, complexes and illnesses, and any other of the religious, mystical and medical theories which Western man has embraced to explain criminality are "bourgeois idealism." Refutation of all these other explanations does not *automatically* lead to long sentences. On the contrary, it would seem a humane approach because it considers the criminal a reflection of his social and economic surroundings, less responsible than society for his shortcomings.

But to say this, and in the next breath to say that there are no objective reasons for crime in Soviet society, seems to me perfectly illogical, pure contradiction. Materialism means that *something* in the objective world, something environmental, prompted the criminal to err, and this cannot be explained away simply by *saying* that Soviet society is now perfect in this respect, that for the first time in history the interests of the people fully coincide with the interests of the state, that socialism has eliminated all objective causes for crime, that in the West crime is a product of the economic system while in the Soviet Union it has nothing to do with the economic system.

This reasoning is disturbing, not because in dealing with Soviet society it jettisons the most fundamental Marxian axiom —that man is a product of material forces—but because it shifts the whole blame to "subjective individual failures"—to the accused. "We have given you a clean society; if you dirty it, only you are to blame." It is unfair nonsense as well as un-Marxian nonsense.

And what will happen to deviants under Communism? Will punishments be more severe because living conditions are more perfect? Will there be still less mercy for transgressors because Soviet society, rich and socialist, will more than ever be *presumed* to be rid of them? The real test will come in two or three decades, and if it turns out that there *is* human nature, and that wrongdoing is part of it, then it will be clear that sordid wrongs have been done again in Russia in the name of a magnificent illusion. It will be the old story of chopping away at man to make him fit a theory and a grand design, of hurting him temporarily "for his own good" so that he will be *happy*.

Or maybe there will be crisis and change in Soviet criminology. Maybe the dogma will be allowed to erode and the causes for crime will be treated again in their baffling complexity. There are hints of this now; the spirit of inquiry is gathering momentum in Moscow. Progressive criminologists have recently stopped chanting that Soviet crime is a survival of capitalism and have begun to search for the *real* causes. So far, they say, the causes are not really understood.

Down the hall was Hooliganism. "Comrade Judges, I don't ask you for freedom, I know I must be punished. But please not for too long; my family needs me." He had been drinking and swearing, and had ripped the collar of a stranger's coat in a fight. He got two years. Further on there was Insult, two civil cases, a court gone on a traveling session, and Hooliganism again. The ordinary cases, the ordinary faces; I had seen them for months every day, Monday through Saturday, in a dozen People's Courts.

Something held me there: the special language and intimacy

of the courts. I felt near to knowing a momentous secret, though I could not say precisely about what. Something repelled me: the gloominess and misfortune. I had seen so many saddening ordinary cases. Still, I lingered that last day until the judges went home. Then it was time for me to go too, to come home from that curious world of crime and punishment in Moscow.

XVII

Summing Up

"Give me the making of the songs of a nation and I care not who makes its laws."
—ANDREW FLETCHER, *Conversation Concerning a Right Regulation of Government for the Common Good of Mankind,* 1703.

ONE QUESTION always stood out in Moscow's courts. What do *they* think about their law?—the people who sit in those drab rooms, hardly ever because they want to, feeling it push down upon them or their mates. Do *they* think it fair?

There was no answer, of course; Russians argue among themselves. And there are other difficulties in uncovering attitudes of this sort. One does not ask a woman whose son has just been sentenced whether her courts are just. Still, I put the question when I could—whenever possible, away from the passion of courthouses—and some common Soviet attitudes spoke for themselves.

Russians do not think their courts are an instrument of totalitarianism, police-state repression, terror, or any of the other dreadful forms of tyranny which some American political scientists equate with Soviet government. They do not think that way about Soviet courts primarily because they do not think that way about Soviet rule. "The Soviet regime," "the Krem-

341

lin," "Communist control," "Soviet rule"—all these phrases which imply oppression to Americans mean something much less sinister to the victims themselves. "The regime" means an apartment, a job, and a good education for one's children—as well as restrictions on travel abroad. It means spectacular progress as well as purges. "You must understand," said Sasha (of the first divorce case), "that even during the worst times of the 1930s, our people were very proud as well as terrified. It was a very ambiguous period." And since the Moscow trials, the balance has swung sharply toward approval of "the Kremlin."

Of course Russians are dissatisfied with their lot—what Westerner is not dissatisfied with his? Of course they want the material plenty they know is much more easily available in capitalist countries. Of course they want freedom to travel, to read and to criticize. But however much they want Western things, they do not want capitalism, and on this question—to them a crucial one—they have no quarrel with the Soviet system. Capitalism is *basically* evil and is destined for disaster; socialism is *basically* good, basically fair, desirable and progressive, and is destined for development. Private ownership of property is reactionary, inhuman and tyrannical; only common ownership can be decent, civilized and democratic. In the great issues that divide East and West, they feel sure that right lies preponderantly with the East.

I heard, therefore (except from occasional young nonconformists from Leningrad and workers from collective farms), few references to tyranny, alien ideology or enslavement. At worst the regime is tolerated disinterestedly. So is the law. Judges are spoken of as *svoyi* ("our own"), not as puppets of an occupying power. Courts are considered courts, not sham revolutionary tribunals.

On the other hand, I often heard resentment about punishment. "Our punishments are harsh," people would say, for some reason apologetically, "our laws are severe, our judges are strict. The courts are hard on people who make mistakes."

But whenever this was whispered about the courts, I was somehow reminded of the legendary and actual harshness of Russian life as a whole. And the Russian attitude toward the age-
old harshness. Like the cruel climate, sparse soil, and poor
peasantry, courts and law seemed to be accepted as features
of the landscape about which nothing can be done because
higher powers have willed them. It has always been so.

But there is a difference between harshness and injustice,
and when I asked specifically whether the courts were
spravedliviye ("just," or "fair"), the answer was usually a
shrug and an uncertain "*Da.*" A shrug because the question
seemed strange to them. Ordinary Russians are passive about
such things, considering the law neither good nor bad, but
unavoidable—not for the likes of *them* to contemplate. This
is to say, they very seldom think about the law. "*Shto
podyelaiyesh?*—What can you do about it?*"

This (Eastern?) attitude implies that love of law as a positive good is not natural to Russians and indeed it was not
spoken of admiringly, even by law students. It is no accident, as
Soviet professors love to say, that law students and the Law
Faculty, have the (deserved) reputation for the lowest intellectual standards at the university. Is this the expression of
Russia's traditional weakness in individualism, rationalism and
legalism, or of legal nihilism due to the law's humble place in
Marxian ideology? Whatever the combination, I met no
young Russians excited by the law. Law as a precious achievement, a distillation of human intellect, reason and compassion,
a protector of rights and dignity, "due process," "equal protection," "the rule of law"—this side of it was missing. The
generosity and creative genius of the Russian spirit flow in
different channels.

I regret, in a way, that professional interests led me to Moscow's courts. Looking at a city through its dark sides can produce discolored images. I saw much of Moscow through its

trials that I could not have seen in any other way, but I hope I shall be able to put this part in perspective. I hope a Soviet visitor who spends his time in a Federal District Court or in the Old Bailey will not come away thinking he has unlocked the soul of "bourgeois" society.

During the year I tried to sample the spirit of ordinary Moscow life outside the courts, as well as the spirit of ordinary cases. I lived with young Russians, joining their pleasures at home and in the city. And it was here that my preconceptions about "Soviet" were farthest wrong. For all my years in Soviet studies, I had had the palest notion about how Muscovites *live*, about the ordinary satisfactions of ordinary people. I had known too little about Moscow's comforts and pleasures. Too little about parks, pensions, prices (of things like books, theater, housing and transportation), promotion of learning and self-improvement, participation in athletics and dancing, principles of full employment, medical care, free education, subsidized vacations—about the hundreds of big and little measures taken by the national and city fathers to make their children happy, without the cheap thrills of commercialism. And too little about Russians' appreciation of these measures, about their patriotism, dignity and self-confidence.

Moscow, the center of dictatorship, censorship, propaganda and world Communist ambitions, was evident too, but I saw only the periphery of that aspect. The inner workings of politics were of course cloistered from me. In any case, militancy was the spirit of Moscow I had expected to see. It was the inner workings of personal and private life that surprised me.

One aspect essential to an understanding of Russia can be learned only by living there. I had known too little about the personal pleasures Russians give one another in their natural habitat, their lack of artifice, their natural wholesomeness, their camaraderie, their contact with one another as human spirits. I knew nothing about their snug private evenings of tea and vodka when they are themselves, unaffected by self-consciousness, self-importance or ownership of *things*; nothing about their generosity and candor, their art of enjoying simple pleasures. About beautiful, flirtatious young *Moskvichki,* and old, bent *babas* in cloakrooms sewing together the weak hook inside my overcoat. (The toothless old philosopher in City Court finally lectured, "Young man, it's time you were married, enough bachelorhood for you. Find yourself a nice Russian girl.") About closeness of families and indulgent love of children. About personal loyalty and warmth —a way of life which still values the senses, sentiment and sincerity more than success. Money talks in Moscow, of course, but off the streets it talks more quietly than I had ever heard. Daily life was so much more *human* than anything I had known.

These are the aspects of Soviet life that most need telling, and I regret that they find no place in an account of criminal trials. After court in the afternoon, I often met friends for skating through the woods and along the river in Gorki Park. Those evenings told as much about Soviet life as my trials. Writers who measure Moscow in terms of work hours, wages, the price of shoes, even the barrage of propaganda, simply miss its spirit. That is why I cannot measure it alone in terms of criminal sentences.

Summing up is as difficult in Moscow as anywhere else. I would like to form some general impression of the whole society, just as the courts are required to judge the whole man. But the whole is contradictory and confusing: construction and corruption, humaneness and harshness, staggering accomplishments and staggering backwardness. If one leaves Russia not confused, he has only confused himself. That is why I do not want to do what I too often saw the People's Courts doing: jumping quickly upon defendants' failures.

Soviet law is a mirror of Soviet life; its administration is an

essential element in the nation's daily existence. But it also re-
flects these sharp contradictions, and perhaps less accurately
than in Western countries. I think it would be wrong to imply
that justice in Moscow precisely equals the justice dealt out
in its courts.

Appendix I

BASIC PRINCIPLES OF CRIMINAL LEGISLATION OF THE UNION OF SOVIET SOCIALIST REPUBLICS AND OF THE UNION REPUBLICS

Article 21. *Forms of Punishment*

To persons who have committed crimes the following basic punishments may be applied:

1) deprivation of freedom;*
2) banishment;
3) exile;
4) corrective labor without deprivation of freedom;†
5) deprivation of the right to occupy certain positions or engage in a certain activity;
6) fine;
7) social censure.

To military draftees, punishment in the form of assignment to a disciplinary battalion may also be applied.

In addition to the basic punishments, the following additional punishments may be applied to convicted persons:

confiscation of property;

---

* From six months to fifteen years; twenty-five years was the maximum prior to 1958.
† A person sentenced to corrective labor continues to work at his normal job and live at his normal residence. A portion of his salary—up to 20 per cent—is deducted from his wages. It is a common punishment in American military services.

deprivation of a military or special title.

Banishment, exile, deprivation of the right to occupy certain positions or engage in a certain activity and fine may be applied not only as basic punishments but as supplementary punishments as well.

Other punishments, besides those listed in the present article, may be established by legislation of the Union Republics in accordance with the principles and general propositions of these Basic Principles.

The death sentence has had an extraordinary history during the forty-six years of Soviet rule. It was abolished in 1917, restored in 1918, abolished again in 1920, restored in 1920, abolished in 1947, restored in 1954, and during all of the time it existed—I refer to the ordinary court system, and not to any of the extralegal state security organs—there has been sharp fluctuation in the kinds of crimes to which it is applicable. In 1947 the Soviet delegate to the United Nations proposed a resolution that capital punishment be prohibited by all states in time of peace. But in 1961 the death penalty was extended in the Soviet republics to economic crimes—an extension considered cruel and unusual by most other states. Murder has sometimes fallen within and sometimes without these fluctuating conceptions of capital crime.

It was the intention of some of the early Bolsheviks to abolish capital punishment from the workers' state, and this intention is still reflected in the writings of Soviet criminologists. Death is not included in the list of punishments given in Article 21 of the present legislation, but is the subject of a separate article:

Article 22. *An Exceptional Measure of Punishment—the Death Sentence*

As an exceptional measure of punishment until its full abolition, the application of the death sentence by shooting—is permitted for betrayal of the Homeland, espionage, sabotage, terroristic acts,

Appendix I

banditism, preparation with the purpose of marketing, or marketing, counterfeit money and securities, speculation in currency or securities in the form of trade or in large amounts, violation of currency regulations by a person earlier convicted of speculation in currency or securities or of violation of currency regulations, intentional murder with aggravating circumstances as indicated in the articles of the criminal legislation of the U.S.S.R. and the Union republics which establish responsibility for intentional murder, theft of state or communal property in especially large amounts, and in time of war or in military conditions, or other particularly serious crimes in instances especially provided for by the legislation of the U.S.S.R.*

The application of the death sentence—by shooting—is also permitted with respect to particularly dangerous recidivists and persons convicted of serious crimes who terrorize inmates in places of confinement who are on the path of reform or commit attacks on the administration or organize criminal groupings with this intent, and also who participate in such groupings.

Persons not having reached the age of 18 before the commission of the crime and women in a state of pregnancy during the commission of the crime or at the time of the sentence may not be sentenced to death. The death sentence may not be applied to a woman in a state of pregnancy at the moment of the execution of the sentence.

The *Commentary* to these Basic Principles (Moscow: State Publishing House of Juridical Literature, 1961) explains that "The Basic Principles permit the application of the death sentence as an extraordinary measure of punishment only for several of the most serious crimes. We cannot yet fully abstain from this measure. The Soviet state is forced to preserve

* Three decrees in February 1962 have added "rape, when committed by a group or causing serious consequences as well as rape of a minor, brigandage [robbery], the giving and taking of bribes or mediation in bribery, committed with aggravating circumstances, attempt on the life of an official of the police or a people's *druzhinik* in connection with their official or social activity in maintaining social order, committed with aggravating circumstances."

the death sentence, although in an extremely limited number of extraordinary cases. Article 22 of the Basic Principles permits the application of the death sentence only for the very most serious crimes (indicated in the article) against the Soviet state and against individuals."

Appendix II

Few Soviet citizens sentenced to "deprivation of freedom" spend their terms, even a part of them, in jail. Jail, *turma*, is reserved for those convicted of "especially serious crimes" and for "especially dangerous recidivists." All others are sent to labor colonies, of which there are four levels: "general," "enforced," "strict," and "special" regimen.

The court decides which of these five forms of confinement will be applied in each individual case and announces its decision as part of the sentence. It may pick any of the five for any convicted person, based on its judgment of the seriousness of the crime, the aggravating and mitigating circumstances, the character of the convicted person, the degree of his "social danger," his behavior in the community and at his trial, and the likely effect of one or another type of colony on the goals of Soviet criminal punishment: prevention of future crime and "correction and re-education" of the criminal. But the Supreme Court of the U.S.S.R. has issued "guiding directives" for judges and lay assessors beyond these personal criteria.

Colonies of general regimen "as a general rule" house offenders sentenced for the first time for minor crimes, and all women not classified as especially dangerous recidivists.

The enforced-regimen colony is the place for those sentenced for the first time for serious crimes. (No definition of "serious" is given.)

Criminals who have been convicted once or several times before, but who do not merit classification as especially dangerous recidivists, are ordinarily dispatched to a colony under strict regimen.

Special-regimen colonies are situated far from settled areas; their inmates—the especially dangerous recidivists, including convicts pardoned from the death sentence—are kept in strict isolation and assigned primarily to heavy physical labor.

Finally, there is jail, also for especially dangerous recidivists, presumably more dangerous even than those in the special-regimen camps. But even jailed prisoners are not shut off to "Soviet humanity." They too—the commentaries explain—are given the opportunity for redemption and improved conditions.

I obtained no firsthand knowledge of what these somber-sounding colonies mean in terms of their inmates' daily lives. In fact, I have not even been able to find any of the U.S.S.R.'s Decrees on Corrective Labor Colonies and Jails, although there are discussions of and references to them in the legal press. Justice William O. Douglas was shown a few of the colonies several years ago, and he reported very favorably on them. I suspect that he was given a carefully selected tour, that a cross section of all colonies would not have merited such warm praise. From the earliest days after the Revolution, Soviet criminologists have always operated a few model reform institutions—the paternal, open-door settlement near Moscow in which most of that city's pre-Revolutionary prostitutes voluntarily remade themselves into useful working women is an outstanding example. But the legendary—and actual—coarseness, ignorance and backwardness of Russian prison guards make one doubt whether that kind of enlightened penology has penetrated Siberia.

On the other hand, I am certain that the cruelty and deprivation of the camp described by Ivan Denisovich no longer exist. The few former inmates with whom I spoke were inarticulate about their experiences—they seemed like combat veterans who are often reluctant to describe life on the front—but they did leave me with the impression that life in the less severe colonies is bearable. Hard, spartan, terribly gloomy—but not barbaric. Soviet texts strongly emphasize that inmates are to be treated not as outcasts but as Soviet citizens who have gone astray and must be reformed so that they may return to their rightful places in society. Recently, considerable stress has been placed on the need to provide them with "the cultural and everyday necessities of life," which can be taken to mean soap, writing paper, good books, even films and theater. And the frequent articles in journals condemning misbehavior by labor colony officials, condemning deviation from the standards of Khrushchevian penal policy, can be taken as a sign that decent treatment is truly the norm just as easily as proof that sinister methods are the rule.

In 1955, the responsibility of procurators in overseeing labor colonies was made much more definite than it had been; they were specifically instructed to inspect all colonies systematically for irregularities, to report and take measures to correct all violations, to insure that socialist legality prevails in all places of confinement (as well as to release all persons illegally confined). A year later, administrative responsibility for all labor colonies was transferred from the feared M.V.D., the Ministry of the Interior, to local soviets, parliaments or county councils. I think it is obvious that these changes were more than administrative; they boded well for the inmates. About that time, the term "labor camp" was revised to "labor colony." Surely that too was more than symbolic name-changing.